AF866610

UNSPLODE

UNSPLODE

THE BOLD NEW APPROACH TO RECONSTRUCT YOUR WEALTHSPAN AND HEALTHSPAN

TREVOR B. HANSON

CALEB O. PINEGAR, D.O., A.T.C.

LIONCREST
PUBLISHING

COPYRIGHT © 2026 TREVOR B. HANSON, CALEB O. PINEGAR
All rights reserved.

UNSPLODE
The Bold New Approach to Reconstruct Your Wealthspan and Healthspan

FIRST EDITION

ISBN 978-1-5445-5376-4 *Hardcover*
978-1-5445-5375-7 *Paperback*
978-1-5445-5377-1 *Ebook*
978-1-5445-5402-0 *Audiobook*

CONTENTS

SIDE 1: UNSPLODE YOUR WEALTHSPAN BY TREVOR HANSON

SIDE 2: UNSPLODE YOUR HEALTHSPAN BY CALEB PINEGAR

SIDE 1

UNSPLODE YOUR WEALTHSPAN BY TREVOR HANSON

INTRODUCTION

"You have a choice in life. You can either live on purpose, according to a plan you've set. Or you can live by accident, reacting to the demands of others."

—MICHAEL HYATT

All guessing. No client-centered purpose. That is how the big corporations within the finance industry operate.

This lack of purposeful planning is rampant, and it's a death sentence for most people's WealthSpan—their financial longevity and well-being. Why? Let me put it this way. Nobody would walk into an open field and start building a structure without a vision, blueprint, or materials. The structure would fall apart during the first storm. But that's essentially what happens in the finance industry.

I see the frustrating results all the time. People spend their entire lives saving money for a nest egg while neglecting their health and quality of living. Then they retire, and in just a few short years, they either lose their sense of purpose or their health goes sharply downhill, and they pass away before living the life they had hoped for.

Working with an advisor to build that nest egg, they've picked one of five portfolio products, limited choices designed by a company looking to make the firm as much money as possible by doing the least work while still retaining the client. To some degree, this corporate thinking is intended to mitigate their own risk, but it handcuffs the advisor. And doing so can hurt the client by limiting choice, opportunity, and flexibility. Ultimately, it's a sickness of the corporate mindset. One I'd like to cure.

Instead, people need specialization based on their immediate lifestyle needs. But that's not how the industry works. There's no discussion about their purpose right now, the future, their dreams, or a desired lifestyle at all! There's no understanding of their passions or aspirations. There's no additional work when it comes to helping a client protect their assets and purpose from a lawsuit. There's no tax planning to optimize the longevity of their WealthSpan. It's just a cookie-cutter, one-and-done deal complete with a once-a-year (if they're lucky) check-in.

Here's a great example; let's call them Bob and Carol. I was working at a big-name firm as a senior vice president wealth advisor. I had many years of experience, and that expertise created a conflict between this couple's needs and the firm. Bob was a very successful CEO. There were certainly complexities to his portfolio and overall financial situation. I knew how to tailor their plan to their goals, but the firm wouldn't let me use the best tools to take those actions.

I wasn't allowed to help Bob and Carol pursue advanced tax strategies, take actionable steps to achieve a lifestyle, or carefully plan for their estate and legacy. As an employee, my duty was to go through my pitch, hook them into one of five portfolio options, and have one call with them a year. I was encouraged to have them sell assets they already owned—for the purposes of getting their money into one of the five portfolio products. Although I'm not a tax professional, I believed that would create large tax liabilities. The institution just did not care.

I believe Bob and Carol could have been living their dream life now while generating an income that would have paid for the future life they chose for themselves. Instead, they'll sit on a nest egg—a cookie-cutter portfolio that is sold to everyone—that a firm uses to collect fees and dues. They'll delay their life into retirement, and they may just miss the boat on having truly lived with purpose.

Why are many big financial firms like this? It's a top-down approach. A small committee of ten people, most of whom have never had experience as an actual financial advisor, tends to make choices for an entire company. Anybody on the board that speaks up about holding assets with large tax liabilities, advanced tax strategies, tax loss harvesting, investment alternatives, structured investments, or anything else that would benefit the client but reduce the company's residual revenue or increase risk to the institution, the institution will shoot down. It creates a culture where advisors are either afraid to speak up or glad to add bulk clients to earn a paycheck.

Bob and Carol were just a portfolio to this firm. Nobody looked at them and thought that they could benefit from a financial plan with purpose. But if you want to live with purpose, you need a financial plan. Most people think portfolios and financial plans are the same thing, but they're not. A financial plan is much broader and more holistic, designed to help you achieve a desired lifestyle. Shockingly, only around 30 percent of investors have one.

The reason why I got into this line of work was to help people live the life of their dreams, but my managers wanted me to fit Bob and Carol into the same portfolio that everybody else had. Eight to ten different mutual funds. Moderate diversification. And giving them a "choice" of conservative, moderate, balanced, growth, or aggressive portfolio growth (a.k.a. risk tolerance). Just another tax-inefficient, cookie-cutter portfolio.

Choosing a percentage of risk is *not* purposeful planning. It is the illusion of planning! One meant to make the client feel like they are getting some sort of personal care and attention (even though everybody gets the same thing). What's worse, Bob and Carol were meant to leave the meeting thinking they had agency in their finances, but it's more accurate to say the firm was deciding for them.

Maximum corporate revenue. The least corporate effort. The big institutions get between the advisor and the client, and only 17 percent of planners offer their clients a proactive approach. And when they do rarely talk about purpose, it's not a system designed to help the client. That's got to change.

That's why I built my own company and financial organization that serves the client first. Independent and boutique financial planners like me can provide the vision and passion—what's needed for true financial planning and wealth management—that larger firms seem to have lost or were never interested in providing.

Now that the veil has been pulled back, I have a crucial question: what can you do to stop the system of guesswork when it comes to your financial planning?

PURPOSEFUL PLANNING

It's time to identify and patch up the gaps in your financial health by being purposeful, strategic, and intentional. Make your ideal life real. Push back against the cookie-cutter portfolio and plan with purpose. *Everybody* needs a WealthSpan—or intentional and lasting longevity for their wealth—built from purposeful planning in order to create a fulfilling life.

You may be a highly successful person, but that doesn't mean there isn't a gap somewhere in your finances that, down the road, could change your financial expectations dramatically for the worse. Do the strategic preventative work to ensure that your WealthSpan can give you a great life now *and* the retirement you want.

What's at stake if you don't plan with purpose? What if you aren't optimizing your taxes? What if somebody slips and falls in your driveway and sues you for two million dollars? Without strategic and intentional planning, your financial future and expected lifestyle could be up in smoke.

And it's not unusual for a family to break up from the aftermath. Here's a great example. A high-net-worth family never bothered to put a trust together or do proper and purposeful estate planning. Despite my encouragement, their financial advisor didn't work with them on it. All hell broke loose after the head of this family passed away. The kids, angry there wasn't an estate plan, went to court. It was a long, drawn-out process. The kids all fought during the years, and even though they all did fine—in terms of inheriting equal shares—they no longer speak to each other. It's an unfortunately common consequence—one that's entirely preventable.

Financial advisors don't get paid for helping their clients be intentional about their strategies or do proper estate planning, so maybe it's only natural that most don't bother to take necessary steps to strengthen their client's WealthSpan to avoid disasters. It makes sense, in a way. Intentional strategies add work to their plate that, from one perspective, dilutes their income. But wealth managers who foster WealthSpan and work on the same side as their clients are committed to *you*. They're going to use purposeful planning that goes beyond the basic features of traditional advice.

But proper purposeful planning is about building a fulfilled life. That concept—of living intentionally now and into the future—is what separates this book from any other financial book you might pick. It's about giving you the confidence that you have a plan and can enjoy your hobbies now *and* when you retire. If you've planned well, it will include reevaluation milestones for changing priorities and modifications in recreational and leisure activities as your body ages.

Speaking of leisure activities in our retirement years, part of your purposeful financial planning is connected to the longevity of your health, but I'll let Caleb handle that on his side of the book. Perhaps you didn't realize that this book will discuss both aspects of your future planning and investments: your finances *and* your health. That's why I'm writing this book with Caleb; he's an orthopedic surgeon with an interest in longevity and injury prevention who can provide you with a very important medical perspective on how to make both your body and mind work best for you now and into the future. So stay tuned for that.

Purposeful planning means thinking about what your goals and aspirations are. Do you want to create a legacy? Do you want to create net worth for a nonprofit? Do you want to spend more time with your family? Do you want more time freedom? What is it that makes you happy, and how can your finances support that? A lot of people don't know the answers to questions like these. I don't want you to be one of them. Because *these* are the questions that set my mission apart from every other financial advisor that you have ever spoken with before. And that is why I am here.

THE NEW PURPOSEFUL PLANNING

It's time to introduce The New Purposeful Planning. Planners who help clients manage their wealth with purpose can create financial longevity where the larger financial industry is currently leaving gaps.

I'm the creator of my organization's Purposeful Planning Process. Part of this book's mission is to clue you into the strategies of purposeful planning. Think of it as your first step working with a planner who sits on the same side of the table as their clients instead of functioning as a corporate Yes Man. This new planner thinks in decades, not quarters. They simplify complexity. They lead with planning, not products. They tell the truth. They are there to give a client pushback even though it's not what the client may want to hear. They say what others won't, ask what others don't, and deliver what others can't. They are there to look at every aspect of the entire financial situation, including tax optimization and building a plan based on client goals and needs to sustain their WealthSpan.

I have two questions for you that any good wealth manager should ask. What does your ideal WealthSpan look like? What is your financial purpose? The following chapters are designed to help you start answering the complexities of those questions. Here's what to expect.

First, you'll explore the concept of WealthSpan in more detail. That will include rethinking the function of your net worth. Is your net worth simply a nest egg you're trying to get as big as possible, or is it a tool for living a fulfilled life? You'll learn that being financially present and focusing on your relationships and daily experiences, not just having an eye to the future, are keys to financial happiness.

That kind of approach will require you to rethink how you approach saving and spending money. That's when I'll switch gears to discuss a New Abundance Mindset of Finances in Chapter 2. Many individuals are asset-rich but cash-poor, which restricts living in the now. A mindset shift can help you navigate a new approach to living your life on your own terms.

But money isn't infinite. In Chapter 3, you'll take stock of your current financial situation while also setting achievable goals. After all, financial planning must account for a lifestyle that motivates action. And it needs to be realistic about goals surrounding physical, cognitive, and emotional health—especially as you reach retirement age.

With those goals in mind, the next step is to help protect the finances your goals require. That's why Chapter 4 will discuss strategies designed to preserve assets, such as insurance strategies, trusts, gifts, retirement accounts, titling, walling off personal assets from business assets, and more. You can build as much financial health as you want, but if you don't take the steps to help protect it, you'll have left an exploitable, fatal flaw that could ruin your plans.

Once done with the preliminary education, it's time to start making the body of your finances healthy again. That means a lot of preventative care to make your money work for you. Chapter 5 will consider how to invest to help prevent the damage of market fluctuations, advanced tax strategies, and more.

One of the most important aspects of a well-functioning and long-lasting financial plan is to delegate to your WealthSpan Longevity Team. Chapter 6 will walk you through the framework of the most successful version of your financial team, positioning the New Wealth Manager as the captain working in conjunction with key professionals like trust attorneys, tax attorneys, tax accountants, insurance agents, and real estate advisors. Each will stay in their lane but clear the fog for you, working with a new standard of transparency.

The right professionals can smooth over problems and, even better, create an engine that can dramatically increase your net worth. I'll coach you on how to hire the best people, identify when somebody is not working for you, and give you permission to fire somebody if they don't have your best interests in mind.

With your individual needs identified and a team is behind you with an aim to ensure your plan comes to fruition, you can live your life and produce income confidently knowing both your present and future are taken care of. But at some point, you can expect to retire, which means you'll need to plan on generating income after you actually stop producing it. In the last chapter of "Unsplode Your WealthSpan," you will plan your retirement with purpose, letting your portfolio do the work for you.

As you move throughout the chapters in "Unsplode Your WealthSpan," there will be corresponding chapters related to your HealthSpan—your physical and emotional health and longevity—in this book's complementary part, "Unsplode Your HealthSpan." There, your financial planning will be balanced by physical and emotional health strategies that you can use your finances to implement. Together, both parts of this book are about finding out what your individual financial and health needs are. You are unique; your plans should be unique, too.

Think of it as a Choose Your Own Adventure. You can read all the way through this part before moving onto HealthSpan, or you can go back and forth between corresponding chapters. It's up to you.

Whatever you choose, don't waste your life wishing for next week. There's a better way. It's time to make your health and wealth work together and bring them into balance so that you can live your life now *and* tomorrow.

LET US BE YOUR NEW WEALTH CEO

You'll be in good hands in the chapters to come. Grounded in principles of the financial organization I built from the ground up, you'll learn practical tools and strategies on how to plan with purpose and build the right team around you to ensure a healthy WealthSpan.

I've been in the wealth-management business for twenty years. When I hear endless stories about client regret, it is always that they wish they'd lived and experienced more. My financial philosophies are geared toward helping clients create meaningful memories. And since I started in this industry before the financial crisis, I know how to shape financial plans that can weather a storm and keep dreams alive. It was some of the best training any financial planner could receive. People like me know what volatility means.

We specialize in leadership and execution. The very nature of being a CEO has to do with finding the right path that fits your needs and helping you stay the course. These are strategies for the now and for the long run, designed by a wealth manager who gives their clients continuous support.

We have the materials; you have the vision. Let's build something special. I want to help you do it the right way. You have the chance to build the life of your dreams with purposeful planning, and we hope to be alongside you to make it happen.

WHAT DOES "UNSPLODE YOUR WEALTHSPAN" MEAN?

As you read on, you'll experience a bold new approach to deconstructing and rebuilding your WealthSpan, a purposeful plan designed to maximize the longevity of your wealth. I'll remove anything cancerous about your current financial situation and build it back stronger than before. And my cousin Caleb will help you with your HealthSpan.

About seven years ago, Caleb and I started to collaborate on this book. We come from wildly different professional backgrounds. I'm a wealth manager. He's an orthopedic surgeon (and a darn a good one). When we'd catch up, we both realized that the people we serve go up against systems not necessarily designed with their best interests in mind. Patients don't go see doctors until they're sick. Investors don't plan with advisors much at all. Too often, this creates an imbalance—

where a person focuses only on their health, only on their wealth, or neither—which causes people to lose their health and wealth needlessly. Unnecessarily losing everything they've tried to work for causes a catastrophic destruction of their aspirations and plans. Their life basically explodes! And it happens all too frequently. How can that be prevented?

That's where Caleb and I started to contemplate a new and improved planning method that flips the script on traditional methods. In our view, traditional planning—for health and wealth—encourages behavior that can actually explode our lives by creating unexpected and devastating changes in our wealth or wellness. Our systems *unsplode* that. What Caleb and I mean by "unsplode" is to reverse any negative impacts that you could knowingly or unknowingly be placing on your personal success with your health and wealth. In wealth planning, we aim for long-term, compounding growth that is tax efficient. In health, the return is more years, more energy, and more time doing what matters. But we build it so that you can live a fulfilling life today *and* tomorrow. It's not good enough to only plan for the future; you have to plan for now, too.

For my part, I want to reduce and then eliminate any damage your finances have incurred because they've been in a prolonged, tax-inefficient, cookie-cutter "plan" not meant for your individual goals or, worse yet, not benefiting from *any* plan. It's time to *unsplode* and take back control of your financial future.

This is a book of nonnegotiables. It is a book meant to help you bring balance back into your life. Use it to create clarity on what you need to be financially successful, how to cultivate happiness alongside your financial plan, and how to build your life with purpose. Look at all aspects of your life—health, wealth, family, hobbies, and everything else—and take the steps required to maximize them.

Although my chapters will focus on finances, WealthSpan also requires you to be healthy in other areas of your life. To maximize your life, you need both to be balanced. Improving your health gives you the energy to gain more wealth. Improving your wealth lets you invest more time and capital into your health. One needs the other. Therefore, utilize the entirety of this book as a tool to rethink your financial and physical health and to seek out the professionals like me who can help you rebuild both.

Let's get started!

CHAPTER 1

WEALTHSPAN: FINDING LONGEVITY IN FINANCIAL WELL-BEING

"No one ever said on their deathbed, I wish I had spent more time in the office."

—PAUL TSONGAS

It's difficult to see people throwing away their lives and a retirement they may never enjoy because they've been pigeonholed into a boilerplate financial plan.

When I see this as a wealth manager, there are certain folks that you remember. A married couple—let's call them Erik and his wife, Sarah—found their way into my office one day. They were going to retire within the year. They'd heard about my company and how we tailor portfolios to fit the needs of the client.

As I do with each of my clients, I started asking them questions to get to know them as unique people. This is crucial for building a tailor-made financial plan.

Their answers were focused on memory-making experiences. They wanted to go to Europe, particularly Italy. Somewhere down the line, they hoped to travel all across Asia in one big, expansive trip. And Erik had his heart set on visiting South Africa. But it wasn't just dream vacations for the two of them. They also wanted to spend time with the family.

Working hard their entire careers meant that they missed out on a lot of their children's lives, and now they wanted to make up for it. They wanted to treat their kids and grandkids to trips to Disneyland and national parks to create family experiences that could act as their teachable legacy. The hope was that the memories from these journeys would generate even more adventure in their family for generations to come. Their passion and excitable collaboration were awesome to witness. They were like a storybook couple.

It got me really excited to work with them. My financial philosophy is to plan with purpose and have the *why* as the central part of the planning process, and they were clear on theirs.

But there was some melancholy in the meeting. They talked about how, although excited about retirement, they hadn't done anything fun like this in the past. Instead, their entire focus was saving money to reach a point of retirement. In other words, they delayed their happiness. Sure, they may have been late to the game, but they were here now and with the means to spend.

All told, they saved eight million dollars in assets. But their assets also included their paid-off commercial building (where Erik ran his company) and house. And their expenses were so low that they'd have to go out of their way to spend their nest egg, which was good because they had plans.

As we started going through the planning process, we decided to front-load their spending to ensure they had the experiences before they became too old to travel and their kids and grandkids got too old to make the time. Erik was on the younger side, in his early sixties, so this plan made sure to prioritize fun now, fun later, and keep them financially healthy for the rest of their lives.

Our meeting ended, and there was joy and excitement in the air.

It wasn't but four weeks later that I heard back from them. Sarah called me and was sobbing, and I couldn't understand what she was trying to say through the tears. The wealth manager part of me dropped, and the human part of me took over: "What's going on? Is everything okay?" Composing herself, she told me that she had called to tell me that Erik had been diagnosed with brain cancer and only had three months left to live. She continued, "My life is over. There won't be any trips. We waited and waited, then ran out of time. That's the part I can't live with." I was stunned.

As a wealth manager, having this experience with a client is the toughest part of my job. Being in their corner, I have a hard time not thinking about stories like these at night—clients running out of time, being too late with living their life now, and fulfilling themselves with purpose. I ache for them—for clients like Sarah. And my own purpose and drive is to help them find a new sense of purpose and planning.

I had to coach her a little bit: "Your life is not over. There are still good things ahead. And you could honor Erik by doing the things you set out to do with him." Despite her grief, she knew I was right. As the years went by, there were still trips with the kids and memories made, but unfortunately Erik wasn't there to impact his family like he'd hoped.

The stinger to this story is that this experience is not unique to them. I've been a wealth manager for over twenty years, and I've seen my fair share of stories like this. When, even as an acquaintance, you witness something so horrific happen to a person, you can't help but reflect on what matters in your own life a little bit.

For me, I decided that I needed to do things with my kids while I'm still here, not when I retire. Like, this year. This month. This week. Tomorrow. Heck, I'll call them right now to tell them I love them. Give me one second.

* * *

Okay, I'm back. Where was I?

Nothing is promised to us. Our time is our most precious commodity, even if we plan for maximizing the longevity of our HealthSpan and think "everything will be okay." Things crop up that we don't expect, and that's when we regret not living sooner.

Just ask Caleb, my co-author and a doctor who's seen it all. He's full of stories where an accident cut a life short too early. Learn from us instead of learning the hard way: you don't need to wait for retirement or to save enough before you're ready to have meaningful experiences.

A well-lived life is about purposeful balance and starting a plan as early as possible, which is now. Plan a WealthSpan to create a fulfilling life now and for every moment for the rest of your life.

WHAT IS WEALTHSPAN?

Most people think financial planning is about hitting a number—some target for retirement. But numbers without meaning can still leave you feeling empty. These kinds of plans are built around projections instead of purpose and the present.

WealthSpan flips the script. "WealthSpan" is a word that combines *wealth* and *lifespan*. It is a brand-new approach that bridges financial freedom and lifestyle freedom. It is a balance. Not between risk and reward but between a life deferred and a life experienced. It is utilizing your finances as a tool to support the people, moments, and memories that matter—*before* you lose your health and energy. It's about leveraging your money to live for today *and* tomorrow with confidence.

WealthSpan is how long your wealth actually funds a life that feels good. It is doing the work now to help prevent the explosion of your financial future while still pursuing a purposeful present by using your wealth as a tool for living right now. In essence, it's *unsploding* any damage you might be unknowingly doing to your financial health.

The Greek philosopher Theophrastus famously wrote, "Time is the most valuable thing a man can spend." *Now* is the time in your life when your money and health are both strong enough to fund meaningful experiences. It's not tomorrow. It's not retirement. It's now.

Money is meant to fund a life that fulfills—physically, emotionally, and relationally. It's not about working forever. It's about living richly and with vitality today and planning to maintain that lifestyle into retirement.

The idea of pursuing a healthy WealthSpan—or sustaining one's finances to live a purposeful, meaningful, and fulfilled life now and forever—changed my perspective on what I do with my time and my kids. It helped me realize that the strongest WealthSpans are built around a *why*. That's different from any financial plan that has come before.

For me, one *why* or purpose that I have is to visit every continent (except Antarctica) together as a family before the kids get out of college. So far, we've been lucky enough to travel to many locations within the United States, Mexico, Costa Rica, Southeast Asia, South Africa, Greece, Egypt, and Jordan. And we have a few more trips on the horizon. When my wife, Kenalee, and I first got married, she had only been to two states. I remember thinking, *We'll change that.* After traveling all over the world with her and our kids, her love for travel has sparked an excitement for life—despite her nerves for the travel days. Sure, you can see she's feeling a bit anxious to get on a plane, but once she's on, it's over. She becomes the most adventurous among us. Nothing stops her.

Planning for a life has had trickle-down effects. For example, my kids now say, when I ask them about gifts they may want, that they would rather travel with the family than receive the latest gadget or popular thing. We are building a life on experiences, not things.

When you don't prioritize living, you're rolling the dice that you might *never* live meaningfully.

It reminds me of a client I had for many years. Let's call him Mike. We worked together for so long that we became friends. He had fantastic balance in his life. He coached his kids' baseball teams, was active in his hobbies and family life, and greeted each day with positivity and gratitude. Come to think of it, he was always a laughing, happy guy.

Even so, he delayed some of his dreams. Mostly travel. In the decade up to his retirement, he decided he wasn't sure if traveling would jeopardize the longevity of his retirement plan. I presented him with some plans that would allow him to travel—and live his life now—while ensuring he had an ironclad retirement. We led with conservative investments, added some guaranteed income, and lowered the overall risk of his portfolio. He had that personality that couldn't handle large market swings. He said, "Thanks, but no thanks. I'll just wait."

Right about the time he retired, he started facing some health concerns and frequently came into my office to make adjustments to his plan (to pay the health costs). He was going through his joints, one by one. Incrementally, they needed to be replaced. In the end, he had his hips, knees, and shoulders replaced—more than half of the possible joint-replacement surgeries that a person can even have.

Even though he had to pull money for these surgeries, he was doing fine financially and could have gone on those earlier trips. But these healthcare costs spooked him a little, and he continued to delay his travel dreams for fear of running out of money.

After about eighteen months, one of his replacements went septic and, being on the unfortunate side of the 10 percent mortality rate, he passed away quickly. At the funeral, Mike's wife said the same things I've heard countless times before. "We had all of these plans, and now my life is ruined," she said through tears. It was heartbreaking.

Part of me wished I had the medical knowledge, like Caleb, to have advised Mike on preventative health measures that would have prevented his need for all of those joint replacements. But it was too late.

MONEY AS A TOOL FOR LIVING

Unlike the rest of the industry, which is focused on bulk clients and collecting fees, I see a financial plan as a way for my clients to confidently live with purpose and budget a fulfilled life.

Plan for purpose, not just preservation. In other words, your money isn't a pile to hoard for later—there may not be a "later." It is a tool for living. What your ideal life might be is up to you. It's different for every individual. Maybe it's spending time with your family, creating unforgettable memories, pursuing passions and interests, building a supportive community around a charitable cause, curating experiences that reflect your core values, or any number of other things.

Whatever's included in the life you want to live, your money is there for you to live it. Stashing it away for later means you are stopping yourself from living now. Instead, purposefully plan to invest in health and joy—not just growth.

But just like any tool, you need to know how to use it. If you use a tool incorrectly, disasters can happen. For example, we don't want you to overspend and run out of money. And if you do have the goal of passing money on, we can help you strategize finding the right balance.

CALEB'S INTERJECTION

Heya! It's me, Caleb, Trevor's cousin and co-author. You may recognize me from writing the HealthSpan side of this book. Get used to me interjecting every once in a while with useful information—I just can't help it. I like interrupting Trevor. Disclaimer over. Now let's get to the useful information.

When we talk about money as a tool, consider that there are a variety of different ways to use a tool. Along the way, we learn that some are useful. Others are less than useful.

For context, I'm a medical professional—specifically, I'm an orthopedic surgeon. During surgery, I'll never use a round burr. It's the worst thing anyone could hand me. I tend to poke holes in things or botch it when wrapping up the drape. Any flat surface will end up looking like a cratered moon. The cylinder-shaped burr, on the other hand, is fantastic for me. I kick ass with that thing. I can make anything look beautiful.

What does this all mean? Success means being able to use a tool in the right way *and* choosing the tool that suits you! If you are putting all your money in one high-yield account for decades, you are probably doing damage to your WealthSpan because there are other better ways you could have maximized your money. But the good news is this: what Trevor has created at the organization he built uses money as a tool to build and grow a WealthSpan unique to an individual's needs.

No matter where you're starting from financially, the methods exist for you to use your money as a tool to scale and grow your WealthSpan.

For the typical person, when they meet with a financial advisor, they are given one of five "options," a framework to use their money as a tool. But by not tailoring that financial plan to the individual's needs, it's like trying to fit a square peg into a round hole. It's not a plan meant for you.

So when you use your money as a tool, you have to do it purposefully and know that *how* you're implementing your tool is appropriate for the job you want to accomplish.

And that "job" doesn't have to be lavish and luxurious. It could be budgeting for a few weekend getaways a year. You can still create fantastic memories with fewer assets, such as camping, going to a national park, a road trip, or visiting a low-cost region of the world like Southeast Asia.

You're only limited by your imagination.

THE EXECUTIVE AND BUSINESS OWNER TRAP: ALL HUSTLE, NO HARVEST

Do any of the following sound like something you might say?

- "I'll slow down when my company hits its next milestone."
- "Once I sell my business, then I'll have the ability to take that dream vacation."
- "This is just a busy season. Next year I can pursue my hobbies."
- "I worked hard to get this role, and now I have to hustle harder."

These are things I frequently hear from business owners and executives. And to a degree, I get where they're coming from. I own my own business, too, and it takes drive to make it thrive. But when you're putting all of your drive into your business or work, that comes at the cost of sacrificing most or all of your time in one area of your life. All hustle means no harvest.

And when you're imbalanced or hyperfocused, that's when things can fall apart. Someone I like to refer to as David was a fifty-eight-year-old retired entrepreneur who built a multimillion-dollar logistical company from scratch. A true success story. But he sacrificed a lot along the way. He skipped anniversaries, missed birthdays, and passed on vacations—always promising his wife, "Just a few more years of growth." In a way, his business was his passion and hobby. But for him it was a sixty-hour-per-week hobby that took energy away from his family—what should have been another source of joy in his life.

David and his wife planned to travel to Europe together once the business was sold. By the time that happened, his health had deteriorated—years of stress, late nights, and fast food had taken a toll. He had high blood pressure, chronic back pain, and fatigue that kept him from walking long distances.

They had $25 million in portfolio assets after they sold their business, but they had to cancel that European trip.

Later, when he set up his first meeting with me to restructure his financial plan, he admitted, "I built the business so we could finally live. But I feel like I missed the life we built it for." Business owners are used to reinvesting in everything but themselves.

WealthSpan planning flips that script. Because your business or work should be a tool to create freedom for *you*, you need to shift your mindset to live for now *and* later. You need a financial plan that reminds you that *you* are your most valuable asset—not just your equity.

WealthSpan planning gets deep, going far beyond basic income and investment decisions. It considers complex compensation structures, including stock options, restricted stock (RSUs), performance-based equity, and many more. Each asset is giving its own timing, tax, and liquidity implications. Because executives and business owners are focused on their roles, many lack a coordinated plan for when and how compensation is exercised, vested, distributed, or deferred—not to mention the tax liabilities those decisions create. As a consequence, important elections and planning opportunities are often overlooked or made by default, which can permanently lock in unfavorable tax outcomes. With WealthSpan, thoughtful planning aligns compensation strategy, tax planning, and cash flow with long-term goals—so decisions are made intentionally, not reactively, and before opportunities disappear.

WEALTHSPAN NONNEGOTIABLES

Even if you're not a business owner or executive, consider that you are the CEO of yourself. You might be in a career position for a company working late nights, putting in the blood, sweat, and tears every day and putting off a life that you should be living now.

If you want a strong WealthSpan that creates a purposeful and fulfilling life and creates a longevity that maximizes your twilight years, there are a series of nonnegotiables you need to proactively consider.

INVEST IN HEALTH

You read that correctly. Good health is essential for longevity of wealth. Don't forget that this is a book about WealthSpan *and* HealthSpan.

There will be a lot of crossover. One is only as strong as the other. Although Caleb will go into a lot more of the health details for you, I have some basics I want to talk about.

You need to start taking care of your health now. That should include proactive checkups, creating an age-appropriate and functional fitness routine, understanding and consuming a nutritious diet specialized to your needs, and improving your sleep hygiene. If you don't take care of your health, you won't be able to use your money as a tool to do the things you want.

A painful personal example is with my dad. He and I were extremely active. We traveled the world. He loved tennis, was a big scuba diver, and included his family. It was part of his big personality. He was the personification of adventure.

Both he and my mom, when I was growing up in Dubai and Muscat, Oman, instilled a love for world travel in me. My mom hardly said no to doing something outside of her comfort zone. Even now, despite her back hurting a bit these days, she's still a kid at heart who's up for the next adventure.

Before I turned ten, we had visited four continents. Everywhere we went, we made a point to have active adventures together. We went on hikes, traveled a lot together, and made a lot of wonderful memories. I am so grateful for the loving and purposeful atmosphere they've always provided for me. They lived with purpose before they had health issues—living life to its fullest.

Unfortunately, all these decades later, my dad's health has gone a little downhill in the last few years. Our family has hereditary issues with arthritis, and his passion for skiing—he was a fantastic skier—took a toll on his knees. His ankles swell, and he has to keep them up. He has a hard time traveling long distances or on planes, and his mobility has slowed. Looking back, based on what doctors know now, there were preventative steps that could have stopped issues that are now showing up in his daily routine.

I'm still incredibly grateful for the time we spent together, but it's been a tough pill to swallow (for both of us) to slow down. It's challenging to have young kids and want them to experience their grandfather the way I got to experience him as a father; I wish they could experience adventures with him the way I was able. It's my drive. Looking at the adventures we had, I'm turning inward to determine the health investments in myself to try and maintain activity with myself and my own kids down the road.

And it's not just my drive for my own family. It's why I'm writing this book. I want to help my clients set themselves up for a life of purpose, fulfillment, and longevity.

PLAN FOR EXPERIENCES, NOT STUFF

We live in a culture where stuff seems to matter most. "How can I get more stuff to show the next person I have more stuff than them?" But this cultural phenomenon is at odds with our human nature. I work quite a bit with retirees, and *all* of them talk about how they wish they had less stuff and more experiences. So start ticking things off your bucket list now.

Quit thinking about retirement as if it'll be exactly like today but with more free time. Don't shoot the messenger, but your body and ability will be *much* different. You might not be able to enjoy in retirement what you can enjoy today.

Further, when we retire, we are making a pretty dramatic transition from a busy schedule to an empty schedule. That can have a negative psychological impact on us. We no longer see our work friends. Our sense of purpose (work) is gone. Meaning can quickly slip away, and it feels like we spent all those decades wishing our weeks away—"I can't wait for the weekend"—only to retire into nothing.

To combat this, establish a purposeful routine of experiences *before* you retire. You will maintain a sense of meaning, purpose, and fulfillment as you make that transition. Make memories now and don't delay moments that create legacy. And when you establish that purpose, you can then build a wealth strategy that maintains that lifestyle. It turns out that longevity is only possible when you have purpose today.

MAKE MEMORIES NOW

When we think of the word "legacy," we usually only frame it in terms of a lump-sum number we are passing on to our heirs. But when we are gone, the money we pass on is likely to be the very last thing on the minds of the survivors that were closest to us. They'll remember who you were as a person, the shared experiences you had, and the memories you made with them. Legacy is really about living life now with the people you love so that they can hold you in their heart forever and continue living in your spirit.

Those people who are hyperfocused on increasing their retirement number will wish their week away, spend less time with their family, and diminish a true legacy. Don't delay moments that create only a financial legacy. Find purpose and happiness now. Start building a wealth strategy to sustain that purpose. Longevity is only possible when you find your purpose today. Wishing for something tomorrow actually shortens your legacy to a really small timeframe at the end of your life.

DESIGN FOR LIFESTYLE

Balance your budgeting and financial planning with real, joyful living. Without doing the numbers and having a plan, you won't be able to set your fulfilled life into motion. You'll be on a trajectory to explode the potential for the life you want. *Unsplode* that by designing your finances to support the lifestyle you want.

Most of the financial industry, when giving you a limited number of options, is helping you budget for your needs, not what you want. Those numbers only consider major expenses, not bucket-list adventures. Well, you can't just sit at home and pay your bills your entire life. You need to live a life, too. Design a model that fits a lifestyle. Nearly half of Americans with significant assets don't have a financial plan. That's absurd to me.

If you wanted to build a home to raise your family in, would you take some tools and lumber into an empty lot and just start building without a plan? Of course not. That house would be unlivable (and take too long to build). But living your life without a purposeful financial plan is like existing without any real understanding of what you're doing or if it's beneficial.

BALANCING WEALTHSPAN AND HEALTHSPAN

Where does this lead us? Ultimately, this chapter is about understanding the need for *balance*. Not between risk and reward but a life deferred and a life experienced. Your finances should support the people, moments, and memories that matter—*before* your knees go, your energy fades, or your window closes. To do that, you need to balance your earning and spending with your physical and mental well-being.

When I see clients regret not living their life before they retire, it's because their WealthSpan and HealthSpan weren't in balance.

Don't be that one client I've seen time and time again. Let's call him Frank. Frank did everything the traditional model told him to do. He cut back spending, delayed travel, downsized expenses, and prioritized saving for the "someday" that would come after work. His retirement dreams were big.

The only problem was that he never invested in his health. In his sixties, he was overweight, out of breath walking through the airport, and lacked the flexibility to enjoy even basic activities. He ate poorly, rarely exercised, and never prioritized preventative care.

His kids would invite him to go hiking in the Tetons, but he couldn't go. He was too exhausted. "I missed those memories. And now my kids have moved on."

His wealth could have bought him plane tickets, guides, gear, and more. But it couldn't buy him the mobility to enjoy it. So consider that if you don't have good health, you won't have a good retirement. Alternatively, if you don't have a purposeful financial plan *but* are extremely healthy, you'll be working for a paycheck until you die.

There needs to be a balance in prioritizing your WealthSpan and HealthSpan.

IT'S TIME FOR A MINDSET SHIFT

Now you know what's at stake. If anything in this chapter has resonated with you and you've been hit with a renewed sense of "I need to start living my life right now," then you'll likely need to change your mindset in order to reposition your financial trajectory and achieve your goals. It's a revelation that you might be asset-rich but experience-poor.

To change that, it's time to start thinking about changing our mindset.

Sure, you don't want to run out of money. Nobody does. But you also don't want to die in a net-worth prison, watching the world pass you by as you add to some nebulous nest egg little by little.

CHAPTER 2

THE NEW PURPOSEFUL MINDSET OF FINANCES: HOW TO RETHINK THE WAY YOU APPROACH MONEY

"Wealth is the ability to fully experience life."

—HENRY DAVID THOREAU

Many people find themselves in a retirement that resembles the life of Disney character Scrooge McDuck.

Maybe you're old enough to remember him. Scrooge McDuck hoards every penny he ever made. He's not interested in living a fulfilled life centered on experiences. His only hobby seems to be quite literally swimming in his pile of money—a pool of gold coins in a gigantic vault.

Instead of swimming in a huge vault of coins, the person with a Scrooge McDuck–like portfolio or business valuation will check their balance each week or maybe daily, looking at their net worth all the time as a kind of scoreboard where the only goal is to increase that number. It's the first thing on their minds before asking their kids how their day was.

At some point, McDuck's mindset surrounding his finances changes, and he instead realizes that he should be prioritizing his family. McDuck was lucky because his mindset change was forced onto him.

Suddenly, he was thrust into a situation where he had to take care of his three nephews. Because of their tenacity, curiosity, and desire for adventure, McDuck slowly learns the importance of connection, experience, and community over counting coins. Because they helped him see the value of family, one could say that the nephews actually took care of him.

That was an after-school special, though. Those shows have to have happy endings. The bad news is that real life doesn't really work that way. In the real world, happy endings are rarer and, more importantly, have to be intentionally created.

Whether we know it or not, our actions tend to tacitly create our own ending (happy or otherwise). We create our own reality. And we personally propel ourselves to our final destination. So if you find yourself asking, "How did I get here?" The answer is you brought yourself here. Ultimately, we are responsible for our own impact and future. So if we want it to be a happy story, we have to change our mindset and tap the right resources (and professionals) to write the story differently.

And sometimes all it takes is a story to create a wake-up call and act as the catalyst we can use to change our real life. If not, we'll learn the hard way through our own pain and regret—that lingering pain of the *should haves* and the *could haves.* Between the two options, I suggest the first one.

Let me share a story with you. Early in my career, when I was still working for a firm, a client of mine, let's say his name was Dan, spent all of his time counting his net worth. Dan read every statement he received thoroughly, filed each statement away according to his meticulous organizational system, and kept a whole basement full of financial documents. That room would have been the perfect room to feature on the show *Hoarders.* I love fiscal diligence, don't get me wrong, but I think that life needs a balance. During his free time, maybe he'd watch finance-oriented entertainment news shows. He also kept a collection of financial articles he'd read, mostly from *The Wall Street Journal.* It was more paper in a basement stockpile—his version of McDuck's gold coin vault.

Dan didn't have joy. His primary, obsessive hobby didn't bring him joy. He never smiled. He didn't have a good relationship with his kids. In my estimation, he didn't have a fulfilled life. He just wanted to talk numbers with people. These habits were exploding his happiness and sense of purpose.

Dan, as we all do, passed away. Unfortunately, he didn't take the time to *unsplode* and find balance in his HealthSpan and WealthSpan. His wife reached out to me to invite me to the funeral. I went. And there weren't too many people there. Those that spoke had very little to say about him because he didn't go out of his way to connect with people or share experiences with them. It didn't seem like he left a mark on the world—no stories or experiences that had a positive impact on anybody in his life. His only legacy was his net worth. And that's not the only legacy you want to leave behind, which is something even Steve Jobs learned as he was dying with a terminal illness. It is reported that, near the end of his life, Jobs reflected:

> Material things lost can often be found again. But there's one thing that, if lost, is gone forever—life. No matter where you are on your journey, a day will come when the curtain falls. So love your family, love your spouse, and love your friends.

Dan's wife was loyal, meaning she put off much of her own life to support her husband's obsession with their net worth. She didn't really go anywhere, and her relationship with her kids was more distant than she would have liked. Thankfully, she was able to create a community of friends through volunteer and nonprofit work. That kept her connected to her community.

CALEB'S INTERJECTION

It's me again! Trevor, let me step in here for a sec.

In my time studying medicine and health, it's become apparent to me how important the roles within a partnership are. They need to be balanced for a strong HealthSpan. If your spouse is doing all of the socializing and networking and you're just the provider without a social support network, there is an imbalance there. Your overall physical and mental health will be negatively impacted by that. Furthermore, your relationships will continue to suffer. And your loved one's health and ability to create relationships will suffer, too.

They will have to seek additional relationships and hobbies outside the ones they had when they met you. Because you've isolated yourself, they won't be able to bring back their social circles to you, further isolating you *and* them. Everything about this imbalance is counterproductive to your health. Actively creating and nurturing supportive networks *and* being intentional about a balanced spousal relationship is essential to maintaining longevity in one's HealthSpan.

After Dan passed, his wife spent the money on experiences with her children. She successfully reestablished relationships with them, filling the family with a sense of community and happiness it had long been without. They started to live purposeful, fulfilling lives. And I could see that every time I met with her.

Dan's funeral and his wife's subsequent change in lifestyle greatly impacted me. First, I spent more time finding balance by being clear about my purpose. Money isn't my purpose; it's a tool that helps me access my purpose. So I work to provide but also take my family on adventures and fill them with experiences. Second, I also understood that I never wanted Dan's situation to happen to any of my clients going forward. That's why I've moved on from a large corporation and now run my own organization where I'm not limited by corporate overlords in how I can help my clients.

So how can you avoid a situation like Dan's? How can you rethink the role of your finances and create balance in your life?

START WITH YOUR PURPOSE—YOUR *WHY*

Living purposefully and in balance isn't just about having more money; it's about using it with intention to live, give, love, and enjoy without regret or fear. It's about investing in your health and joy—not just growth.

But let's be clear: living purposefully doesn't mean spending every penny today. It's about alignment with your purpose, not indulgence. You don't need to burn through your bank account to enjoy life. Instead, you need to figure out how to fund a life that feels meaningful and joyful.

It's time for your mindset shift. The old mindset said, "Save everything, spend nothing, and maybe retire someday." The new mindset says, "Use my money to live purposefully today while I am still planning wisely for tomorrow."

In order to live with purpose today and align your financial plan with your whole life in mind, your first order of business is to define your *why*. When I first meet with new clients, understanding their *why* is the very first thing I do. Not only does it let me get to know them a little bit, but what they tell me is vitally important for structuring their finances.

Enjoying your wealth—responsibly and intentionally—is part of your financial health. You don't need to feel guilty for spending on things that bring you joy. In fact, everyday enjoyment can be a sound financial strategy. It builds joy into the budget. Add a "Lifestyle ROI" column to that budget and track how your spending adds to your physical and emotional return. Think of it as an investment in yourself.

Enjoy the twenty-dollar cafe outing with a friend if it deepens the relationship. Take the spontaneous weekend away if it recharges your spirit or connection with your partner.

Just do it with guardrails, something I call "planned spontaneity."

That's an amount you can set aside annually as a lifestyle reserve for fun, flexibility, and freedom.

Of course, balance is key. You don't want to overspend and compromise your future, and you don't want to underspend and miss out on your life. When setting an achievable *why*, the goal is to find the personal equilibrium between purpose and finances.

CALEB'S INTERJECTION

When budgeting for joy, don't forget to budget for your health. That could be fitness classes, nutrition seminars, wellness retreats, personal trainers, preventative care, or other action items that increase your HealthSpan longevity. You want to be around to enjoy what you've earned. A strong body fuels a long, purposeful financial life.

Too many times it is apparent that my patients have not spent the proper time, effort, and budget on taking care of their health. In my heart of hearts, I hope patients never get to the stage where they have to come into my office. And a not insignificant percentage of them might have been able to avoid needing my services had they invested in their health. I have so far never met a doctor that actually "talked his way out of business by preaching health," so I feel confident to tell you that I truly do want that for you. But if I can convince even a few of you to live your life with better purpose and longevity by committing to your health, then this is a win!

FINANCES, HEALTH, AND PURPOSE IN ALIGNMENT

Life happens now. Plan for experiences, not just expenses.

When purpose directs your financial plan and guides your investing, balance becomes less about guessing the market's next move and more about living with clarity and confidence for today and tomorrow.

When your money and your health align with your values, your entire life gains clarity. Ask yourself: Does your financial plan reflect your values? Does your lifestyle support those values?

Here are some guiding questions that can help you determine whether or not your finances, health, and purpose are in alignment:

- Am I hoarding money or multiplying meaning?
- Is my financial plan allowing or limiting my joy?
- Is my health gaining momentum or slipping in silence?
- Is my wealth serving my purpose or just sitting on paper?

It's not just about having the ability to spend. It's having the energy, wellness, and mindset to enjoy what you've built. Prioritizing your physical and emotional well-being alongside your financial life creates true balance. Your calendar, spending, and habits should support your lifestyle and health, not just what you want to own.

When that doesn't happen, an imbalanced life leads to a life unfulfilled. I've unfortunately seen it numerous times with clients. One that will live with me forever was...let's call him Bob.

THE GOLDEN SARCOPHAGUS

Bob ran a printing company—local magazines, leaflets, sometimes clothes, and whatnot. It's all he could focus on or talk to others about, and he did that until he was ninety. Just obsessed with his business. He would come into my office every day (I'm not kidding) to go over numbers. That daily obsession, anybody could tell, was having an effect on his appearance. He always wore off-white shirts. Well, their original color *was* white but were dirty because he would wear them days at a time. His trousers were similarly soiled. His hair was always a mess, and it was clear that he wasn't aware of how he smelled. It all added up to one thing: he had no love for himself, just love for his business.

To Bob's credit, he took great care of his employees. He gave them retirement packages—a pension program that guaranteed 7 percent returns. During bad markets, it really made his business struggle.

But even the employees that loved him for his retirement package were miserable to point out that Bob had no life. All he did was go to work six days a week. Bob wasn't creating an environment where the business could run itself. Nobody was self-sufficient.

In fact, not unlike Scrooge McDuck, he literally started hoarding gold in an underground vault. He was afraid of all the negativities in the world and thought gold would be secure. I would always lightly joke with him that if the apocalypse did happen, people would be searching for food and shelter and basic essentials, not gold. It was like he was building himself a golden sarcophagus—a coffin from his net worth.

There was an imbalance in Bob's life. He spent too much time focusing on finances and neglected his health and purpose. He never used his wealth to pursue experiences. In fact, he didn't have a *why*. He had no balance between earning and spending. He just wanted to earn. He just worked six days a week. Several decades went by, and then he died.

I advise my clients to rethink their relationship to their net worth. I might be the only wealth manager out there that actively encourages you to intentionally use some of your income a little bit so that you can go on vacation and enjoy your life now (and later). Sure, I'll get paid less. But you'll have more balance to increase the longevity of your WealthSpan and, just as importantly, your HealthSpan. And consider this: the more time you spend dwelling within your purpose, the more you give yourself the opportunity to contribute and impact the world—which often leads to making even more money. This is an investment in yourself that might pay off in a way you never imagined.

CALEB'S INTERJECTION

In the process of writing this book, I've spoken to numerous colleagues and people in my circle about Trevor's concept of wealth as integrating a wealth of lifestyle and purpose into the more traditional concept of growing one's net worth. That they can *unsplode* their lives with the principles of WealthSpan. Trevor wants people to go on vacation *this year*, not ten years from now. He doesn't want us to postpone our purpose or our sense of fulfillment. Sure, working eighty hours a week technically increases our bank account, but at what cost? Why feel burned out? Why damage your body and mind if you're saving for an imagined day in the future that might never come? What Trevor points out is that we should be planning for *both today and tomorrow.*

Whenever I come back up for air in the middle of one of these spiels, the person I'm talking to automatically says something like, "Can you please give me a copy of that book right now?" Despite the fact that you, dear reader, are reading this from the finished book, I am writing these words during the production of it. So I unfortunately had to tell them that it was forthcoming. But that universal reaction told me how unique it is for wealth managers planning with purpose that doesn't delay gratification. Instead, plan on present and ongoing gratification aligned with purpose. Trevor lives that life, and he's ready to help you do the same.

DON'T GAMBLE YOUR FUTURE

We've talked a lot about people who hoard their net worth and don't plan for a *why*. Within that group, there's a specific niche of people that take a lot of unnecessary risk.

For this set of folks, one of the biggest inhibitors of a fulfilled life is that dopamine rush of investing. I call these people "gamblers." They thrill-seek on short-term investments, almost treating markets like a casino. Maybe they've gleaned "insight" from a popular talking head that hosts an entertaining and graphics-laden financial talk show, and now they want the adrenaline rush of quick wins while ignoring risk management.

This kind of behavior can explode a sound financial plan quickly. Why? It ignores future obligations, confuses convenience with contentment, and evaporates cash flow. It's a breeding ground for anxiety at every level.

It doesn't take long before this type of person anchors their identity to the next big score. They keep thinking that all they need is that next win to set up the rest of their life. "Just one more trade." "Just one more crypto spike." The problem is it's a volatile mindset that usually ends in losses, stress, and shame. And the pattern becomes so habit-forming that it usually doesn't end until there's very little left (or worse).

A lot of people want immediate gratification and to get rich quick. If this sounds like you, keep this in mind: Warren Buffet once remarked that, "The stock market is a device for transferring money from the impatient to the patient." He was spot on.

And here's some more advice. Don't get sucked in by anybody who brags about how well they've done with their individual trades. The thing is that they'll never talk about all the things that went wrong between those individual deals. They'll present themselves like a genius, and if they do discuss a failure, it will always be somebody else's fault. If they have a partner who is interested in their financial survival, it won't be long before that spouse drags the gambler by the ear into my office.

Purposeful investors, on the other hand, are goal-seeking and think long-term. They will take steps designed to prevent that portfolio explosion—they will *unsplode* their finances. They have a *why*. They use a disciplined process, diversify their allocation (more on that later), create a clear time horizon, and build in the freedom of flexibility to their plan.

They measure success by progress toward goals. There's that word again, *goals.* By having their goals top of mind, they keep their values aligned with their finances. For most, that could include college funding, sabbaticals, and legacy gifts.

Those sorts of building blocks let you approach your financial plan with passion. You aren't just trying to hit a number, you are making choices that enable you to live your life now and in the long term. That sort of mindset—one that balances their financial plan, their purpose, and their health—builds a fulfilled life.

The outcome of being a true investor is compounding confidence and capital, freeing up their time for relationships and health.

DESIGN A LIFE, NOT JUST A PORTFOLIO

Financial planning is really life planning. Like the best kind of healthcare, it's proactive, not reactive—it starts with purpose. Numbers and money are just the tools. Rethinking your finances means that your wealth should be mapped to your dreams, not just a retirement date.

Sure, we've gone over the basic importance of your *why*, but now it's time to take stock of all of your wealth goals. Living with balance by seeking clarity, intention, a realistic vision, and alignment between your wealth, health, and values.

As a wealth advisor for over twenty years, I've seen the difference between planning with intention and planning only for numbers. People with purpose make better decisions and find joy sooner. They regret less, live more fully, and feel confident about their legacy.

And what's legacy? It isn't what you leave. It's how you live now.

CHAPTER 3

WHAT'S THE PROGNOSIS? TAKING STOCK OF YOUR WEALTH GOALS

"It's good to have money and the things that money can buy, but it's good, too, to check up once in a while and make sure that you haven't lost the things that money can't buy."

—GEORGE LORIMER

My early career goals were pretty straightforward and vague, and yours were probably similar: make better money incrementally over time.

Starting my career as a planner for a financial firm, my own upward trajectory at that time was tied to selling as much as possible. That was my drive, and I was really good at it. That moved me up the corporate ladder pretty quickly. But I didn't go home thinking I had made a difference in somebody's life.

I was almost like a robot. I had okay relationships with my clients but didn't find any deep connections with them that created a mutually beneficial collaboration.

Over time and in a business like mine—one that depends on strong professional relationships with clients—connecting with my clients helped me understand that I'm not just in this for me; I'm also in this for them. That's when my goals shifted to include actually planning for my clients, too. Rather than sell, sell, sell, I was trying to figure out ways for my clients to retire on time, not run out of money, or prepare for major life events like car accidents or getting sued. These things don't earn a wealth manager more money, but they help clients.

As I developed more and more ways to help my clients, I realized that my wealth management style was more tied to life goals and less tied to corporate needs. I was trying to sit on the same side of the table as my clients. I started meeting with my clients more, building out their planning process, and helping them find meaning and purpose in their financial approach. I was done with trying to sell them a plan on the first day and never meet with them again.

But there was a problem. My firm was most interested in revenue. Because of that conflict—and despite being a senior vice president in charge of $1 billion with eighteen years of experience—I left and opened up my own office. And I wanted my professional goals and purpose to be aligned with my practice.

Now and throughout my career, I've found interesting parallels to my story with my clients. Most enter my office without a true understanding of their purpose—the life they want to live. They may have a general, vague hope to increase their net worth. That's a fine place to start, but without a clear direction, they'll end up living an imbalanced lifestyle chasing money first and last.

Instead, a purposeful life needs something more defined and planned. When it comes to your own financial goals, you might have been like me: a robot without much purpose and just trying to maximize earnings. It's time to change that.

Creating a WealthSpan that lets you live your life today and tomorrow starts with taking stock of your wealth goals and making sure they are infused with your *why*. At the company I founded, I call this the Purposeful Planning Process.

It includes strategies not available at boilerplate firms looking to drive revenue, and it helps bridge the gap between where clients are and where they want to be. Now, my experience with clients is totally different than when I started my career. They love planning with purpose and receiving a blueprint centered around their values.

THE PURPOSEFUL PLANNING PROCESS

The proprietary process for the financial organizations I built is the Purposeful Planning Process. It's a multistep methodology that helps clients first (re)discover the nuances of their life's purposes and, from there, helps them create an intentional financial plan tailored to those goals.

Let's go over the steps in this process to give you an idea of how you can clear the fog—that uncertainty that comes with mindlessly earning as much as possible and hoping that your portfolio will have enough for your "someday" retirement. And don't forget, it's this same "fog" that prohibits you from enjoying the present moment, strips away the health of our relationships, and damages the body intoxicated with stress.

STEP 1: DEFINE YOUR *WHY*

We're back to your *why*. In the last chapter, we reset our mindset by understanding that having a *why* is vitally important. That was a good start. Now it's time to define it. Before you can begin, you need to set the vision, name the value, and use that information to anchor the plan. It's the carrot and the stick. There's nothing as motivational to live your life as when you set that clear goal in front of you.

What should your goals be centered on? Begin with what matters most: your life, your values, and your legacy. Wealth isn't just about what you've built; it's about where you're going, who you're impacting, and how you want to live. And, to borrow some phrasing from Benjamin Franklin, if you're not planning for these things, you're actually planning your own failure.

Here are the questions I usually ask, questions that you can ask yourself to help you determine your *why*:

- What does a fulfilled life look like to you?
- What experiences would you like more of?
- What legacy do you want to leave?
- What values would you like your money to represent?
- What type of health are you hoping to achieve?
- How do health, energy, and time factor into your definition of freedom?
- Are there any health matters that may modify what a fulfilled life looks like for you, long-term?

What did you come up with?! Do you want to road bike across the country? Hop across Europe? Volunteer at the local food bank? Something else? How are you going to factor in your health (and your hopes for your health) into your *why*? True wealth is measured in memories, time, health, and experience—not just dollars. Don't travel more when you retire. Travel now, and you can still travel when you retire.

After these preliminary questions, there are a few follow-ups that can help you have a clearer understanding of living daily with a sense of purpose:

- Who do you want to spend more time with?
- What do you want to spend your time doing?
- What does freedom look like to you?
- What does your ideal day look like right now? One year from now? Five years from now? Ten years from now? In retirement? How might your purpose shift in your future?

Most of the time when I ask my clients these questions, they are a bit befuddled and admit they haven't really thought much about their *why* before. That blows my mind. Part of my purpose is to change that, and it makes me happy that I've asked the questions.

Your purpose becomes your North Star, a pathway or lens through which every financial decision is made. It's the carrot on the stick that determines your direction. When your financial plan is grounded in purpose, every step forward feels (and is) intentional. The longevity of your WealthSpan is fueled by your multiple purposes.

STEP 2: TAKE INVENTORY

With your purpose(s) determined, you need to clear the fog and get a full picture of where you're at today. It's important to chart a proper path forward by not missing anything. That way, everything can work in sync.

That means it's time to get into some nitty-gritty details. As you take inventory, you need to assess the full financial picture of the following things.

Net Worth

Your net worth is a consolidated view of your assets, liabilities, and overall financial position.

Starting with your assets, make a complete list of your holdings. Some common examples include your bank account, stocks, bonds, retirement accounts, the fair market value of any real estate you own, and, for business owners, the value of your business. This is the fun part of determining your net worth because it'll be your biggest number.

After that, it's time to list your liabilities, or money that you owe. Again, it's best practice to start with the most common types. These include mortgages, car loans, student loans, any business debt, and personal loans. It's also credit card debt. (Taxes are complex enough to require some separate inventorying, which I'll talk about below.)

Once you've inventoried your assets and liabilities, finding out your net worth becomes a simple math problem. Simply subtract your liabilities from your assets and, ipso facto, you've landed on your net worth.

Knowing this number will help you set and achieve financial goals that are aligned with your values and purpose. It'll inform your investment decisions and help you understand how you can be flexible and find freedom.

Taxes

Taxes are a liability. The most obvious part of taxes-as-a-liability is an answer to this question: how much of your income do you expect to have to pay back in taxes? That's what most of us pay our CPA to determine each year.

But there's much more to it than that. It's critical to understand potential future tax exposures that could increase your overall tax liability. These may include capital gains taxes from the sale of assets, taxes on IRA distributions or other retirement programs, gift and transfer taxes, state tax, or business-related taxes. Business taxes can include payroll and employment taxes, self-employment taxes (for certain business structures), sales and use taxes on taxable goods or services, and, in some cases, excise taxes. Depending on the state and industry, there may also be additional business-specific or inventory-related tax considerations.

Things can get into the weeds pretty fast, so I don't want to overburden you. Furthermore, you need to work with a tax and legal professional—both things I am *not*—when making these considerations. The takeaway here is having a full snapshot of your tax situation is the only way to create opportunities to limit tax liability and adjust your overall financial plan.

Estate Planning

When you know your *why*, a natural component to that is preparing for how your remaining assets will enact your values and purpose after your pass.

Do you have a will? A trust? Any gifting strategies? Estate planning is a legacy design meant to help you understand what will happen to your wealth after you pass away.

Without this in place, there could be legal battles and choices made about your money that end up not reflecting the impact you wanted to leave on the world.

In general, I've found that when people take inventory of their hopes and dreams for their legacy, they are more likely to sleep well at night and maintain a focus on themselves and their plan—maximizing their WealthSpan and HealthSpan for a fulfilled life.

Cash Flow

How much income do you receive monthly? Do you receive it as business income, real estate rental income, or others? How will retirement affect your income? If different, is that a tolerable change? What are your expenses (budget)? How much are you saving after income and expenses (positive cash flow)?

And how much monthly income do you want to have to pursue your life purpose? These are crucial elements that shape a financial plan because cash flow is how you use money as a tool to live your life.

Without cash flow, you're just playing the waiting game. What do I mean by that? For example, business owners will keep all of their assets in the business itself rather than cash that they can spend. It's value in theory, not in cash. Similarly, real estate investors will keep much of their equity in the tangible assets themselves. That means less cash flow to spend on life right now and, instead, waiting for these assets to grow over time to liquidate later.

Included in this process is listing your nondiscretionary and discretionary spending. Those mandatory, nondiscretionary bills—mortgage payments, utilities, and so on—must be factored into your cash flow. The essentials have to be covered.

And as you start to list your discretionary spending—streaming services, dining out, and things like that—you are essentially making a list of things that you could consider cutting to maximize your financial plan and aim it back toward your purpose. You may, for example, find out that paying for a streaming service and watching shows every night is actually taking away from your ideal day. Or maybe that is your ideal day. You have to figure that out.

This discretionary list will help you determine what you can substitute to boost your savings. As you make your spending list, feel free to modify them. Experiences are nonnegotiable, as I'll continue to preach. Making memories is crucial to a fulfilled life. But maybe camping or going to Thailand will be a less expensive vacation than the Maldives or the Swiss Alps.

When looking at your income, don't forget to inventory the guaranteed portions, such as Social Security benefits, future pensions, deferred compensation, and annuities. These are all income amounts that need to factor into a purposeful plan.

And while you're taking stock of the possibilities that Social Security will have on your cash flow, also consider the importance of Social Security optimization. There are several ways to make sure you're getting the most out of this program. Let's look at them.

Social Security Optimization

Social Security is a guaranteed, lifetime income for retirees. It makes sense, then, to plan with purpose and optimize your Social Security income to secure not just a stable future but your healthiest future—boosting your retirement lifestyle to meet your life and longevity goals.

Let's consider a few crucial points about how you can optimize Social Security.

Full Retirement Age Matters

Full retirement age (FRA) matters more than you might think. FRA is usually sixty-six or sixty-seven years old, depending on your birth year. This number is critical to Social Security planning, as it determines *when* you can receive 100 percent of your earned monthly benefits. If you start collecting Social Security benefits before your FRA (they can be claimed as early as sixty-two years old), then your benefits will be reduced by up to 30 percent. On the other hand, if you delay taking benefits until after your FRA, you stand to increase your benefits.

Delayed Credits Are Powerful

Delaying your claim earns you what are called delayed retirement credits. For every month you are eligible for benefits but do not receive them, credits accumulate after your FRA and until the age of seventy. If you delay your claim until the age of seventy, you could increase your benefits by as much as 8 percent per year. This can be an important strategy to help protect your lifetime retirement income from inflation.

So, hypothetically, if your full FRA benefit would be set at $3,000 per month, waiting three years would increase that monthly benefit to approximately $3,720—a 24 percent increase (8 percent multiplied by three years).

The Break-Even Point

A key question to ask while considering delayed credits and *when* to claim benefits relates to break-even point analysis. How many years will it take for delayed, increased benefits to start earning more than taking less at the FRA year? While the monthly check at seventy will be higher, you'll forgo three or four years of payments.

Taking the higher payment generally breaks even with FRA payments around eighty to eighty-two years of age. If you have a clean bill of health and expect family longevity into your eighties, then delaying often makes sense. If you have health concerns and nobody in your family has ever lived into their eighties, or if you have cash flow needs, then claiming FRA benefits might be the right fit.

Spousal Strategies

If you're married, you have optimization options, too. Spouses can earn up to 50 percent of the other's FRA benefits (a figure reduced if taken before their own FRA). And the higher-earning spouse must file for their own benefits before the spousal benefit can be claimed. Otherwise, if the lower-earning spouse claims early, the spousal benefit is permanently reduced.

When one spouse passes away, the survivor receives the higher of the two benefits. This creates another important reason to optimize: maximizing the higher earner's benefits by delaying claims until the age of seventy will secure a higher survivor income. This household strategy can materially change lifetime income.

Insurance and Asset Protection

Asset protection is so important that it will get its own chapter. But for the purpose of taking inventory of where you're at financially today, make sure you have a clear picture of how you are protecting yourself.

From an insurance point of view, that means inventorying any life, disability, property and casualty, or umbrella coverage that you have.

For business owners, real estate investors, or those whose assets themselves could create some sort of liability, you should also make note of any legal structures and titling you use (or don't) to protect yourself.

You may have gaps in this area that, once identified, can help you better plan with purpose.

Business Interests

Some often overlooked assets include business interest. You need to include these in your inventory. A common asset in this category is equity ownership in a business—the total value of an ownership stake after liabilities have been paid.

A little bit more complicated than that is a business valuation. Let's say that you fully own your business. A business valuation would be understanding the company's total economic worth by analyzing all aspects of its operations, finances, assets, and market position. If you were to sell, that valuation would determine the price. And that price should factor into your financial planning.

Or maybe your business has buy-sell agreements and/or succession planning. In these contracts, certain triggering events will determine what will happen with the business if a death, divorce, or voluntary exit occurs. This information will have a profound impact on how your financial plan needs to be built to serve your *why*.

Putting It All Together

We'll cover many of these pillars of financial planning and ways to help you maximize your finances in greater detail in subsequent chapters, but for now the goal is to make it an action item to inventory them.

With an easy-to-understand snapshot inventory of your finances, you'll be cleared of any clutter and ready for action, in terms of forming your financial plan around your *why*.

STEP 3: PLAN WITH PURPOSE

With your purpose clarified and financial inventory in focus, you can more easily build a personalized strategy to connect the two. I custom-build plans that support the life my clients want to lead while allowing enough flexibility to evolve with any changes.

Designing a plan aligned with your purpose has many benefits. They include but are not limited to:

- Long-term cash flow and retirement income modeling
- Investment strategy built around goals and risk preferences
- Tax-efficiency strategies and proactive planning windows
- Estate, trust, and wealth transfer design
- Business exit or liquidity event strategies

- Charitable giving or legacy structures
- Intentional family planning, vacation planning, purposeful discretionary spending, investment in health, investment in self, etc.—all those longevity-increasing elements that let you life a fulfilled life right now *and* tomorrow

The result is a clear, actionable strategy that creates momentum, reduces guesswork, and brings every financial decision into alignment with your purpose—and this kind of WealthSpan work sets itself apart from any other financial planning out there.

And get started as soon as possible. Get started now, regardless of where you might be in life. Because the earlier you start, the more benefit these investments have for your future. It's because of the concept of compounding interest, which is a finance concept that has to do with the time it takes for your interest made on your money to help you start making more money! This is more clearly defined by a concept that we refer to as "The Rule of 72." This investment tool is used to understand how powerfully money can grow over time.

Here's what the rule states: when you divide seventy-two by your annual rate of return, that's how many years it will take to double your money. So if your annual rate of return is around 8 percent, your money will double in about nine years. For somebody who starts investing at the age of twenty-five, they can only expect to double their money about five times by the time they are seventy. Somebody who starts later will double their money less within their lifetime. Let's try a hypothetical example, such as $100,000 growing at 8 percent. What will it look like when it doubles? And how will starting earlier land you at a specific amount when you are in your seventies?

- First double: $200,000
- Second double: $400,000
- Third double: $800,000
- Fourth double: $1,600,000
- Fifth double: $3,200,000

Take a moment to look at the stark difference between doubles and what you stand to miss if you don't get started immediately. Let's say you aren't able to make it to the fifth double. That means you'll miss out on $1.6 million. If you only make it to the third double, you'll miss out on $2.4 million. That would be a hard pill to swallow—just from not starting as early as possible.

Once you have your purpose and actionable strategy that reduces guesswork, then let your financial plan gain enough momentum to reach your financial goals. This is *exactly* what we mean when we teach people to invest in a way that allows you to let your money work for you. Your money, when used properly, can actually build your wealth for you.

STEP 4: ADJUST WITH INTENTION

Circling back to your purpose, think of it as more than a starting point. A strong WealthSpan reconnects with and reevaluates your purpose, modifying and adapting your financial planning as needed. This helps design a lifestyle that motivates action (not just financial independence).

Beyond that, there are three primary reasons why it's important to adjust our financial plan with intention. The first is market change. Let's face it. The economy shifts and can be unpredictable. When the market shifts, your investments will need to shift, too. Second, legislative changes. One year, a certain asset might have fantastic tax advantages due to specific laws or policies. What if those laws are changed, and all of a sudden, a large part of your plan becomes tax inefficient? It's time for an intentional adjustment. Lastly, you might have to make changes to your spending. That could be a good thing or an unexpected thing. Maybe a market upturn gives you a windfall that you aren't spending to live the life you've always dreamed of. Or, alternatively, maybe a market downtown requires less spending to meet certain targets.

If you're working with a wealth manager worth their salt, you will have an ongoing partnership with them that includes strategic clarity and zero guesswork.

Why an ongoing relationship? Well, life doesn't sit still. And neither should your plan. To accommodate that fact, a purposeful plan should lead with proactive support, strategic updates, and consistent communication. You shouldn't have to wonder what's coming next or whether you're on track.

You deserve regular reviews and timely course corrections on evolving goals, strategic coordination with a CPA and attorney, and clear next steps every step of the way.

That's a high-challenge, high-support partnership. In a later chapter, I'll coach you on cultivating that relationship with your wealth manager and creating a team of financial professionals that works with your best interests in mind, one that offers you bold guidance, a steady presence, and a plan that stays aligned with your *why* so you can focus on what matters most: your life.

DESIGN YOUR IDEAL DAY, NOT JUST A VAGUE FUTURE

Financial planning that *unsplodes* the ticking time bomb that is your traditional portfolio is a full reverse engineering process. You have to start with your purpose and work backward from there. Only when you have the correct information can you create a purposeful financial plan that makes sense for your dreams and goals.

Without planning, you have no idea what your future will entail. A traditional plan is about financial independence and paying bills only. I would go so far as to say that if you have a traditional plan, you've done no planning. There is nothing anchoring the plan to purpose. No carrot and stick creating motivation to stick to a plan. That type of situation leads to credit card fat, overspending, or gambling-style investment moves—moves that could threaten the strength of your finances.

Let me give you some alarming statistics. Two-thirds of Americans have no financial plan for their net worth or retirement whatsoever.

For those that do, the majority simply bought one of five cookie-cutter portfolio products that all fit within the boundaries of a traditional, cookie-cutter financial plan that does not make adjustments for their desired lifestyle.

Designing a plan around your unique life means achieving more than just financial independence or paying bills. It's about designing your ideal day.

What do you want your day right now to look like? What about five years from now? Ten? When you're retired? What daily activities will make you happy? Try to answer those questions, and then build them out.

What would your ideal week look like? Month? Year? Fill your imaginary calendar with your life to understand that there is a financial plan out there that can help you achieve that life. And when you see that hypothetical future—one that will adjust as your purpose adjusts—you will be more apt to stick with a plan that can ensure you maintain a fulfilling lifestyle. You will be more likely to *unsplode* and maintain a balance of HealthSpan and WealthSpan.

With your carrot clearly dangled in front of you, it creates two important daily habits: (1) with your plan in place, you will start living for today instead of wishing your week away for the weekend, and (2) you will start saving and spending according to the plan that allocates you your dream life.

CALEB'S INTERJECTION

Trevor, I just wanted you to know that I waited as long as I could for my interjection in this chapter. You're welcome.

My cousin raises an intriguing challenge here about envisioning our ideal day both today and in retirement. I know one answer I'd give: "I want to play golf at least once a week with my kids when I'm retired." Sounds fun, right? As the resident doctor, I feel obligated to connect this to our HealthSpan. Something we don't often think about is that our body and overall health in retirement is not going to be the same as it is when we're younger. Right now, I could golf multiple rounds a week and only feel minor back pain. But what about the future? I will have to take active steps now to ensure that I can hit the links regularly with my kiddos when I've been "blessed" by Father Time.

That brings us back to the idea of daily habits. Trevor knows that if you develop good daily habits to maintain the health of your financial plan, you will have a long-lasting WealthSpan. Call him the yin to my yang, because keeping your finances healthy is an idea complemented by and only enjoyed if you also take the time to maintain the opposite area of your life: health.

Daily habits in health include things like exercise, nutrition, mindfulness, gratitude practice, flexibility, and proactive healthcare. You'll read more about those in my chapters.

Whether finances or health, the later you start, the harder it will be. And developing tiny daily habits takes time. You can't go from zero to a hundred push-ups in a day. Regaining flexibility takes years. And you can't go from saving nothing to saving your entire paycheck in one pay cycle.

So get started now. Today is the day. Don't put it off.

And don't forget to read my side of the book when you're done with Trevor's. Or just go there now. Trevor won't mind.

Let's not mince words here. What's at stake is your dream life. When it comes to your finances, it should be related to designing your life around moments and memories, not milestones or material things.

Why? Experiences are known and proven to make you happier

and more successful. Not only will you feel like your money is working for you to give you a fulfilling life, but that joy you receive from taking the time now to take care of yourself will motivate you to do the work necessary to maintain (and reevaluate) your financial goals. The joy you feel will be habit forming, helping you take one step at a time toward happiness for the rest of your life.

THE SIDE EFFECTS OF HAVING A PLAN

For those looking to reduce stress, having a plan is the antidote. What's more, it gives you confidence, enhances your focus and clarity, and improves your resource management. You won't be spending on things that don't align with your purpose.

Over time, it will create a sense of accomplishment and control over your life. On a smaller scale, think about finishing that yard project—like reseeding the lawn, building a garden, or installing a new feature. The end result is imagined and idealized, but the purpose is clear and motivates you to finish. When you're done and look at this completed endeavor, you can't help but point it out to your guests. You did that. On your own. (Hopefully I'm not the only one who takes pride in that sort of thing.)

Getting back to your financial plan, you'll be experiencing something very similar but on a much grander scale. You'll be living your life now with a sense of confidence that later, when you're in your twilight years, you can sip on that French wine in the Rhone Valley (or whatever your retirement dreams are) while reflecting on the purposeful life you lived (and are still living).

When you plan with purpose, everything is in balance. And if one thing's off-balance, then everything's off-balance.

CALEB'S INTERJECTION

Side effects? I'm a medical guy. I can talk about those! There's a bridge here with HealthSpan, where regardless if you are looking to improve your health or finances, hitting milestones—however small, medium, or large—gives you accomplishments to acknowledge. As you start stacking accomplishment, that fires off the reward systems in your brain—neurotransmitters I'll talk about in more detail on my side of the book.

But every time your brain triggers the chemicals associated with success, your body and mind will train itself to be more committed to the cause. When at first a little pile of snow comes down, soon it's an avalanche.

BEHAVIORAL FINANCES: FINANCIAL IMBALANCE MEANS MINDSET IMBALANCE

Another crucial side effect of planning with purpose and taking stock of your wealth goals is that it helps you stay balanced with the mental side of investing.

When you have the right plan, you have the right mindset. Your emotional health shouldn't be spiking all over the place, triggering emotional habits that tell you to get upset when the market's down or lagging in some benchmark indicator. You won't get rattled into selling everything off or making a risky, fast-money investment while sacrificing your long-term purpose and plan.

People without a purpose-driven financial plan are setting themselves up for cognitive biases or preventable errors in judgment. Here are some of the more common biases:

- **Loss aversion:** Losing money on an investment is said to have twice the damaging psychological impact than equivalent gains.

This can create errors in judgment that lead to further losses, such as holding onto losing investments too long, selling winning investments too early, taking excessive risk to recover losses, becoming overly conservative and stripping away your *why*, and generally making choices that ignore your long-term strategy. All of these choices can lead to devastating financial consequences.

- **Overconfidence bias:** This is when an investor thinks they can "beat the system," and it can lead to a lot of bad choices that blow up their financial plan, including excessive trading (which leads to lower net returns), under diversification (which increases risk), and ignoring professional advice.
- **Herd instinct:** There is a perceived safety in numbers and a "social proof" when a lot of investors start jumping on a bandwagon. A problem here is that such choices actually increase volatility and increase the losses associated with buying high and selling low.
- **Mental accounting:** When we don't take inventory of every piece of our financial lives, we might be intentionally playing into the mental accounting bias. That's when we evaluate money differently depending on its source or intended use. For example, we might treat a cash bonus differently to our regular salary, being more apt to spend that bonus instead of aligning its use to our purpose.
- **Emotional gaps:** These gaps are financial decisions based on extreme emotions like fear, anxiety, or excitement. These extremes overtake rationality or the balanced, healthy mindset of making a plan and sticking to a plan.

There is a direct correlation with the clients of financial wealth managers: the worse or more volatile the clients' cognitive and physical health, the more they want to live outside their means, pull out of bad markets, and/or take on risky investments—all of which are actions known to, time and time again, explode a portfolio.

So *unsplode* your portfolio and alleviate these issues by going through the Purposeful Planning Process and designing your wealth and health around a *why*.

MAKE YOUR PLAN, THEN PROTECT IT

Living a fulfilled and purposeful life is as simple as creating a plan that serves your *why*. That sets you on the right path to accomplish what you want to achieve, but there is something else you need to consider: protecting yourself.

If you build a net worth and have purposeful goals, what if something happened and you were not properly protected? What if you are faced with expensive hospital bills? What if somebody sued you? Everything you planned and built could be destroyed in an instant.

Protecting your assets is where we'll turn next.

CHAPTER 4

ASSET PROTECTION: SAFEGUARDING YOUR PERSONAL FINANCES

"Money does not dictate your lifestyle. It's what you do to get it and how you manage your finances that determines your lifestyle."

—WAYNE CHIRISA

One day, I had a new client come into my office. It was kind of a sad deal. She knew she'd be passing on soon. She was there to solidify her legacy. She was at peace, thankfully, having lived a great life.

For her, legacy specifically meant leaving her money to her kids with airtight conditions. (You don't want kids fighting over an estate. It ruins families.) The good news was that she had a clear understanding of her *why*.

The bad news was that she waited too long to plan for her *why*. What made her situation unique? First of all, she was worth a substantial amount of money, around $40 million. But the kicker was that most of that wealth was grown from *within* the estate. The majority of her net worth was in portfolio assets and real estate, all of which was titled in a revocable trust.

At that point, there was nothing I could do to help mitigate estate taxes. There wasn't any time to implement WealthSpan strategies. For individuals like her, the more money you have, the more complex options there are to help maximize things like legacy.

Had she come to me earlier, ideally when she was starting to grow her wealth, she would have been able to plan with purpose and pass on most of it. But it was too late. Her net worth would be subject to estate taxes.

I made it clear to her that $12,060,000 (the amount allowed in 2022) could be passed on free and clear. Everything else was subject to a 40 percent tax. After the complicated math was all said and done, the government walked away with over $11 million—or about 28 percent of her entire net worth was liable to estate tax. That jaw-dropping amount went poof, as if it never existed. Nobody within the family, not even the person who earned it, would ever be able to use that money as a tool to pursue purpose and fulfillment.

Despite her best intentions to plan, the result was exactly what she was hoping to avoid: her kids started fighting. One was grateful for the amount they received, but most of them fought with each other and lashed out at me, even though I was late to the game. They began to distrust advisors and ended up adopting the same non-proactive approach to their inheritance money that she adopted in growing her net worth. Unfortunately, they'll be subject to the same tax situation in a few decades' time.

She and others like her could have taken steps designed to help protect her assets. For her, the goal should have been to get her money outside of her estate and grow it as much as possible as early as possible. But that didn't happen.

And it's not just legacy planning. Assets are lost despite preventative measures all the time—and for all sorts of reasons. Most people have no idea about the liabilities their net worth is subject to, a kind of "ignorance is bliss" that allows them to sleep at night until one day the unthinkable truth comes down on them.

For me, I prefer that my clients be educated on the liabilities surrounding their assets and, in coordination with their purpose, plan on mitigating factors that are designed to help them protect themselves from various events that would otherwise take large chunks of their hard-earned money.

And to be clear, when Caleb and I use the phrase "asset protection" or "asset planning" in this book, we are talking about something specific. We don't mean it in some sort of traditional way—like the legal process of entity formation for businesses. Boring! Instead, we're using our poetic license to refer to an "asset protection" that means something more profound. What we mean by "asset protection" is the consideration of steps designed to help you maximize the longevity of your HealthSpan and WealthSpan.

PROTECT YOUR NET WORTH

A person spends most of their time growing their net worth. That's it. What is often left behind in that equation is the need to take steps designed to protect their net worth.

Here's a wake-up call: your net worth is only as good as the planning you set up to guard it. You can brag to me about the size of your portfolio, but if left to chance, all it takes is something like one lawsuit, one accident, or one bad decision to reduce that number to zero. But asset protection isn't paranoia—it's smart, strategic planning.

A lack of asset protection and asset planning is the most common gap I see when assessing the financial plan that new clients walk in with.

The most common gap is insurance. Four out of five insurance policy structures I see are not done correctly and don't contain the proper coverage based on the client's needs. Part of the reason why is because the majority of the insurance industry, like the financial planning industry, just wants to lock the client into a policy and then never talk to them again.

Agents get paid more for larger policies and premiums, but they have to deal with bulk, so the real incentive is acquiring as many clients as possible and locking them into the basic plans that are known to sell. We'll talk more details about insurance shortly.

It's not just insurance that can protect you. You can also protect yourself by making smart liquidity decisions.

LIQUIDITY EVENTS

It's common for business owners to reinvest all of their money back into the business in an ongoing cycle. They never take anything out. That's great for growing a business but bad for using the business to earn you money to live your life.

But it's not just about taking liquidity out to experience your life. You also need to consider the role that diversification plays in helping to protect your assets.

Think about this. If you are constantly reinvesting in the business, you open yourself up to a huge liability: what if the business goes downhill fast? Having your net worth tied up into one asset is a ticking time bomb for disaster.

I knew somebody in the radio business in the early 2010s. It was very lucrative for him, but with the invention of the podcast, his expected growth sunk, and he turned to damage control. Podcast platforms started offering similar services as his independent radio station but with around-the-clock access. Ultimately, this cost him a lot of revenue. Having not taken any liquidity out of the business to diversify and create a foundation of wealth, he ended up losing it all. Things just fell apart as he couldn't compete with the sudden market changes.

Or I'll occasionally run into a real estate investor whose preference is to do 1031 exchanges—a tax-deferring strategy—to build their portfolio with fewer assets that grow from purchase to purchase. Most end up regretting this strategy, because they'll own mostly real estate assets, be subject to more legal liability and less diversification, and learn a hard lesson when the market goes south or when they finally face those big tax liabilities instead of taking money over time.

I'm here to tell you that any market is vulnerable to similar stories. Taking liquidity out of your assets to live now can give you the freedom to live the lifestyle that you want instead of waiting for a promise that might never come.

Liquidity events are a specific type of equity event where parts of a company's shares or value is converted into liquid cash. It creates freedom. Keep three-to-six months of planned cash needs in low-volatility reserves. It buys discipline when markets misbehave. Also, diversify into stock, bonds, and alternative investments, giving you more control when the markets change.

Track net-worth trends and goal funding ratios quarterly. Small, consistent upticks matter more than beating a benchmark every month.

THE ASSET PROTECTION PYRAMID

Growing wealth is only half of the equation. The other challenge is preserving it by shielding it from lawsuits, taxes, and unexpected life events. That's one thing that sets apart the organization I've built from other service providers.

You will benefit from "restructuring" your financial plan. Choosing that word isn't an accident. Like sound structures, you need to make sure every component of the structure—from the bottom to the tippy top—has the strength and integrity to withstand any market earthquakes.

To build a structure that can provide protection, think of it as a pyramid that must be built first from a robust foundational layer and then add strength upward from there. Here is how it would look.

BASE LAYER: INSURANCE

A majority of people need to start with simple insurance.

I say "simple insurance," but it's probably more than what most people already have. Home insurance and auto insurance are common.

But insurance should also include proper umbrella insurance, life insurance, and long-term care insurance to fit the nuance of your net worth and purpose. In fact, the biggest gaps I see in this layer are underinsured umbrella policies, outdated life insurance, and no long-term care plans.

Let's break down the nonnegotiable insurance protections.

High-Limit Home and Auto Insurance

These policies will cover property damage and liability. Keep in mind, they must reflect your net worth and the true value of the property itself. For example, many homes increased in value during the COVID-19 pandemic, but very few homeowners increased the coverage to reflect that value—a big problem. Never carry insurance with outdated values.

Last thing: if your house or auto are titled in a trust name or an LLC, that will need to show on the insurance policy itself as an additional insured.

Umbrella Liability Insurance

Most umbrella policies will add around $1 million in extra liability coverage above home and auto policies. If you have a higher net worth, you'll need much more than that. Holding these policies is critical in preventing high-risk exposures. And in the event you're sued, you can let the insurance company attorneys fight on your behalf.

Umbrella policies themselves require minimum coverage for home and auto, so make sure you're meeting those minimums.

Life Insurance

These provide tax-free liquidity if someone dies. It can also pay for estate taxes in advanced trust structures, wealth transfer, and trust funding. It needs to be an amount appropriate for your net worth and income. If you're making $400K a year, a $1 million policy will only cover expenses for two-and-a-half years. It simply won't be enough. What about college tuition for your kids—if you have kids? What about debts? What about retirement for your spouse? There are so many factors to consider here that might add to the appropriate amount of life insurance. Talk with your Wealth Manager to find that number.

Long-Term Care Insurance

This will cover the growing expense of certain treatments like Alzheimer's care or nursing home or in-home care costs, which can run into the thousands per month. The earlier you set this up, the better (and cheaper). What is the risk, exactly? It helps pay roughly $4,000 to $8,000 per month for regular care—things that help with personal care and daily living. If around-the-clock care is required, that price is much more substantial—think tens of thousands of dollars per month. This insurance will cover those bills.

For those with enough net worth, consider choosing to self-insure this risk. The benefits of doing so are two-fold. First, you'll likely end up paying lower premiums. And second, self-insuring allows for greater flexibility when it comes to options and limitations.

Costs will vary depending on options for in-home care or assisted living communities. Consider your purpose here: Do you want a policy that gives you the option of staying in your home as long as possible? Or are you okay with joining a community?

For some, medical conditions require them to live in specialty nursing homes that can provide the specific care they need. Monthly costs range depending on whether you want a semi-private or private room, with the highest costs potentially exceeding $12,000 per month.

My advice is to set up long-term care insurance through your trusted financial planner rather than using an agent, as your planner *should* have more trusted connections in this industry.

Putting It All Together

When it comes to this base layer, not only will insurance do the bulk of asset protection and asset planning for you, it's also the cheapest and least complex protection to implement.

What's more, you need to regularly evaluate your insurance needs. What if you bought your dream vacation home and insured it at the purchase price, it doubles in value in a decade's time, and then is destroyed in a fire? Your insurance may only reimburse you for half its real value.

MIDDLE LAYER: LEGAL STRUCTURES

Next, consider how your various assets might be creating liability for you as a legal entity. For example, maybe you have a rental property in your own name. That looks good for your net worth, but you're liable for *anything* that happens at that property.

What if somebody trips and falls there? What if you are sued by an amount that goes over and above your insurance? In that situation, *all* of your other personal property, expected income, and assets would be on the line.

The biggest gaps I see in this layer are improper titling, such as no LLCs for rental or vacation properties and outdated or missing estate documents. There are ways you can use legal structures to your advantage, though. Let's look at a few.

LLCs for Real Estate

As I mentioned, the owner of a property is liable for what happens on that property. It's therefore a good idea to keep real estate holdings in separate LLCs to wall your other assets off from the liability rental properties would otherwise expose you to. Or consider Series LLCs, which is one entity but can have multiple assets within it that are all shielded from each other.

Proper Titling

If you are married and your home is jointly titled, you are actually opening yourselves up to additional liability. If one spouse is sued, the other spouse's assets are vulnerable. With proper titling, assets are owned in a way that aligns with the estate and liability plan and lessens the liability you can be sued for. Additionally, if one spouse is in a high-risk industry, where there is a higher chance of being sued or held personally liable, the asset should be in the other spouse's name. Doctors do this often.

Buy-Sell Agreements and Succession Plans

As a business owner, what if you were to unexpectedly pass away? Would your business partner receive your portion of the business? Would it pass on to your kids or spouse? Your business partner probably didn't join the venture to be in business with your spouse. Is there no plan, and everyone will be going to court?

Buy-sell agreements and succession plans are crucial legal contracts so that owners know exactly what will happen to the business after a divorce, death, disability, or departure—the "triggering event." It prevents unwanted outside parties from trying to take control of the business but also the finances involved. Also consider incorporating a key man insurance policy that pays out the family of the partner that passed away.

Revocable Living Trusts

These documents let you manage and transfer assets during your life and distribute them after you pass away, avoiding probate, maintaining privacy, and ensuring a smooth wealth transfer.

It doesn't protect these assets from creditors, but the details of the trust aren't public record (like a will), meaning that you'll be less of a target from lawsuits.

Putting It All Together

For this layer, structure is everything. If you layer your assets smartly in separate LLCs and create airtight legal documents, then your assets will be walled off and protected.

TOP LAYER: ADVANCED STRATEGIES

As you continue to build protections, you can place firewalls *within* your structures so that liability doesn't bleed into other areas of a structure.

Irrevocable Trusts

This is where trusts come in, for example. Trusts create a legal barrier that shields assets and make them inaccessible to creditors or lawsuits, helping you direct your money in a manner (and at increments) as carried out by the trustee. They also move money out of your estate for an advanced tax strategy.

A trust has to be properly structured and irrevocable, meaning that it generally cannot be changed once it's established.

Asset Protection Trusts

An asset protection trust (APT) shields your wealth from future lawsuits or creditors. It can be domestic or offshore, and each has their own benefits and drawbacks. There is often a mandatory waiting period before the assets are protected, and different states have different rules.

Family Limited Partnerships (FLPs)

These entities are created to keep central control of and hold family assets. They help in the gifting of equity to heirs and create specific roles for family members in the facilitation of wealth transfer. They can offer tax advantages for estate planning.

Charitable Trusts

These blend philanthropy with tax efficiency and income planning. Some people can reduce their tax burden while also arranging for a trustee to manage funds for charitable purposes. Additionally, certain structures can help with income during retirement and pass any remaining money over to a charity (or charities). This is a legacy strategy that helps a person give back to causes that matter to them while also protecting their own assets.

Strategic Gifting

You can gift up to a certain amount—to your kids, grandkids, or spouse, for example—to separate yourself from assets, thus preventing those assets from being accessed through litigation if you were to be sued. The level of protection depends heavily on timing, structure, and the intent for making the gift.

Perhaps more commonly, using annual and lifetime exclusions can reduce your estate size, which is an important thing to do if you are over the estate limit. As I've written elsewhere, at the time of writing (2026), anything over $15 million per person (or $30 million per married couple) will be taxed at a rate of 40 percent. Those estate tax figures could change in future years. One of the many ways to get money out of the estate to avoid this tax is strategic gifting.

Each year, you can give $19,000 to your spouse and each child or grandchild. If you're married, you and your spouse can give that amount. So one child, for example, might receive up to $38,000 that is no longer subject to the estate tax (and won't be taxed upon transfer).

Some "gifts" are unlimited. Tuition and medical bills fall under this category since they don't count, from the point of view of the IRS, as a gift.

Irrevocable Life Insurance Trusts (ILITs)

This legal arrangement lets you transfer a life insurance policy for the purposes of keeping the proceeds out of the estate and tax-free. These provide significant tax savings, especially if you're over the estate limit. This will help you pay for estate taxes that you assumed in the estate because the proceeds from the life insurance were outside of the estate.

Putting It All Together

Advanced strategies such as these are only really necessary if you're approaching the estate limit, in terms of your next worth. In 2026, that limit is $15 million for an individual or $30 million for a married couple. If you're over that limit, you'll be subject to a 40 percent tax on your estate. Keep in mind that legislation can change these details at any time. Nonetheless, you should implement these strategies to maintain your wealth and desired legacy.

Very few people will need these advanced strategies, but even those that do will often have gaps that need to be filled. Common gaps are no irrevocable trusts or gifting strategy to lower their tax burden. Or there will be no multigenerational governance plan in place.

THE TOP FIVE LAWSUIT TRIGGERS

It's time to talk about the most common ways that unprotected people lose their money from lawsuits. Keep in mind, the more affluent the person, the more they will be a target of litigation.

Don't believe me? Here's an example. It used to be common practice for doctors to acquire special license plates that identified the car as being owned by a doctor. This was done in case of an emergency. Called out to help somebody, the doctor could park quickly (and illegally) to rush to a patient's aid. The license plate would indicate to the meter maid (or whoever) that this car, in fact, had a reason to be there.

Over time, it was shown that, of all the doctors who were being sued, a growing majority of them had this special indicator on their license plate. The thinking was that these plates marked them as potential targets for more "accidents" that made them, high-net-worth doctors, the defendant of a lawsuit.

The point is that your net worth, especially if it is significant, makes you a target. And the US has the most lawyers per capita in the world, thirteen times more than the second most.

1. DRIVERS IN THE HOUSEHOLD

Car accidents happen all the time. In fact, Caleb will tell you that it's far more likely that you'll die from a car accident on the way to a surgery than a complication from one of his surgeries themselves. But among those driving in the household, teenagers tend to lead the pack because of their riskier behavior.

Cars themselves are expensive, as are the medical bills involved with injury. Add it all together, and drivers create a major liability. Through friends of mine in the financial field, I hear all of the horror-story examples.

One that stuck with me was a woman who, unfortunately, passed out while driving. She sadly passed away and killed the teenage driver of the car she hit. Her husband, who was in the passenger's seat, survived. A head-on collision.

Even though he had nothing to do with the causation of the accident, his assets were tied to hers, and he was sued for over a million dollars. They didn't have any umbrella insurance, which would have covered the payout and attorney's fees.

He wanted to focus on the grief of his wife passing, but instead he was fighting for his financial survival. He ended up losing everything, both his wife and his money.

For any drivers in the household, you are responsible for them as if you were driving.

2. RENTAL PROPERTIES

I talked a little bit about this already. But just like you are responsible for drivers, so too are you responsible for what happens on any property you own. Accidents on rental properties become another major source of lawsuits.

Somebody fell off the roof of your rental property? You're getting sued. Somebody tripped going up the stairs? You're getting sued. The causes are really endless. Hopefully, if you've structured things right, your LLC is getting sued and your other assets are protected.

Fault doesn't really matter here. It's easy to think, "Hey, this wasn't my fault. That guy climbed up to the roof and made a reckless choice." Doesn't matter. It's your property. You are responsible. So make sure you carefully vet your renters.

3. PERSONAL EMPLOYEES

Whether you own a business with paid employees or hire a contractor to come out to your house to work on something for you, they can sue you if they get hurt.

It's the same story as rental properties, in a way. That story is when somebody is employed by you and directed by you, their actions, in many ways, are now your actions. If a judge determines that the circumstances were preventable and largely created by the employment conditions, then you might be out of luck.

4. RECREATIONAL TOYS

Boats, ATVs, trampolines, and pools are really, really fun. They are also lawsuit magnets.

These are things that make us social, right? We want to buy a boat to enjoy a nice day on the lake with our friends. So what happens when, while skiing, your friend's cord gets caught on a rock, falls off their skis, and suffers a debilitating injury? You're going to get sued.

Here's a thought experiment. Imagine a teenager's birthday party.

It was supposed to be a day where everyone (parents and kids alike) could focus on the important things like connecting, having a good time, and cake. But an accident is looming. This particular party featured four wheelers, and the kids were having a ball tooling them around the property.

One unfortunate kid was on a four wheeler that, unbeknownst to him, was in need of some maintenance work. While on it, and going very fast, the column broke, and he flipped over the handlebars and suffered significant injuries. Thankfully, he didn't suffer life-threatening injuries. However, long-term, he will have problems for the rest of his life.

Unfortunately, there wasn't *any* insurance on the four wheeler. That meant, too, that there was no umbrella insurance meant to cover large liabilities like hospital bills and any litigated penalties (and the attorney fees associated with litigation).

What would happen next? The father, a high-net-worth individual with millions in assets, will get sued. When the dust settles, nearly half of his net worth will disappear just because he didn't have a simple and relatively cheap (compared to his net worth) insurance protection in place. We're talking about a $115 per-month insurance policy that could have protected millions.

And let's not stop there. Through the whole process, the father would have had to miss a lot of work to focus on the court battle of being sued, which would further drain his expected income.

These kinds of financial headaches are extremely preventable.

Sure, as the wealth manager, I might not be the right guy to set up specific insurance policies, but managers often act as the quarterback of a larger team. Since I have an understanding of your *why*—and we've built your plan to serve your purpose—I (or someone like me) would flag these gaps and connect you with insurance agents or estate attorneys that can shore up your WealthSpan. I'll talk more about your financial team in a later chapter.

5. BUSINESS OWNERSHIP CROSS-CONTAMINATION

Business owners and entrepreneurs tend to excel in their specific expertise. They are really good at making a product or service that customers love. Maybe they can market and scale growth a little bit, but they are not a business person first and foremost. Their passion, generally, is their service or product.

That usually leads to improper business and entity structuring that can create problems later. Without proper titling and the wrong number of LLCs, business owners may be pooling too much of their assets in one place and opening themselves up to liability.

Once, I found $30 million in a client's business accounts. There was nothing walling it off. Most of it wasn't FDIC insured, for one thing. And since it was all just sitting there, he was slowly losing money to inflation (despite earning a small bit of interest from the bank). This guy was in the construction industry, meaning the many employees he put on (dangerous) job sites and the lucrative projects themselves were all magnets for accidents that would put those accounts in danger.

I moved quickly, keeping operational expenses in his accounts but moving other funds out to set up a few layers of much-needed protection.

PROTECT YOURSELF BY TRUSTING YOUR TEAM

It's so important that you build a team of financial professionals that, as I previously mentioned, I'll devote an entire chapter to the topic later. But I do want to return to the client I spoke about in the introduction of this chapter, whose net worth shrank by over $11 million after she was subject to estate taxes.

Situations like hers happen to wealth managers and financial planners all the time. Then the kids come to us and, somewhat angry at us, ask us why their parents didn't implement a variety of strategies to mitigate estate taxes. We get blamed.

The problem, of course, is that wealth managers can only lead a horse to water, but they can't make the horse drink. We are advisors. And many clients don't take the advice of their advisors, their CPAs, or their trust attorneys. They don't delegate things to the professionals. They do their own research. Or they put off planning for years. These are all ingredients for a bad situation.

Ideally, wealth managers or financial advisors need to holistically plan for the client, helping them mold a unique plan centered on their *why*. (Most don't help protect a client's assets because they don't get paid to do it.) That means clients are responsible for finding and vetting proactive and trustworthy wealth managers so that the client can delegate and go live their lives.

CALEB'S INTERJECTION

For a second, I thought Trevor was talking about the medical industry. Let me explain.

The same general principles Trevor outlines here are also true in medicine. I should know; I've been a medical practitioner for almost two decades. Financial advisors are only incentivized to grow wealth because that's all they are paid for—not the extra steps to help protect assets. Most doctors, too, are only incentivized to *treat* their already sick patients because that's the only thing they can get reimbursements for. Doctors, generally, are not paid to practice proactive, protective, or preventative medicine. In my half of the book, I'll talk to you about building a health team designed to focus on functional, proactive medicine so that you can beat the system and maximize your HealthSpan. And while you wait for that very exciting read, please consider finding someone like Trevor that actually does care about all of these various aspects of your WealthSpan. Because if your person is not looking out for you in these various categories, then you're not maximizing yourself and your potential.

ASSET PROTECTION IS A NONNEGOTIABLE

There are too many liabilities for you to ignore asset protection. It needs to be nonnegotiable. Know your goals, inventory your net worth, and take steps to help protect yourself with the right strategies based on that information.

Once you dig into the numbers, you can create the foundational and layered strategies that will help give you confidence in the longevity of your WealthSpan. When you have a solid plan, you can feel reassured and turn your attention back to doing what you need to do to balance your earnings and live a purposeful life today and into the future.

CHAPTER 5

PREVENTATIVE CARE: HOW TO KEEP YOUR FINANCES MAXIMIZED

"A man who does not plan long ahead will find trouble right at his door."

—CONFUCIUS

As the saying goes, pigs get fat and hogs get slaughtered. I'll translate for anybody not from the country: getting greedy leads to negative consequences.

So anytime there's a runup in the market, many investors—hogs in this situation—want to be all in on certain stocks. They don't want to be properly diversified. Chasing returns using this kind of bandwagon mentality usually leads to one of two results: (1) they are late to the game, missing out on the returns and lowering their overall return rate (buying high and selling low), or (2) their lack of diversity exposes them to a downturn in the market. Both can explode and destroy the value of their portfolio.

I had a friend who practiced this chase-returns strategy. When the market was in a downturn, his limited stocks were down 50 percent. His financial plan called for a steady monthly retirement income from selling stocks to supply that cash. Well, during the downturn, he had to sell twice as many stocks just to provide his monthly cash needs.

For those who are in the upper echelons of net worth, that might not be a big deal. But for most investors, selling double your expected assets will greatly diminish the life of that portfolio's WealthSpan. Unfortunately, for my friend, his financial plan blew up. He had to go back to work during his planned retirement. Finding that work to make ends meet proved difficult. He confided in me that he believed his age made it so that very few people wanted to hire him.

As a wealth manager, I *never* want that scenario to happen to one of my clients. That's why it's a nonnegotiable at my practice that clients have intentional planning, proper allocation, and time horizons. If they aren't interested in mapping those out, then I'm not interested in working with them. So when I tell you that it's a nonnegotiable, I want you to realize that I mean it. If it's not something that you can commit to, then I am not your guy. I am here to take you to a new level of preparation and planning, which you won't regret.

CALEB'S INTERJECTION

Trevor can really lay the hammer down sometimes, can't he? But he makes a good point. I'm a doctor, but sometimes the occasional stock chase makes me fancy myself a professional investor.

The truth is, though, I don't have a degree in finances. I have a medical degree. So I need to be clear with myself: I'm not a professional investor. Just because I went to school forever and accrued a lot of student loan debt doesn't make me a genius at everything. But guess who is a genius at investing? My wealth manager.

If I didn't delegate those finances to somebody trained in that area, I would expose myself to a greater chance of ruining my finances. Similarly, thinking we know how to treat a serious medical condition better than a medical professional can also ruin our health—destroying assets essential to living a purposeful life.

FINANCIAL HEALTH AND YOUR BODY OF ASSETS

When talking about markets during a ten-year period, we'll probably have three bad years. Those *will* be years where our assets (and net worth) stand to lose value. Market fluctuations are an inevitable truth that nobody can completely avoid. But we can invest in prevention by mitigating and lessening the damage caused by these market downturns.

In other words, planning for "bad years" will help you maximize your WealthSpan and overall financial health. We need to have a plan in place that can weather the storms as well as promote growth during the sunny days—that sort of plan becomes the ideal tool for living a purposeful life.

There are, of course, many ways to plan for preventive action in our finances. One of my philosophies when I work with clients is that everything needs to be in balance and aligned with a purpose. It might be helpful, then, to think of our finances as a living body, where interconnected systems—like the circulatory, immune, and skeletal systems—thrive if they are all working together and kept in tip-top shape. Let's look at preventative systems that help maximize our WealthSpan.

1. CASH FLOW

Think of cash flow like your circulatory and respiratory systems. They are the oxygen and lifeblood of your financial life. Without them, there is nothing. Even the most sophisticated investors and highest-net-worth individuals can suffocate themselves without healthy circulation of cash flow.

And when people run out of cash, at best, they usually need a transfusion of cash by selling off another asset. At worst, they'll have to file for bankruptcy—closing the book on their portfolio.

Cash flow, of course, depends on the financial plan and the budget—and the client's ability to stick to their plan. The budget and cash flow needs are determined by the *why*. What experiences will make them happy? What kind of life do they want to live? How can they live within their means? These are the types of things that will determine a healthy cash flow.

There are many things that can cause cash flow to dry up. Straying too far from the plan and spending more than budgeted—such as through an irregular distribution—will burn assets and implode the portfolio. An example of an irregular distribution might be needing to pull out cash to pay for a new car. If the investor is in private equity, capital calls can create a demand that the investor produce $50,000 to $100,000 dollars for the investment and drain cash flow expectations quickly. Another example would be irrational liquidity decisions, such as selling when the market is down.

When cash dries up and needs to be replenished to pay the bill or maintain the lifestyle, that's when assets have to be sold at a loss, which diminishes your net worth and WealthSpan. It's like a double-loss. Reluctantly selling that rental property or luxury car will also have a major impact on your emotional health—those things sting.

Cash Forecasts

Although the long-term financial plan will set much of the cash flow needs, that doesn't mean adjustments can't be made to fit a modified purpose and maximize the health of your WealthSpan.

This can be accomplished by twelve- or eighteen-month rolling cash flow forecasts. Combining these with the overall financial plan will ensure you have both short-term and long-term views of your cash flow. Maybe you need to remodel your kitchen this year, but that wasn't in your financial plan when you set it up ten years ago. By forecasting your needs, you are keeping everything balanced. If you own investment real estate, map out when you might need to replace the carpet, roof, cabinets, etc. Incorporate those items into the forecast to improve accuracy and have fewer surprises.

Tiered Liquidity Buckets

Investments can be categorized by how easily they can convert into cash. They are put in different "buckets" or categories and utilized to ensure funds are readily available. More accessible tiers can meet short-term needs while helping less accessible assets hum away for higher, long-term returns.

It's about having the right type of investment for the right period of time. For short-term needs, that would typically be more bonds. Mid-term needs would typically be stocks and bonds mixed together. They are built to keep up with or outpace inflation slightly, but they grow enough and can be converted into cash. Long-term investments would be more stocks and other assets meant to grow and outpace inflation over time.

Guaranteed Income

More and more workplaces are getting rid of pensions—monthly guaranteed income after working. Do you like the idea of a pension? If yes, then you also like the idea of an annuity. Every product has a place, even if you don't like the word "annuity." I'm here to tell you that annuities are essentially like pensions, and you have the opportunity to pay yourself a guaranteed income for the rest of your life—cash straight into your pocket.

Although you'll be paying an insurance company for an annuity, your money will grow with tax-deferred benefits. During the payout phase, usually during retirement, you'll get fixed payments for a set of years or the rest of your life.

Ultimately, these are not usually suitable for high-net-worth investors unless you are really risk averse. Why? Usually, it's because high-net-worth individuals find it worth it to let their assets grow while tolerating the risk in favor of lower distribution rates. They're not worried about running out of money. They want their money to work for them.

But for some folks, maybe they are worried about having enough money in retirement. Annuities are a form of guaranteed income if that's the case.

Putting It All Together

You need cash flow for a healthy WealthSpan. If you are a status spender who blows up your budget, you've got some work to do. Shift into meaning-spending by going back and doing the mindset shift to focus your financial plan on your *why*.

You have permission to have the things in your life that bring you joy. You have to choose to make this a nonnegotiable, but do it responsibly within your budget and plan. Use your discretionary spending to improve your passion, drive, and other elements of your mental health that will actually grow your WealthSpan over time rather than diminish it.

The good thing about cash flow is that, like blood and air quality, it can be predictable, flexible, and aligned to an individual.

2. DIVERSIFICATION

Properly and purposefully diversifying assets within the financial plan is like a body's long-term nutritional health. If you start early, it'll pay major dividends later. If you neglect it, you'll open yourself up to unnecessary liability that could jeopardize your future.

Further, too much of any one asset—no matter how "healthy"—creates an imbalance. Diversification helps your wealth absorb shocks, support growth, and stay resilient.

And there are clear signs when you're not diversified enough. If you are overconcentrated in one area—like a business, real estate, or public equities—then you lack diversification. For example, a friend of mine dabbled in fix-and-flip real estate investments. He wanted to save money on labor, so he did all of the work himself. Needing access to these homes meant he bought in his local area, which opened himself up to the market fluctuations of that microclimate. When home prices plummeted, he wasn't just going to lose money on one of them—he lost money on all of them. If he had owned properties in different cities, counties, or states, the losses of having one of them slide in price could have minimized loss from being protected by the other unaffected markets.

Another problem you might run into is high correlation, or assets that all behave similarly. When things are going good, high correlation feels great! It's like you're winning the lottery. But what happens when there's a downturn in the market? Gains go kaput. It's better to have a mix of assets to help prevent the drawbacks of high correlation.

There are other prevention and maximization strategies to consider.

Blended Portfolio

I've already alluded to the concept of a blended portfolio. But this is when the portfolio includes different types of assets from across public, private, and alternative markets (and many different kinds of markets) to protect against market fluctuation. If one type of asset suffers a setback, the others are there to keep the portfolio moving toward its goals.

Real Estate, Bonds, and SMAs

High-net-worth individuals can create a diversified portfolio with appreciation potential, reliable income, customization tailored to their purpose, and tax efficiency when they combine real estate, municipal bonds, and separately managed accounts (SMAs).

In these situations, real estate usually acts as the long-term anchor for growth and cash flow. In turn, the bonds provide a lower risk and tax-advantaged income stream to fund lifestyle expenses while also providing reinvestment opportunities.

And the SMAs customize everything for individualized plans. That's because SMAs give you direct ownership of individual stocks and bonds, providing precise control to align the portfolio with your purpose and goals. You own each holding, not a pooled vehicle like a mutual fund. You have similar customization with your tax considerations, as owning securities directly allows somebody to harvest tax loss as an individual, creating a customized tax exposure and aligning.

Alternative Investments

Well-diversified portfolios usually utilize alternative investments to play an important role in pursuing long-term growth while managing and taking steps that can help protect oneself from risk. Used well, they are a great diversifying complement to the portfolio or plan. Why? Quite simply, they used to be available to large institutions, huge endowment funds, and ultra-high-net-worth individuals. Now things have changed. You can access these as part of a broader investment plan.

Diversity with alternative investments—such as structured notes, structured ETFs, and private equity—is possible because they tend to behave differently than traditional investments. The end game of that scenario is less volatility.

Taking a position on alternative investments can be a natural next step once a portfolio grows, more net worth is accumulated, and new investment opportunities should be looked at to implement a broader investment approach. And while I'm here to focus on alternative investments as a diversity play, that's not the only purpose. Some provide defined outcomes that may be advantageous to growth while never appearing in public forums, such as a stock exchange.

As your alternative investment strategies take shape—and as you become a more sophisticated investor—consider the different purposes of structured notes, structured ETFs, and private equity within a well-designed portfolio.

Structured Notes

For investors who are looking to hedge against the uncertainty of the rising and falling of traditional investment markets, structured notes are an investment strategy designed to create specific outcomes over a defined period of time. Rather than experience the volatility of a regular market, notes create more defined parameters of risk and return. And they are offered by financial institutions, such as investment brokerages.

The way in which they are structured can vary wildly depending on the particular strategy, but they may offer enhanced income potential and a buffer against a certain level of market losses. For example, a structured note can provide a defined buffer against market downside. Let's say a particular note offers a 15 percent downside buffer. That means that the investor may not experience a loss in the investment if there is, let's say, a 10 percent decline in the market.

Structured ETFs

Sometimes known as buffer ETFs—*an* "exchange traded fund"—the idea here is to provide some downside protection to hedge against loss while also capping the potential upside within a defined period of time. Like the structured notes, structured ETFs have defined investment parameters. Essentially, you are agreeing to a limitation on upside in order to receive limited protection from downside.

This option provides liquidity since it is traded on public exchanges. For times of market volatility where investors want to participate but are looking for a little bit more risk management, the structured ETF is a useful strategy.

Private Equity

Public markets are only a small portion of the business world. The truth is that more than 99 percent of businesses in the US are privately owned. And over 80 percent of companies generating more than $100 million in annual revenue are held privately. Even though public stock exchanges and markets let investors participate, the vast majority of economic growth is fueled by private companies that exist outside the public markets.

That's where private equity comes in, which allows investors to directly participate in private business by providing capital in varying investment capacities, including growth capital, buyout funds, venture capital, and secondary investments. Two things here that you need to keep in mind if you're considering private equity as part of your plan. First, private equity usually requires longer time horizons, typically lasting between five to ten years.

Second, private equity is usually only available to accredited investors. What is an accredited investor? Usually, it means a net worth of at least $1 million (not including primary residency), and an annual income of over $200,000. This requirement exists because of SEC regulations designed to protect individual investors from risk. Regulators assume that accredited investors have the financial savvy and ability to sustain any possible downside from the investment.

Portfolio Rebalancing and Risk Alignment

If one asset goes down, the others tend to stay put. When you rebalance, the usual move is to sell assets that are higher in value, buy some asset classes that have gone down a little bit (and can be viewed as at a discounted price), and then wait for those to rebalance.

Periodically, you should work with your financial advisor or wealth manager to consider rebalancing your portfolio to reflect your overall financial plan, your purpose, and your risk tolerance. Your team of professionals will be able to consult you on how and why certain allocations of assets present risk, what those risks are, and how those risks align with your time horizon and needs.

Putting It All Together

Just like a varied diet supports immune health and energy, diversified wealth fuels both opportunity and well-being.

3. INSURANCE

I talked at length about the need and purpose of insurance in the previous chapter, so I'll make an effort to be brief here. But I return to it to emphasize insurance's preventative role (not just protective role) in maximizing your WealthSpan. To keep the extended metaphor going, insurance acts as the immune system, that thing lurking in the background as a defense against catastrophic attacks.

One uninsured event can erase decades of planning and earning. Insurance is not just a policy; it preserves the health of the entire system.

The uninsured or underinsured, as you now know, are subject to lawsuits and liability. Without coverage, especially for high-risk or specialty assets (recall the ATV story?), your entire net worth could be lost with one accident.

Let's look at some prevention strategies.

Annual Policy Review

It's important to schedule a comprehensive policy review annually. This encourages proactive and preventative measures to make sure that policies meet the needs of your financial plan and provide you with the necessary coverage.

These reviews will also help you make sure that the policies are clear, compliant, and align with strategic goals, adjusting as necessary.

Customized Insurance

Future NFL Hall of Fame tight end Jimmy Graham, you may or may not know, is an avid pilot. If you followed his career at all, you understood that he played football to essentially fund his dream of flying various aircraft every day of his life.

Jimmy Graham has a unique purpose driving his financial plan. Part of maintaining the health of that WealthSpan is customizing his insurance needs. Guess what that means for him? Aviation insurance.

Are you going to need aviation insurance? Probably not. But there are other customizable insurance policies you need. The most common will be umbrella insurance to cover what regular insurance doesn't to limit liability. You might also own a collector's item or unique valuable that requires its own insurance. Or if you run a large software company, you may need cybersecurity insurance to protect you against the liabilities from a cyberattack or data breach. These are just a few examples, and the takeaway here is that there might need to be a customized aspect of your insurance policies.

Consider Your Net Worth

One of the biggest gaps I see with insurance is that a client's policies do not provide an appropriate amount of coverage compared to their net worth.

Go back to Chapter 3 and inventory your net worth, then combine that with the comprehensive policy review. Standard insurance policies might not cover enough for your entire net worth to be protected in the event of an accident. That might mean adding additional policies to cover that gap.

Putting It All Together

A healthy immune system doesn't prevent every risk, but it ensures you survive, recover, and remain intact. Insurance does the same.

But insurance isn't just a catastrophic event in the present. It's also preventing challenges in the future. As we age, insurance provides long-term care plans that most medical insurance won't cover. I've talked about that elsewhere, and it is worth noting.

4. TAX STRATEGIES

Taxes quietly erode the financial plan you've put in place. For the body of your financial health, then, taxes are like inflammation that erodes the body silently over time, diminishing what should have otherwise been very healthy.

When you turn over your portfolio a lot—buying and selling and buying and selling—that creates short-term capital gains, which are all taxed at ordinary income rates. That's tax drag. If you hold on to an asset for more than a year, it is likely to be taxed at a lower rate, minimizing the negative impact of taxes and maximizing your WealthSpan. If not managed properly, tax drag will be the biggest fee you pay.

There are many symptoms that could tell you if you suffer from tax drag. The most painful are the large, unplanned April tax bills that come from not planning for a tax event properly. Maybe you sell your business, thinking only of the large number you've sold it for and not the tax liability of selling it.

Difficult-to-spot symptoms include missing a window for deductions or gifting. Depending on your situation, there may be a slew of tax strategies and deferrals that allow you to keep more of your money now to grow and compound. Or, somewhat conversely, you might be missing opportunities to get your net worth down to avoid estate taxes.

How you invest your money could also be creating financial inflammation, tax-wise. REITs (real estate investment trust) and high-yield bond funds are highly susceptible to taxes, whereas tax-efficient asset locations like Roth IRAs might be right for you to create tax-free growth in retirement.

These are just a few examples of what may happen. But there are many prevention strategies you can implement.

Tax and Bracket Planning

Starting in November at the latest, start looking at your tax liability. Find out your job's income, the portfolio's income, and anything else that might bump you up into a new tax bracket. You need to know and plan for what bracket you'll be in. If you are able, you should do projections for as many years forward as you can to help you prepare.

Tax planning helps you be more proactive instead of reactive, helping you identify any opportunities to implement strategies and reduce what you owe.

Equity Events

An equity event is a significant financial transaction that allows an individual to convert their ownership or position in a business into liquid assets. This can include the sale of a business, cashing in stock options, or receiving a stock payout.

They are often once-in-a-lifetime opportunities, but they also come with major tax and legal implications. To reduce or defer the tax burden of an equity event, you could implement strategies like capital gains optimization, qualified small business stock, charitable planning, installment sales, and residency planning.

Entity Structuring

For business owners, how you structure your entities has a major impact on your tax liability. If you choose an LLC, your entire net profit will be subject to self-employment tax (15.3 percent). If you choose an S-Corp, you can pay yourself a "reasonable" salary, pay regular taxes on that salary, and distribute the rest of your profits, which are not subject to FICA taxes.

What is best for you depends on a lot of factors, but your entity structure will be a tax-preventative measure.

Gifting Strategies

In 2026, if you want to lower your estate tax burden or avoid wealth transfer taxes, you can gift up to $19K (or $38K per married couple) per person to any number of recipients. That includes a lifetime exemption of $15 million per individual. If you're reading this in the future, these numbers have likely changed slightly.

You can also donate appreciated assets to avoid tax liability on the asset's value while simultaneously writing off the entire value of that asset. For example, let's say you buy a stock at $10 and donate it while it's valued at $100. You will not be subject to tax on the $90 increase but be able to write off the entire $100 on your tax return.

Asset Location Reviews

As we discussed before, your assets may not be in tax-efficient places. Make sure you do regular reviews with your CPA and wealth manager to make sure you are maximizing your HealthSpan by keeping a healthy balance of asset allocation.

Tax-Loss Harvesting

In some situations, it is actually better for your tax plan to sell some assets at a loss to offset capital gains to reduce your tax liability.

The win-win here is that it allows you to use underperforming investments in an advantageous way, increasing your after-tax returns.

There is a caveat to keep in mind when seeking out tax-loss harvesting. It's called the "30-day wash-sale rule." Essentially, it prevents somebody from claiming the loss of a stock or security if the same or "substantially identical" stock is purchased thirty days before or after said sale. It's a somewhat poorly named rule because it's actually a sixty-one-day window: thirty days before the sale, the day of the sale, and thirty days after.

Income Layering

This is primarily a retirement-income strategy that draws money from various "tax buckets," or accounts that are taxed differently. For example, your financial plan might call for your monthly retirement income to draw from taxable accounts, tax-deferred accounts, and tax-free accounts to keep you in a lower tax bracket and/or minimize your lifetime tax burden.

Common taxed accounts are things like brokerage accounts (stocks, bonds, etc.), CDs, high-yield savings. You'll pay traditional taxes on these earnings. Tax-deferred accounts could be traditional IRAs or 401(k)s. And tax-free accounts include Roth IRAs and Roth 401(k)s.

Strategic Asset Location

You can reduce annual taxable income and optimize capital gains through this strategy. Essentially, the idea here is to put tax-efficient assets in taxable accounts and vice versa. So if you were to put municipal bonds (which are tax-exempt) in your brokerage account (which is taxable), you'd be reducing the taxes associated with the brokerage account. Or you could put a REIT investment (which is subject to regular tax) in your IRA (which defers taxes). Strategies like these are designed to minimize your "tax drag" and keep more of your money to compound over time. But most people will want money in tax-deferred accounts, taxable accounts, and Roths to create tax diversification and prevent a required minimum withdrawal problem.

Withdrawal Order Optimization

Similar to income layering, this strategy is instead defined by timing and sequence. From which retirement accounts are you going to draw from, how much will you withdraw, and when (and how often) will you draw from them? The common way to go about this is to draw from taxable accounts first to encourage the tax-advantaged accounts to compound your money in a more tax-friendly way. This all depends on your tax bracket, if you're retired, if you're drawing (or not) social security, and other factors. Be tactical about this and work with your team.

Bracket Management

Sometimes it can be advantageous (from a tax point of view) to strategically plan *when* income is received in order to avoid moving into a higher tax bracket. There are other bracket management strategies at play in addition to potentially shifting when you receive income. For example, contributing to retirement accounts will reduce your taxable income and potentially bring you down into a lower bracket.

Roth Conversions

Let's say that you expect to be in a much higher tax bracket in a future year than you are this year. A Roth conversion is a tax strategy where you move money from your retirement account (which are usually "pre-tax") and convert it into taxable income. Converting it and paying taxes on it now could save you money on future taxes, when you expect to be paying a higher rate.

A good strategy would be to convert a certain amount every year between when you retire and when you start social security and/or are required to take minimum required withdrawals from retirement accounts. You could be at a lower tax bracket than you were in when you first started your career.

1031 Exchanges

This is a real estate play where, upon the sale of your investment real estate property, you defer paying capital gains tax on your earnings *if* you use that capital gains to purchase a "like-kind" property. People use this strategy to use the appreciation of real estate value to access more valuable properties. An investor friend of mine used this strategy to gradually increase the size of his Airbnb. He started with a cookie-cutter suburban investment property and, by the time he retired, ended up with a beautiful $5 million investment property overlooking the Puget Sound.

This can be great for legacy planning because heirs receive a "step-up in basis," where their real estate inheritance is viewed to have been "purchased" at market value at the time of ownership transfer. So the original deferred amount and any appreciation that occurred during your lifetime would pass onto your heirs tax-free.

Depreciating Investment Property

Tax deductions are one of the major benefits of owning investment property. In particular, depreciation is a significant tax deduction that allows investors to recover the cost of a building over its "useful life." That "useful life" is generally set at twenty-seven-and-a-half years for residential property and thirty-nine years for commercial property. Here's how it works: the cost of the purchase, minus the land value, is spread over its useful life using IRS depreciation schedules, and you can deduct that amount from your taxable income.

In some cases, it may be tax advantageous to front-load your investment property depreciation. There are three ways to accomplish that: cost segregation, component depreciation, and bonus depreciation. A cost segregation study identifies certain components or improvements that qualify for five-, seven-, and fifteen-year depreciation (such as fixtures, equipment, or landscaping), separates them from the standard useful life, and accelerates those deductions into earlier tax years. Certain components, like appliances, specialized lighting, or HVAC systems, may also qualify for faster depreciation. Finally, bonus depreciation is a tax incentive that allows businesses to immediately deduct a significant portion of qualifying property costs in the year the asset is placed in service, subject to current tax law limits. At the time of writing, bonus depreciation is being phased down, so make sure you check the current rules.

After-Tax Return

Sometimes it can be better to pay tax later rather than pay tax now, or vice versa. There is a point where deferring taxes or taking liability as you go will help ensure the lowest tax liabilities incurred on the financial plan.

Saving a lot of money on taxes this year looks great on paper, but how does that affect after-tax liability twenty years from now? There has to be a balance to maximize net worth.

Putting It All Together

Chronic tax drag, like inflammation, often goes unnoticed until significant damage has occurred. That's one reason tax strategies should be ongoing, integrated, and forward-looking.

5. ESTATE PLANNING

Your estate planning is like your genetic blueprint, determining your legacy by passing on your wealth in a systematic and defined way. It not only defines who gets what but how and why they carry it forward.

Without proper estate planning, lines can be broken and generational legacy doesn't happen. It usually comes as a shock to most people, even though the symptoms of dysfunction were right in front of them the whole time.

Problems arise when wealth is transferred without meaning or guidance. Family members fight. They go to court. They never speak to each other again. Families are broken up and lost. This is something you will want to avoid if you care about your legacy.

Ensuring a proper estate plan means that your documents are *not* out of sync with your current family or goals. It means that your heirs are aware and prepared for the responsibility of your legacy once you pass on (or while you are here, such as through a trust).

Let's explore some actions you can take to maximize your WealthSpan through estate planning.

Coordinated Titling

You can legally title your assets, such as your real estate holdings or investment accounts, in a trust. Investment real estate should be owned by an LLC, and the LLC owned by the trust. This crucial aspect of estate planning ensures the legal ownership of your assets, but make sure they are coordinated with your will or trust (and your overall intentions).

In most cases, titling overrides any will or trust for nonprobate assets, so you'll need to make sure that there aren't any conflicts between them and your wishes.

Keep in mind, you can't retitle retirement assets. Accounts such as IRAs and 401(k)s must remain in the individual's name during their lifetime. However, you can designate beneficiaries on retirement accounts, and these assets will pass directly to them at death, bypassing probate. And if the beneficiary is a spouse, the account can typically be rolled into the surviving spouse's own IRA and treated as their own.

For non-spouses, things change, and taxes play a role. The assets will transfer into a Beneficiary (Inherited) IRA. Under current rules, the funds must be withdrawn within ten years, and distributions will have to be carefully managed to mitigate potential taxes. The beneficiary could also be a trust, but this is generally not recommended unless there is a special situation like protecting minor children or beneficiaries who may not be financially responsible.

Legal Letters and Purpose-Driven Trusts

These complement a standard estate plan, acting as tools that direct your assets to specific endeavors or missions.

The main difference between the two is whether or not they are legally binding. A legacy letter is a nonbinding document that shares your values, life lessons, and wishes to your heirs. They are still free to do whatever they want with what you've passed on to them, but the letter will act as a guide for them to honor your wishes.

A purpose-driven trust, on the other hand, is a binding entity that directs a trustee to use assets for a specific purpose rather than general benefit. The trustee is the designated "enforcer" rather than the beneficiary. These can be customized around pretty much anything. For example, maybe you are designated as a beneficiary but cannot access the entire value of the trust until a certain amount is donated or spent on humanitarian causes.

Scheduled Family Meetings

It is imperative that you set up regular (annual) meetings with your family to go over your estate plan, including any governance structures that go with it. This prevents any surprises, negligence from heirs not understanding their responsibilities, and a host of other potential problems.

The biggest benefit is that these meetings, more than anything else, can prevent families from fighting over your net worth after you're gone.

Putting It All Together

Just as DNA carries your genetic history forward, estate planning carries your generational intent forward. If it's not coded clearly, the future gets rewritten without you.

6. ASSET PLANNING

Your net worth has to hang on something. It's the framework that gives your portfolio strength. It's designed to help with shielding and protecting your wealth, much like our skeletal systems give us our structure, strength, and protects our organs.

Your wealth needs that solid framework to absorb ongoing complexity. It needs to be flexible enough to adapt. And it needs to be structured to help protect you from external threats.

You will know if your assets are threatened if, say, there is no separation between operating and holding entities for your business—an example I covered earlier. Another way is titling high-risk assets, like rental properties, in your personal name rather than an LLC. When you don't take steps to help protect yourself, your business liabilities can bleed into your personal estate and take an unnecessary (and usually significant) chunk from your net worth.

Beyond what I've already discussed, here are proactive, preventative measures you can take to help protect your assets and maximize your WealthSpan.

Charging Order Protection

These protect an LLC and its members from the personal debts and liabilities of a single member of the LLC. If the LLC were sued, the creditor's rights would only be for the member's interest.

Consider that there are state-specific rules for charging orders. Some states allow for the force of a sale of an LLC to pay back the creditors. Others do not.

State-Specific Entity Layering

Have you ever heard that Delaware leads the nation with registered LLCs? From one point of view, it would seem like that would be impossible, given that it's not a state with the most industry (or even the most space for industry). But LLCs are allowed to operate out of the state they are registered even if the members run the business from a proxy, out-of-state location.

Different states have different strategic advantages, liability protections, operational flexibility, and tax benefits that may warrant that your plan calls for state-specific entity layering, where your entities are registered in the most advantageous-to-you locations.

Putting It All Together

Bones don't just hold you up—they protect your most vital systems. Likewise, strong asset protection can give your wealth the structure to endure pressure, impact, and time.

The best way to take steps to protect yourself is to create a clear delineation between your personal, business, and investment holdings—with more complex options within that general framework.

DELEGATE

You have to do the preventive care that not only *unsplodes* but also maximizes your WealthSpan. Break down your financial situation to its most basic elements and consider all the factors that contribute to it. Understand that this number is the most raw version of what you are working with. *Unsplode* it. That is to say, maximize the possibility of this number by utilizing the information and tools that we are discussing here. This is how you maximize the longevity of your WealthSpan. It's a nonnegotiable. Why? Your present and future happiness is what's at stake. But finances are so complicated, it's important to understand not everything rests on you. You have to free yourself up to live your life, not just work or work on your finances.

Working all the time and not taking time off is a mistake. Just as much as maximizing your finances, your purpose is an asset that you shouldn't neglect. Don't miss your kids' baseball games. Don't miss the opportunity to go on vacation.

That mentality of not delegating will ruin your health, destroying an asset essential to living a purposeful life. You can create an automation that generates Experience ROI. You'll be more available to do the things that bring you joy, that align with your values, and let you live for today *and* tomorrow.

What do I mean by "automation"? We can think of that in a couple of ways. First, you could hire people. Let's say you want to retire early but not let go of owning the business just yet. Pay somebody to run it for you. Your business will be running on autopilot while you free up a lot of your time and still reap the business's financial benefits. Or consider the ways in which apps can help you organize your life. Caleb uses the Fyxer app, which helps him filter and automate his email. He's "hired" this app to do that work for him, which he desperately needed. I love Caleb, but the guy was really bad at email for a while there. With that time saved, he's freed himself up to get the ultimate Experience ROI: more time with his kids.

Delegate so that you can free up your time. If you can pay somebody less to do it than it would cost you—and can do it at the same level or better than you—then do that every time. Don't mow your own lawn.

CALEB'S INTERJECTION

I absolutely hate this concept, but it's correct. It is necessary for you to visualize what you are capable of and commit to giving up what does not contribute to the success of your plan. Delegate what holds you back so that you can live a purposeful, fulfilling life now *and* tomorrow. Sometimes, we can let somebody else mow the lawn so that we can cash in on experiences.

I say this as a former teenage lawn-mowing entrepreneur. My friend and I mowed lawns for a living—or, at least, to satisfy our cravings for Mexican food. When you're a teenager and can put away endless amounts of food, that's no small budget. And I say this as somebody who still loves to mow lawns. I love that fresh smell of cut grass. And it looks so good when it's done! And I did that work! That's something to be proud of. Nice work, me!

But the honest truth is that, during the week, there are other things I'd rather do that more align with my purpose. I want to be with my kids and spend time with my family—family like Trevor. To continue gaining that Experience ROI, I need to delegate that weekly ninety minutes it takes to mow my lawn to somebody else so I can spend time with my family.

What is your version of "mowing the lawn"? What can you delegate to realign with your purpose and increase your WealthSpan?

CHAPTER 6

THE WEALTHSPAN LONGEVITY TEAM: COLLABORATING WITH A NEW KIND OF WEALTH PROFESSIONAL

"If everyone is moving forward together, then success takes care of itself."

—HENRY FORD

It's nonnegotiable for me to design my client's financial plan around their purpose. That's why when clients I like to refer to as Charlie and Roberta came into my office, I started asking questions.

Charlie wasn't really interested in what I was asking at first. He simply wanted to open an account with me and invest $1 million. I was open to the idea, but I started to ask them about their goals, purpose, estate plan, tax situation, net worth, and everything else.

As Charlie opened up and gave me a bit of information, it turned out that the estate plan was over a decade old, and the attorney who put it together was retired. Their net worth had passed the estate limit, opening them up to huge liability. We looked at the tax statements. There was no tax-loss harvesting.

They put me in touch with their CPA so that I could get a better understanding as to the tax strategies that were being utilized—all important details to maximize the WealthSpan of a financial plan. Well, the CPA didn't want to talk to me. I got the impression that, in his mind, he knew it all and I knew nothing.

During our next meeting, I asked Charlie and Roberta if they'd be comfortable with a partner CPA looking over their last two tax returns. They agreed. I conveyed their goals and potential financial plan to the CPA to help him in his work. When the report came back, the partner CPA identified tens of thousands of dollars worth of tax savings that *hadn't* been taken and, perhaps worse, several errors that might have triggered an audit.

Right then and there, Charlie and Roberta knew they were in the right office. They asked me to proceed.

With their taxes in better hands, I started asking them about their estate. Without annual reviews, they had no idea what was in it. So I contacted my partner attorney, since their estate attorney was retired, and told him about Charlie and Roberta's goals, and the attorney reviewed their decade-old estate plan. The attorney's recommendation was to completely restructure the plan, and he also identified that the trustees were wrong—old family friends that were no longer in their social circle. Money and items weren't passing to the appropriate people as they indicated their wishes were in our conversations. The partner attorney fixed all of that to align with Charlie and Roberta's modified and current goals.

This sort of thing continued with Charlie and Roberta with every aspect of their overall financial plan. There were gaps, I identified them, I passed what I needed off to other providers I trusted, and Charlie and Roberta's WealthSpan improved because of it.

This is just one story about one set of clients. But this happens *all the time*. Charlie and Roberta thought they were getting good advice and service from their previous providers. But the providers themselves either didn't regularly communicate with the clients or collaborate with the other providers.

When I received Charlie and Roberta's holistic picture, anchored by their purpose and goals, I was able to help guide other trusted service providers to work with them to customize and maximize Charlie and Roberta's financial plan.

To say the least, Charlie and Roberta were extremely grateful. They're now lifetime clients of mine. And what started out as a potentially small (for them) account with me has transformed into maximizing their generational legacy—something that wouldn't have happened if they didn't walk into my office. They opened their eyes and benefited from doing so.

This kind of experience is exactly what gives me a sense of purpose and satisfaction as a wealth manager. Helping them *unsplode* and build a purposeful and fulfilling life now *and* tomorrow through a strengthened WealthSpan—that is what I seek out when I work with my clients. That transformation that Charlie and Roberta went through is what I offer my clients and work so hard to achieve.

Among the many morals to this story, there's one I want to highlight: when you plan with purpose, there needs to be consistent teamwork, collaboration, and communication. The quarterback of this WealthSpan Longevity Team—the one who sees the whole picture through the client's eyes—is the new wealth manager, a term I use to convey an elevated financial advisor.

A FAILURE TO COMMUNICATE

When investors enlist a bevy of professionals to help them with their finances *but* those professionals don't work together or circumvent each other, bad things can happen.

One common form of backdoor communication I see is when a specific service provider—like a CPA or attorney—gives their clients investment advice. That in and of itself might not be a bad thing, depending on the advice—although they are not licensed to give advice—but the real issue is that they speak directly to the clients instead of conveying their ideas to the wealth manager. That creates a system of broken communication—like the children's game "telephone."

If the attorney gives the client financial advice, the client takes it, and then no other service providers are notified, a domino effect of problems could have a negative impact on the overall plan. The CPA will be blindsided by new earnings that might actually diminish or eliminate returns (making the investment moot). The insurance agent might not realize that there are new assets that need to be protected, and the client could be opening themselves up to needless liability. And the wealth manager (me) not knowing will prevent them from adjusting the turnover of the portfolio, possibly increasing the tax burden.

There are countless other negative possibilities when communication is poor. CPAs might convince their clients to defer taxes—thinking they are a genius for reducing the tax burden for this year. But having a nice return—a sudden influx of cash—is a sparkly jewel that creates a blind spot to the shackles of that sort of move, such as losing accessibility to and liquidity in funds in the future. If the CPA worked *with* the financial advisor when talking to the client, the whole picture would be known, not just the narrow idea of this year's tax return, and the client could make a decision that best aligned with their *why*.

THE NEW WEALTH MANAGER

If you want to increase the strength of your WealthSpan, it's time to enlist a new kind of wealth manager.

What does this new wealth manager look like? They are actually wealth longevity specialists, and they should be the leader of the team of professionals that enact your financial vision and WealthSpan. They should be the CEO of your wealth management.

You'll recognize a quality wealth manager immediately if they begin by getting focused on your purpose—your *why*—such as how you want to live now, your goals for retirement, how you want to continually seek growth and experiences, and everything else that makes up a purposeful life.

With that information known and cataloged, the wealth manager can then convey that information to every other service provider. The entire WealthSpan Longevity Team will take the new wealth manager's lead to operate with the *why* as the driving force of the plan and all decisions—keeping the client educated and informed about those decisions, of course.

Wealth managers speak a language that is fluent with every other provider. We have to be educated on every aspect of the plan. We can talk about taxes, estate planning, real estate, investing, and everything else that allows us to stay in dialogue with and ask questions of the other providers. This collaboration means that, with healthy pushback and different perspectives, the team can work in unison to ensure the success of your financial plan.

Here's something else to consider. There are two primary ways that financial advisors get paid: they can get paid for each transaction within a portfolio *or* based on the value of the portfolio annually. Those that get paid per transaction are more incentivized to create high turnover (and tax liability) for their clients in order to get paid.

I, and the new wealth manager, sit on the same side of the table as the clients. I should only get paid if I'm doing my job for my clients, guiding them through market fluctuations, and helping them avoid the wrong moves as per their purposeful plan. I win when you win. That ensures objective advice that's meant to find the best strategy and long-term focus.

You deserve more than a money manager. You deserve a thinking partner. A strategist. A guide. Wealth managers like this are unicorns. We're hard to find. The organization I built is among them.

And some say it's a bad business model to get paid annually, but our clients are so satisfied with the holistic work that we do that referrals come our way. The other side of that coin is that boilerplate financial advisors will warn that the fees of wealth managers will be higher. That's true, but we are proactive, looking to save our clients more on taxes and do more to help protect their assets against liability. When you look at the time horizon of the financial plan, the clients have a financial plan that is built around their purpose and goals, one that reflects the lifestyle they've chosen.

It reminds me of a high-school friend of mine. We were going on a camping trip, and he talked me out of buying bargain-bin gear. "You'll never regret paying for quality," he told me. And he was right. It was an amazing trip, and I still have that camping gear all these decades later—it's that superior. The same principle holds true for higher quality and for more deeply invested wealth managers. You will not regret recruiting the right team.

WHY IS THE WEALTH MANAGER THE LEADER?

Once, I actually had a CPA ask me where to put the tax liability for a structured alternative product on my client's tax form. It blew my mind. CPAs tend to look backward, not down the road. It made me realize that the wealth manager really needs to be the architect of the financial plan. They can zoom out on the holistic picture and foresee gaps or problems that might explode the financial plan—thus unsploding it and keeping it aligned with your goals. As they do that work, the wealth manager will enlist the other providers as subcontractors to keep everything running smoothly.

In another instance, I had an attorney push back on my financial plan for a client. But then I showed him my charts and how my long-term plan projected a return that exceeded their expectations. That opened the attorney's eyes, who immediately changed their mind and came around to my strategy.

Each provider has their own specialization, their own lane that they should stay in. The best CPA will tell you, "I'm just the tax person." That's their specialty. Same with the others. But wealth managers are, by design, specialized in understanding the entire picture of the financial plan and are therefore primed to be the coordinator between the team of professionals.

Think of it like owning a business. If the business owner did everything, they wouldn't have time to live their own life. So when the business owner delegates, they don't give every employee equal power. A CEO is put in place who specializes in guiding the vision of the entire company. Then there are CFOs, department heads, and other strategy leaders who have their narrow role and work with the CEO to make decisions.

If the client-investor were to take charge of their financial plan instead of collaborating with a wealth manager, analysis paralysis usually sets in. Inaction and a lack of preventative and proactive care, as we learned, lead to the death of a financial plan's time horizon.

A good wealth manager will clear the fog of the complications and complexities that make up a customized financial plan. They'll also convey a simplified (but not in a reductionist way) understanding of the action steps to the clients so that the client understands and gets an education that doesn't require a financial degree. That education will help the client keep their *why* top of mind and stick to the plan. They'll be proactive and frequently collaborate with you. Otherwise, the plan will most likely be on autopilot, with nobody seeming to bother to check in and confirm that the plan and the why are even in the same room as one another, let alone sitting on the same side of the table. This is complacency. The easy road. Proof of a lack of purposeful planning. And this complacency is the cancer of WealthSpan.

The new wealth manager and the rest of your team needs to commit to staying in their lanes while communicating with each other. The primary facilitator should be the wealth manager, as they'll know how everything ties into the financial plan's purpose.

THE REST OF THE WEALTHSPAN LONGEVITY TEAM

While the new wealth manager might be the architect of your financial plan, you are ultimately the architect and GM of your WealthSpan Longevity Team. You get to hire and fire whomever you wish. That onus is on you.

That can be a little daunting, can't it? Who are you supposed to hire? How do you know if somebody doesn't have your best interests in mind? The vetting process for your financial professionals can be difficult to navigate.

I'm not saying I have all the answers, but I can point you in the right direction by going over some traits I see in the most effective service providers—while also going over some red flags.

CPA

Taxes touch every part of your financial life—yet many people choose a CPA based on proximity, price, or convenience.

The CPA needs to be proactive with tax advice and have an understanding of how the financial plan and portfolio will create tax liability or returns. And they need to be proactive about strategizing ways to save more money on taxes (without undue risks), which could mean collaborating with the wealth manager to adjust the plan.

The ideal CPA not only works well with a team but can take feedback. Again, communication is key. You want your CPA to be agreeable to being a collaborator with the WealthSpan Longevity Team. You don't want them to be somebody who exclusively communicates to you.

I once had a CPA approach me claiming that I owed a percentage of the client's revenue of the portfolio every year because my financial plan was similar to the tax advice they separately gave the client. I was dumbfounded. I'm all for CPAs who are proactive and getting paid for their work. But in this particular scenario, it was clear they were just trying to shake down the advisor to get kickbacks. That's not somebody who cares about their clients first.

Find a CPA who understands your level of complexity, too. Many people will outgrow basic tax prep. If you are a business owner, have multiple income sources, or hold significant investments, make sure your CPA is experienced with business ownership, entity structuring, real estate, RSUs, retirement planning, Roth conversion timing, charitable giving, and donor-advised funds.

Here's another situation. In my experience, CPAs who also get licensed as a financial planner don't generally work out for the client. I'm not saying there are *no* success stories out there. But in general, trying to be an advisor *and* tax professional at the same time means there are fewer opportunities for pushback and different perspectives. A safety net gets lost.

ESTATE PLANNER/ATTORNEY

Sometimes I hear these stories where a client met with their estate attorney once to sign paperwork and never talked to them again. That's unthinkable to me. In reality, most estate attorneys don't meet with their clients regularly. In fact, you'll be hard pressed to find one. But at a minimum, they will meet with you every few years to review documents.

This is why it's critical for your wealth planner to be well-versed in estate planning fundamentals. When something changes—a liquidity event or tax law update—your wealth planner should recognize it and coordinate with the estate attorney to ensure the legal strategy stays aligned with the financial plan's purpose. Without that coordination, even well-drafted plans can quietly become outdated. So when you're choosing one, they need to be willing to work with the wealth manager, take constructive feedback, and be a team player. Estate forecasting, tax implications, and the financial plan are interrelated, so teamwork is essential.

This will be your go-to person to coordinate gifting planning for tax strategies in the estate plan—collaborating with the wealth manager and CPA.

When it comes to attorneys, you should be looking for somebody who is willing to educate you on anything and everything they are doing. Have them walk you through the plan, what makes it unique to you, and why it's right for you. Otherwise, you stand to hire a cookie-cutter attorney who won't be doing anything special or tailored to your needs. Most, quite honestly, will just plug your information into a LegalZoom-like system and then send you a bill.

INSURANCE ADVISOR/AGENT

I won't name names, but many big-name insurance companies are dealing with bulk, meaning they want to accumulate as many clients as possible, put them on standard plans, and "communicate" with the client by sending them a monthly bill. That's a recipe for disaster.

Instead, you need an insurance advisor or agent that regularly meets with you to discuss current values on your major assets, like your homes and vehicles. Most people are still carrying insurance on their house for pre-COVID-19 valuations. Well, homes have appreciated since then, and a lot of people's insurance policies might not pay for the disasters they think they are protected from.

Then, you need an agent that gets more aggressive with often overlooked liabilities. That could include casualty insurance (which protects against injury and property damage) or umbrella insurance (which covers above what regular policies won't, including attorney's fees).

Like the other providers, a good insurance agent is also *proactive*, meaning that they will look for gaps in the policies as they relate to the financial plan. For example, they will recognize the discrepancy if a home policy is titled to a personal name but the home itself is titled to an LLC. (If the agent leaves this discrepancy, the company can get out of paying.)

By coordinating insurance with the wealth manager, it keeps two sets of eyes on things, creating a checks-and-balances situation.

REAL ESTATE ADVISOR/REAL ESTATE ATTORNEY/REAL ESTATE AGENT

Real estate, much like taxes, is its own complex world of rules and regulations. The good news is that your wealth advisor will speak that language. A good real estate advisor will coordinate with the wealth manager and CPA to ensure the client's real estate holdings and future investments are aligned with the purpose of the overall financial plan.

The most common misalignment I see is that, sometimes, clients will end up with 95 percent of their net worth (or a large portion) tied up in real estate. Then, when the client turns seventy or eighty, they regret having all of their net worth in one type of investment because it doesn't have much liquidity and can create taxable events. So for clients who want to live their life now, putting all of their money in real estate and waiting for it to appreciate is not the best way to access cash to create freedom and experiences now.

The ideal real estate advisor will also have a mind for diversification, encouraging their client to mix asset types and market locations to help protect investments against fluctuations.

Something else to think about is estate and legacy planning. The real estate advisor, wealth manager, CPA, and estate planner need to work together to figure out your plans for your real estate holdings. There are a lot of complicated reasons why. One is called the "step up in basis," which is a rule that lets your heirs inherit the appreciated value of a property tax-free.

YOUR SOCIAL CIRCLE

Your friends and family have a profound effect on the health of your finances. But let's be clear. Unless they are professional wealth managers or any other service provider I've mentioned, that doesn't mean you should rush out and share your financial information with them.

The reason why your social circle is part of your team is because they *should* be instilling good habits in you. Who we are as individuals rubs off on others. That means that you should be making more plans with anybody you enjoy spending time with that actively practices good financial habits. Let them rub off on you so that you grow and become better.

ADJUSTING YOUR TEAM

Nobody on your team should be a know-it-all. They all need to have a sense of collaboration and open-mindedness that allows feedback, differing perspectives, and the ability to see what others are trying to convey. If, in basketball, you have one person hogging the ball, that team is not going to be able to walk away with a win. Go look at Michael Jordan's career, if you don't believe me. He didn't win his championships by himself. He had key players and stars in their own right like Scottie Pippen, Steve Kerr, Toni Kukoč, Dennis Rodman, Horace Grant, B. J. Armstrong, Jerry Stackhouse, and Charles Oakley. So don't be afraid to fire somebody on your team if they are not willing to be a team player.

The best professionals provide pushback, which is hard for a lot of clients. People want their hamburger made and delivered in five minutes. They don't want to know how it was cooked. But if you care about your WealthSpan, you need to fight that feeling of instant gratification that has a hugely negative impact on your financial health. Sit with your professionals, be willing to be educated, and listen openly when they give you advice that aligns with your purpose but goes against such-and-such investment idea you have. Don't shoot yourself in the foot; you're part of the team, too.

As your business or net worth grows, you also need to adjust your team to have service providers that are appropriate for your size. You may have started with a CPA you loved when you had no money, but when your business grows to $30 million in revenue every year, that original CPA is likely way out of your league—by not being accustomed to filing such complex taxes—and doing you a disservice.

And stay away from narcissistic advisors. Identifying them is *not* easy. But here are some questions you can consider:

- Do they have boundaries?
- Do they help you and not themselves?
- Are they proactive instead of reactive?
- Do they communicate with you during times other than when things are going well or in crisis?

If you can answer "yes" to these questions, they are likely on your side and not looking at you like a payday.

And reevaluating your providers to create the best team should start from the top. Here's a short questionnaire designed to help you determine whether or not your wealth manager is working in collaboration with you and your purpose or is putting you on a set-it-and-forget-it, cookie-cutter plan.

- Do you understand exactly how your advisor gets paid?
- Has your advisor explained why each investment or product is in your portfolio?
- Do you feel like your advisor is trying to sell you something?
- When was the last time your advisor reached out proactively to review your plan?
- Does your current plan address more than just investments (taxes, estate, business, income, etc.)?
- Are your strategies personalized to your goals and life, or do they feel generic?
- Do you know the plan for your money for the next year, the next five years, and the next ten years?
- Does your advisor challenge you or just agree with whatever you say?
- Do you feel confident that your current plan supports the life you want to live?

If the answers to any of these questions create doubt that your advisor has your purpose and best interests in mind, then it might be time to look for a new wealth manager.

THE NEW STANDARD IS TRANSPARENCY

Way more often than not, clients have no idea what fees they are paying their financial professionals. Your Wealth Longevity Team has an obligation to be transparent and consistent with making sure you understand not just your plan and how it's being executed but also how your team is being paid. Ideally, the pay structures themselves incentivize the professionals on your team to sit on the same side of the table with you.

And this will all come down to simple education. How proactive are the members of your team to meet with you, collaborate with you, and educate you? That is a big indicator as to whether or not your team has your WealthSpan in mind.

When you go to a member of your team, part of their response should be "let me go find out more by connecting with the rest of our team." That will indicate that they seek collaboration, are transparent that their perspective might not be the only "right" plan, and have a growth mindset primed to create financial success.

CALEB'S INTERJECTION

Teamwork makes the dream work!

A collaborative spirit is necessary for your HealthSpan Longevity Team, too. (You can read more about that on my side of the book.) More times than not, because of complex reimbursement issues and legalities, primary care providers will err on the side of doing less and making a referral as opposed to being proactive because that's what reimbursements policy tells them to do.

They're not incentivized to take that extra step. Since they won't be providing that next step of care, they aren't very inquisitive about it. They don't get to know much of the other specialists' motivations or duties, nor do they understand it. Ideally, these individuals work together, and in that spirit of cooperation, these individuals should all operate with your best interests in mind. They might read some of each other's notes (very unlikely that they read all of them!), but they otherwise stay a disbanded group of providers working independently instead of together. Long-term, that has negative consequences for your health...something you need if you want to enjoy your hard-earned money.

Without a team, your purpose gets subsumed and lost. Without an engine underneath the hood, the car won't start, much less run. The best wealth managers will demonstrate transparency *and* have the proper connections to let you build out a team that creates a strong, long-term collaborative relationship.

Your goal should be to set up this team and your financial plan *now*, or as early as possible. Get that engine humming to help you reach your goals and maximize your WealthSpan for a purposeful life today and tomorrow.

Speaking of tomorrow, as you reach retirement age, part of that plan will be your retirement and exit strategies. Proper planning is essential for a good retirement. Because our business exits and retirement tend to come last in your life, they've come last in my conversation about WealthSpan. They are big life changes and something that needs to be done properly. That's what we'll talk about next.

CHAPTER 7

EXIT STRATEGY: PLANNING FOR INCOME AFTER YOU STOP PRODUCING IT

"The gratification of wealth is not found in mere possession or in lavish expenditure, but in its wise application."

—MIGUEL DE CERVANTES

Retiring is nothing that should be taken lightly. It needs to be carefully planned.

And now that you know how to create a trusted WealthSpan Longevity Team, you'll know when to spot narcissistic professionals who don't have your best interests in mind. That's important because too many people blow up their retirement unwittingly, transforming what was supposed to be the crown on a fulfilled life into something unexpected and anxiety inducing.

That's what happened to somebody I knew who was working with a young advisor promising 15 percent returns on their portfolio. Fifteen percent is an impossible number. If somebody is telling you they can get you 15 percent, that's a huge red flag.

What the advisor did, I came to find out, was essentially manipulate the plan so he didn't have to push back on the clients to tell them that their desired monthly retirement income was too much relative to their net worth. The clients wanted $1 million a year in distributions, when $700,000 would have been far more appropriate. Instead of proper planning, the advisor just wanted to appease his clients.

Anyway, the advisor's plan to achieve his unfeasible promise was to get really aggressive and raise the portfolio's risk tolerance. You can guess what happened. A market fluctuation started tanking the portfolio's value quickly. They had to sell off stocks at major discounts to withdraw the cash needed to sustain their lifestyle.

Within five years, their net worth went from $20 million to $14 million.

If they had come into my office with that financial plan, I would have asked them, "Do you plan on dying in ten years?" Their answer, of course, would be "No! We have at least twenty years left." But that shiny object—a promise of 15 percent—blinded them from their purpose and *why*.

Now, they've lost control of their plan. Because they didn't properly plan, they've had to dial back their distributions well below their expected lifestyle. They worked all of those years and did everything right, then one inexperienced advisor comes through who doesn't give them pushback or educates them, and, poof, everything changed very quickly.

When thinking about retirement income and exiting a business, we have to be as careful and thoughtful as when we design every other component of the financial plan. With one block out of place, the whole wall can come crashing down.

USE PURPOSE WHEN DEFINING THE EXIT OR RETIREMENT STRATEGY

Do you remember when we planned with purpose in Chapter 3? We thoroughly determined a *why* and inventoried your net worth as the foundational component to a financial plan that promotes a healthy WealthSpan.

For this chapter, we're going to strip away the concept of living for today (which you are hopefully already taking actionable steps to achieve) and instead focus on what you envision as your *why* for retirement.

Revisit your purpose and values, then apply them to what you want an average day, week, month, and year to look like when you retire. What does it include? Are you traveling? Spending money on grandkids? Going to your favorite restaurant each week? Buying a boat and sailing around the world? Golfing weekly at a country club? What does your social circle look like, and what type of activities will that entail? What hobbies will you pursue? Are you retiring immediately, or will you slowly work your way into it? For example, will you continue to work part time? Consulting? Assisting? Auditing? You don't have to go from working forty hours a week to zero. There are other transitional options.

Give yourself a crystal clear look into the future. Having a clear sense of what you want will act as the carrot on the stick that motivates not only the structure of your financial plan but also your drive to stick to that plan. If you plan on retiring in phases, carefully plan what roles you will be giving up as you do so.

In most cases, our ideal future is a little bit more than we expect to have. That's a good thing because we can use that aspiration to be proactive, preventative, and maximize finances to achieve those goals. Of course, there needs to be a level of realism—goals need to be achievable.

Not many people plan their retirement with purpose. It's extremely common for people to just think that they'll have one lump sum of cash—either through a portfolio, the sale of a business, or some combination of things—that they can be conservative with. The problem is that being conservative with cash won't outpace inflation. So another key reason to be motivated by your purpose is to take on the tolerable risk required for a financial plan to earn money over a long-term time horizon.

THE PSYCHOLOGICAL GAP

Most people I work with think of retirement as this natural transition in their life. The truth of the matter is that it is a huge, abrupt, jarring, and difficult transition to make.

Think about it. A person goes from working each weekday for their entire life, having their purpose partially fulfilled by executing their job well and being congratulated by peers and through their ongoing paycheck. Maybe they even go out for beers and socialize with their colleagues are part of that purpose-driven process. Then one day, that person retires, and that consistent sense of purpose vanishes.

They quit socializing with their work friends. They don't wake up in the morning with a sense of purpose. They don't feel fulfilled after a day's work. Their sense of accomplishment is gone. And their self-worth deteriorates. In other words, their life explodes. It's no wonder that depression spikes in people after they retire. They have not properly *unsploded* that transitional event by preparing other social circles for their retirement.

CALEB'S INTERJECTION

Hi there! It's me again, Caleb the doctor, interrupting my cousin. Trevor is making a great point about the commonality of depression in retirement. Depression stems from an imbalance in our mental health. And since health is *my* subject, I wanted to add a few things for your consideration.

In addition to your mental health, you also need to plan for your physical health. Don't expect to be as fit at seventy as you were at twenty. Sorry if that comes as a surprise to you.

If I were you, I'd add this purpose to your planned retirement activities: prioritizing your physical health. You're not working anymore! That means you should have the time to create quick, regular, daily exercise routines that keep you fit enough to enjoy the things you've saved your money for.

Think about planning ahead. In the years leading up to retirement, you should be exercising regularly (maybe not daily) so your retirement health can hit the proverbial ground running.

When you make a financial plan with the idea that, when you retire, you'll be traveling or golfing or pursuing some sort of hobby, then that otherwise difficult transition is far easier. Instead of work friends, you'll be grabbing a beer with your new golf buddies.

This psychological gap is especially acute for business owners and entrepreneurs. These are individuals who exerted almost complete control over their lives and feel a much larger sense of being self-made. When *that* purpose comes to an end, they can feel isolated and without purpose quickly. These folks really need to plan out their activities and hobbies after they exit that business.

THE RED ZONE

Throughout the book, I've been preaching the need to constantly reevaluate and, as needed, adjust your purpose (and therefore your financial plan). Maybe you want to buy a sail boat and travel the world today, but ten years from now, you instead want to take up photography. Just one example.

As you near retirement, there is an important timeframe called "the red zone," which is five years prior to retirement. This is when you want to solidify your retirement purpose and goals, including how you will maintain your health and social circles—not just fun activities.

This should also include spousal dynamics if you're married. Have a clear picture of how much you plan to do together. And no matter how close a couple is, it's always best to plan a life outside of the spouse to give them and you some space. This is especially important if your spouse is the first to pass away. That event is itself another jarring transition—one where the empty house will perpetuate an unhealthy grief if the surviving spouse has not planned for and set up their individual purpose or any additional support to keep them going during this difficult time.

Making sure you have these things planned *before* retirement will help ease the transition and prevent those jarring adjustments that can take a toll on our mental health and sense of well-being.

THE ENTREPRENEUR'S RETIREMENT VS. THE DELEGATOR'S RETIREMENT

For a lot of my entrepreneurial and business-owner readers, I can feel the wheels turning in their head. I can hear them thinking, "Well, if Trevor says I *need* a hobby in retirement, then I'll just start a new business from scratch and make that my hobby." I respect that thinking.

I'm not here to tell you what you should or shouldn't consider a hobby of yours. But let's just be clear, a hobby is defined as something done leisurely and for pleasure. Most of the business owners I know are Type A personalities, meaning that they don't know the meaning of the word "joy" when it comes to running their business—only "growth" (and maybe "control").

My whole philosophy is to encourage my clients to live their lives now and tomorrow. Find the joy of experiences and create memories that lead to a fulfilled life. The biggest regret I hear my older clients talk about is how they worked their butts off their whole life, thinking they were proud to have created the valuable company they slaved over, to only have no relationships or hobbies to spend their money on. The work becomes their destination rather than the vehicle or tool that should have served a real purpose.

The entrepreneur's retirement is one that gives the retiree another gray-hair-producing project. It's a retirement that can, as Caleb already alluded to when he interrupted me earlier, greatly diminish the longevity of your HealthSpan.

Those business owners that have an exit strategy tend to have more fulfilling lives in retirement. That might mean selling the business. That might mean delegating to family or business partners via a succession plan.

Those entrepreneurs that adopt this delegator mindset tend to, in a healthy way, transfer their acceptance of delegation to their WealthSpan Longevity Team, trusting and collaborating with their financial professionals to keep the financial plan on the pathway to success. Once the portfolio is built, they know that it will be properly managed.

Letting go of complete control will also prevent self-inflicted volatility. Half of the stock market's returns over a ten-year period are made in ten single days. Let your team carefully guide your plan so you're not missing out on those days.

It seems counterintuitive, but a delegator's retirement is actually more selfish (in a good way) than an entrepreneur's retirement because the delegator is actually putting themselves first.

FOCUS ON YOURSELF BEFORE YOU FOCUS ON OTHERS

Another thing that separates my companies apart is the emphasis on planning for *you*, planning for purpose, and letting those two act as your spending guide rails. Before anyone else, you have to plan for *your* purpose in retirement. After that, you can add things to your goals such as spending money on your kids or grandkids.

And when I say "spend money," I don't mean get them a small gift for their birthday or something like that. It's common for people to blow up their retirement planning by suddenly deciding to pay for a grandchild's college tuition, taking care of their child's new monthly car payment, or bailing them out of a bad financial situation. These are the types of spending that not only takes away from you, but they tend to compound the child's problem, crippling them because they never learn how to manage their money smartly.

This can be a difficult thing to avoid because we all want to be there for them. But in the end, this kind of spending—impulsive and indulgent spending that goes against a financial plan—tends to cripple the development of the kids.

One of my retired neighbors is going through this right now, and he won't take my advice (unfortunately). He's a widower living with his adult grandson. (The grandson is in his thirties.) About a year back, he agreed to buy his jobless grandson a new car to help the job-searching efforts. For reasons beyond me, they purchased a tricked out, high-end Honda that isn't so much a means of transportation as a toy meant for somebody with excessive funds, funds which my neighbor does not have. It's been a year since that car was purchased, and his grandson still doesn't have a job. Something tells me that the grandson coaxed the car from his grandpa under false pretenses—and feels entitled to continue living there for free.

This is just *one* thing that he is paying for. There are other gifts and payments he's making for his grandson, and an entire different set of things for his adult granddaughter.

Anyway, the other day, my neighbor complained to me about all the things draining his finances. He was worried that he faced the very real possibility of needing to sell his home and, after his debts are paid, only being able to afford to rent a small studio apartment. Even then, he was afraid he might not have enough money to sustain the rest of his life.

I can't help but feel bad for the guy, but I pushed back on him, telling him to get rid of all of these payments, kick the grandkid out unless he gets a job and pays rent, and a number of (seemingly obvious) fixes so that he can focus on himself in retirement. He wasn't really pleased with my response, apparently just wanting somebody to complain to without a real desire to get solutions-oriented.

In my line of work, this kind of thing happens all the time and at all levels of income. Even those with tens of millions of dollars in assets destroy their own retirement by making choices like this. And I don't want my clients to self-implode their retirement plans.

Don't get me wrong, it's not a bad thing to pay for college or new cars. But that needs to be in the plan as early as possible, utilize gift exclusions and tax savings, and be executed in a way that keeps the WealthSpan healthy.

THE NITTY-GRITTY OF RETIREMENT PLANNING

The fun part of retirement planning is determining your purpose—imagining traveling to Europe or getting a pilot's license is just exciting. That's the first important step. A foundational step.

After that, you and your wealth manager will work closely together to make sure you are sculpting the financial plan to make those things come to fruition. That will include getting clear with you about a number of important data points and behaviors that are universal to successful financial planning.

CASH FLOW

Cash flow is vitally important. You need cash to pay for your retirement.

Although clients don't often think in terms of cash flow, the good news is that they are linear numbers that, when presented, are straightforward and paint a clear picture of retirement. (Make sure you work with your wealth manager to make these numbers clear to you.)

Think of your cash flow as the opposing force of your budget. You set up your purpose, and that purpose will cost a certain amount of money each month in retirement that is achievable within the plan. That's your budget. Then, you'll receive monthly cash flow based on your monthly budgetary needs.

Retirement cash flow is also determined by your legacy goals. If you want a certain amount of money or assets set aside for heirs, then you need to carefully budget and spend as to not overspend and dip into their planned inheritance.

How much money you can spend each month in retirement can be a big sticking point with clients. Many want to increase their cash flow and spending—we made the money to spend it, after all. But that gets people into trouble, much like the clients of the young advisor I opened this chapter with.

A good way to wrap your head around the importance of what an appropriate amount of cash flow will be for your retirement is to do a Monte Carlo stress test, which simulates and evaluates the durability and longevity of your retirement plan. It does this by testing it against a thousand possible future scenarios, including extremes like financial booms or crises.

RISK TOLERANCE

I've alluded to this in some of my examples, but risk tolerance is how a portfolio is positioned to earn. The more conservative the risk, the less volatile the return at a smaller rate (on average). The more risk, the more volatile the returns are, meaning they could be higher or lower on average than conservative risk. The allure with more volatility is the potential for much higher earnings.

There are reasons to position a retirement plan in any risk category. But most people will need to outpace inflation with their return percentage to not run out of money, which means they'll be taking on some risk.

A good wealth manager will also take their client's personality into account when retirement planning. If they are conservative in their risk tolerance and won't budge, that's when the wealth manager needs to explore a variety of products made just for that type of personality. Because a regular portfolio mix won't necessarily help that conservative client overcome inflation risk, that's when annuities and other forms of lower risk income can enter the conversation.

STICKING TO THE PLAN

Speaking of personality, many investors lead with their emotions. It's hard not to. When the market's up, it's easy to feel ecstatic. When it's down, it's easy to feel upset. Feeling those emotions is fine in and of itself, but the problem occurs when those emotions are driving financial decisions.

People who spend money (above and beyond their retirement plan) when the market is good because they see a larger number in their portfolio stand to damage the longevity of that portfolio. Similarly, people who sell assets during a downturn out of fear that their assets will continue to plunge is the equivalent of selling an asset too cheaply; in the long term, that asset should come back up and maintain its upward momentum. Take a snapshot of the life of any market in the US. When you look at its past performance, you can see that it goes up over time. For every ten years, on average, only two or three are bad (on average). That's why it's important to stay invested, grounded in your purposeful plan.

Leading with emotions rarely ever adds value to a portfolio and, in the worst-case scenario, will derail the retirement plan. That's when people have to return to work to make ends meet.

PASSIVE INCOME OPTIONS

The most traditional retirement plans generate their monthly income and cash flow by taking regular distributions from a stock portfolio.

Beyond living off of dividends, there is another way to sustain a retirement through passive income.

Many people, for example, will choose to incorporate rental properties as part of their retirement income. They draw on the monthly rent payments—after any mortgage payments, property tax, insurance, and repairs—and use the rest like regular income. For those nearing retirement age, mortgages are more likely to be taken care of, and the rental payment is primarily going to maintenance and repairs.

On average, you can expect to spend around 30 percent of rental income on taxes, insurance, maintenance, and repairs. So when you see how large that rental income number is, don't let your eyes get too big. You will need some of that to keep the investment healthy.

DIVIDEND INCOME OPTIONS

A self-sustaining portfolio is one where the retiree can live off the dividends and earnings of the portfolio alone, never dipping into the starting value of the portfolio at the time of retirement.

Essentially, this will mean that the retiree's dividends will act as monthly income, money generated from their existing money. For this to work, the distribution rate needs to be pretty low, around 1.5 or 2 percent. But when it works, it works. These retirees don't have to worry much about risk.

Another iteration of the same principle—using dividends as income—is called a balanced portfolio withdrawal strategy. With this approach, the emphasis is on a carefully diversified portfolio that usually mixes stocks and other investments. The withdrawal rate is higher—around 3 or 3.5 percent of the portfolio annually. That rate will be adjusted to account for inflation and to ensure that purchasing power is maintained.

Since this particular strategy increases the rate over time, the portfolio's value will decline over time, especially later in retirement when the rate is much larger relative to the starting rate. The goal isn't to preserve the original principle but instead to create a sustainable stream of income throughout retirement. Ultimately, the balance is between growth potential and income generation, funding a lifestyle while still maintaining long-term investments.

LEGACY OPTIONS

Perhaps a small but important consideration when it comes to retirement and legacy planning is the nature of how your heirs will receive their inheritance. We've talked about some options already—the various trusts that allow you to distribute your assets how you want.

When you're thinking about the legacy aspect of your retirement, how do you want to pass your portfolio on? Do you want it in the form of a portfolio or in the form of income? If the first, your heirs will get a lump sum.

Every parent knows the personality of their children and heirs. They might decide that a lump sum would encourage an heir to spend recklessly and endanger their own future. This parent could instead choose to distribute the inheritance in the form of monthly income to the heir to foster a lifestyle-maintaining approach to using the funds.

EXIT PLANNING FOR BUSINESSES

When it comes to exiting your business, you really have two options: selling it or have somebody run it for you and take a yearly distribution (business succession planning).

If you choose the latter and pick somebody to run the company—maybe a child or employee—it's wise to put golden handcuffs on them. What that means is some sort of incentive for them to run the company well and to not leave. That could be a benefit like a cash balance or percentage of stock in the company that, if they leave, reverts back to you.

For those owners getting ready to sell their business, don't forget about taxes from the sale nor possible estate taxes. Most people do forget. Business owners are focused on the day-to-day stuff and don't always realize they may be opening themselves up to huge tax liabilities without enough forethought.

THE FAILED RETIREMENT

Okay, we've covered a lot of the nuance that goes into planning a retirement around your purpose. But what happens if you spend all of that time planning and then deviate from your plan? In many cases, the dreaded "failed retirement" happens. This is when the retiree has run out of money and now needs to go back to work.

There's one simple rule that can help you avoid a failed retirement: don't forget your retirement goals. Write it down on a piece of paper and tape it to your mirror—or some place where you will be constantly reminded.

When a person doesn't lead with their purpose, that's when people guilt themselves into paying for their grandchild's fancy car, spend too much cash when the market is strong, and other risky behaviors that implode a plan.

Think about your retirement the same way you would think about a business. Successful business owners go out of their way to grow their business and to *not* run it into the ground. Successful retirements operate the same way.

As you plan for your retirement journey, know what you can afford, set clear boundaries and expectations, stay disciplined with executing your plan, and don't delay your retirement goals or ignore your healthcare needs.

Part of maintaining the success of a retirement is accepting that, sometimes, things change. Think about that couple who lost $6 million of their $20 million net worth in five years. In order to not go back to work, they had to accept a change in their plan, modify their purpose, and take a lower monthly distribution than they hoped.

Part of preventing this kind of thing is building backup plans and parachutes into the retirement plan. But changes could be more subtle. Tax law will change. State laws will change. Inflation will give rise to budget adjustments. There will always be new wrinkles and nuances that require the retirement plan to slightly shift to keep everything operating as desired. Your WealthSpan Longevity Team will work with you to make sure your plan is updated and aligned with your purpose.

YOU NEED TO BE A PROACTIVE PART OF YOUR RETIREMENT

Successful retirements are properly planned, carefully considered, and centered on a purpose. *You* are a crucial collaborator in creating and being proactive about the retirement plan because the purpose emanates from you.

With that said, there are so many variables in the air that we must acknowledge that delegation is required to keep a retirement afloat. The critical thinking skills of you, your wealth manager, and the rest of your Wealth Longevity Team are required to make sure every gear is working together to keep the momentum of your financial life operating smoothly.

Without an exit strategy for retirement, you'll be paying more in taxes, will be exposed to more lawsuit liability, and, worst of all, you might run out of money. In my mind, those aren't risks that anybody should be willing to take.

Don't forget that the central thesis of this book is to *unsplode* with a combination of purpose and planning to live a fulfilled life. Without the purposeful planning of your retirement, you stand to lose out on a fulfilled life.

And that's what I'm here to help you avoid. I want you to *unsplode* your WealthSpan. It gives me the most satisfaction to know that I can help guide regular folks who deserve happiness and joy fix their financial planning to experience just that.

CONCLUSION

"Money grows on the trees of persistence."

—JAPANESE PROVERB

My hope for you is that you are completely rethinking the way you look at your wealth and retirement and are ready to build your WealthSpan using proactive and preventative steps, designed to protect.

Don't wish your week away and live for the weekend. Don't delay your life now for retirement later. Don't just match your 401(k) and expect everything to be fine. Don't just think that the sale of your business will take care of you. Don't explode your life while you're still living it.

Instead, unsplode it. Plan your financial WealthSpan to accommodate a purposeful and fulfilling life today *and* tomorrow. Make an impact on your life by giving yourself the time and freedom to choose how to use your wealth as a tool that creates memories, experiences, and joy.

FIND BALANCE TO ACHIEVE JOY

Your day should not just be spent hyperfocused on earning money, advancing your career, and increasing your net worth. Life is about so much more than that, and money is just a means to that end. Take all aspects of your life—health, wealth, family, friends, hobbies, and so on—evaluate them to find your purpose, create financial goals around them, and keep them in balance.

Finances are meant to serve your life's purpose, no more and no less.

Clients come into my office all the time and express that there was something missing in their life. They didn't do enough. They didn't experience enough. They just worked and worked and forgot about the fact that they were alive and, with that gift of time, spent their most precious resource unclear about what gave them joy. They regretted not experiencing life.

For better or worse, American society is one that values production. We too often think of our identity as being led by our net worth, our professional field, our business' size, or our career level. When we define ourselves this way, we end up lost. There are many reasons why, but the two primary reasons are that (1) it ignores our family, friends, and connections that make us feel secure and celebrate us, and (2) we will, one day, stop working and lose that part of our identity.

I no longer want that emptiness for my clients. That's why I'm writing this book—to reach as many people as possible and enact my own purpose.

DEVELOP NEW HABITS OF MIND

Change starts with you. It's hard to develop new habits, but that's what you need to do. My biggest fear now that you've read this book is having New Year's Resolution motivation.

Here's what I mean by that. Each January, the number of gym memberships across the country skyrocket. By February, they'd dipped back down to normal levels. Most people start the year with big aspirations to turn their health around by going to the gym, and in three weeks' time, they fizzle out and revert back to their normal habits. When it comes to your WealthSpan, don't be that person.

Build yourself from the ground up anew, formulate a plan with your WealthSpan Longevity Team, create new habits with their support, *unsplode* your WealthSpan, and build yourself a long-lasting, purposeful, and impactful life.

You might not know what's truly possible for you. For that reason alone, I encourage you to get into contact with a wealth manager who leads the meeting with questions geared toward discovering your purpose—your *why*. That bird's-eye view—that foundation—can help me engineer a financial plan for you that you never thought possible.

If you don't have a purpose, then there's no benefit to financial planning. I mean, you can go through the numbers. An advisor can do the financial plan. But by not focusing on any sense of purpose, there is nothing to look forward to—no carrot on the stick motivating you to stick to the financial plan. At that point, the plan essentially becomes throwing your hands up and hoping it works, which, I'm here to tell you, is not an effective strategy.

REACH OUT TODAY

Meeting with a wealth manager instead of a financial advisor might mean a few more meetings and phone calls a year. It might mean learning something about money. It might mean that this isn't only a money discussion, which is why it might cost a little bit more.

You'll learn more about your life's purpose. When we know more about that purpose, we can design a portfolio around *you*—adding value. Your investment portfolio will be invested in your life that will create purpose and fulfillment and prevent those end-of-life regrets you didn't even know you were on trajectory for.

People like me are here to help you. Take advantage of us. Start living your life today and build out the plan for your future. If you collaborate with us to become an active contributor to the health of your own WealthSpan, I believe you will have a higher probability of success because you will have a structured plan and a committed team.

SIDE 2

UNSPLODE YOUR HEALTHSPAN BY CALEB PINEGAR

INTRODUCTION

"To sustain longevity, you have to evolve."

—ARIES SPEARS

Hyperfocus leads to an imbalance.

And in the hustle culture of our modern world, that hyperfocus usually involves us putting our heads down and spending day in and day out building our business or career. One of the things that commonly gets left behind is investing back in our own health.

Sure, we may exercise a couple times a week. Maybe we even hit the gym occasionally. But in my medical experience, most people ignore their plans for health (strength, flexibility, nutrition, rest, etc.) the same way they avoid understanding their financial plan. That health-impacting imbalance might not seem like a big deal, but it's actively diminishing our longevity and, just as importantly, crippling our sense of happiness, fulfillment, and purpose.

What's worse, people don't usually come to see me until they're really sick and hurting. As a doctor, I see folks with horrible joint pain, sudden loss of limb function, serious illnesses, and more. Each and every one of them wants to be fixed immediately so that they can get back to their lives—and to live out their goals and dreams. But for far too many of them, they've passed the stage of genuine fixing and rebalancing. Their health habits worked against them over time until, eventually, they brought themselves to my office for major repair.

To increase longevity and avoid the health pitfalls of an imbalanced life, we must evolve our understanding of our health. We must plan our health with purpose—just like Trevor taught us to do with our finances. If we don't, we'll just become another patient in a doctor's office. And for doctors, many patients become cases and numbers. The days just blur together. But for me, Charles, as I will call him, was different.

It was December and nearing Christmas. The air was filled with the hustle and bustle of the holidays. The spirit of the season decorated the halls of the hospital and, frankly, the entire town in wintery Ohio. In a healthcare office like ours, it's a time of year when, in the face of all the sickness around us, there's a little more courage and positivity than usual.

When Charles checked himself in, he brought his own radiance and warmth that compounded the hospital's cheerfulness and made him an instant favorite among the doctors. As we got to know him, he told us that, before checking in, he was making Christmas preparations. What made him proudest of all was the fact that his toddler grandson would soon be in his house, and they were going to play trains together.

Beyond his extremely likable qualities, it was a pretty routine evaluation, and something Charles had done before. He was overweight and felt a little unwell. His shoulder hurt. He had chronic issues with his heart not pumping strongly enough to keep fluid going to his legs and lungs. He had shortness of breath. His expectation was to receive some diet recommendations and adjustments to his medication and maybe, at worst, be monitored for a day or two before being sent home.

That was the expectation of the hospital, too. But unfortunately, when a person has a lot of health problems and is on the older side, it makes them more vulnerable to other issues.

As it pertained to his shoulder pain, he had recently fallen and popped something in his shoulder trying to brace his fall. I was among the first to visit him, acting as his orthopedic doctor and surgeon who had come in for a consultation.

"Do you have any questions, Charles?" I asked after going over the simple surgery for his shoulder.

"I just want to make sure I'm able to get home for Christmas" was Charles's response. "I'm gifting a new toy train to my grandson." That's all he could talk about. He was a kind old man full of life and vitality, which made him the type of patient that every doctor in the hospital found an excuse to "check in" on because they just wanted to talk with him and receive some of that positive energy for their day.

"That should be no problem," I said. "There's plenty of time on the schedule for you to recover and be discharged before Christmas."

He received his IV, and it was time to go to bed.

For Charles, there was a complication with his IV. It's not uncommon for IVs to cause issues, especially at his age. This time, a change in the IV left a large blood blister on his hand. Typically, a healthy body is capable of resolving that. One seemingly normal night later, that blood blister soon turned his entire arm red, an arm that was hot to the touch.

The next morning, an infection was identified, and ICU was paged. His hematoma was opened, and a significant quantity of pus and infection poured out. By that time, he was on the brink of needing to be put into a medical coma to continue his various treatments, slow down the body process, and beat the infection.

Now his minor issue was huge. We took him into surgery a couple of times to try to scrub and clean the infection, but it was rampant through his body. We never stopped trying.

While we were fighting to keep him alive, his grandson was too young to visit the ICU. Between procedures, Charles pleaded with us, "I don't care what you do. Go ahead and cut off my arm if you have to. Just get me home."

Charles wouldn't be making it home for Christmas. Charles

wouldn't be making it home at all. The infection had already spread through his entire body, cutting off blood supply to vital organs, and ultimately, it took his life.

It's a heartbreaking story. One of many I carry with me. Charles *should* have been able to have many more Christmases with his family. He should have been healthy enough to have withstood the issue. But by that point, his habitual and general lack of health gave his medical team very little ability to control common complications.

THE NEW PURPOSEFUL PLANNING

Charles died that day. And there were two truths during his visit. First, what happened to him was not his fault. That IV infection, while unpredictable and uncommon, would not have happened to him if he hadn't left home. Second, he was not taking care of himself properly. He was morbidly unhealthy. He was obese, struggled to walk, made terrible diet choices for decades, and sought to treat debilitating symptoms rather than make major changes. When minor issues run into major health problems, bad things happen.

I say that because Charles was different than most grandparents. Most are a little heavy around the midsection. Maybe they are taking one blood pressure pill, a prediabetic medication, and a thyroid supplement. Smaller interventions that are, to some degree, attempting to be proactive. Charles, on the other hand, had a host of issues working against him.

For grandparents and for all of us, our bodies are ticking time bombs. We don't get to decide when the cumulative aspects of our health add up to the unthinkable.

Instead, we prolong our longevity by maintaining a healthy base, a purposeful plan for maintaining that health base, and a proactive mindset.

So much of our health is outside our control—like getting a minor infection or respiratory illness. It could be a random cold you caught in public that sends your body into an autoimmune response that you now have to treat for the rest of your life. It could be Charles getting an infection during a hospital visit. It could be anything.

But here's the stinger: there is *a ton* that you can control. And for what you can control, it all contributes to creating a HealthSpan—or your holistic health snapshot and your associated life expectancy—that maximizes your longevity. It's time to create a new purposeful planning system that optimizes your HealthSpan.

Americans live in a medical system that is reactive and not proactive. If it ain't broke, don't fix it. And even then, there are a lot of factors deterring patients from reacting to their health issues. Copays and deductibles lessen check-ins with primary care physicians. But even when patients come through the door, the role of the healthcare industry is to treat an illness or issue, not to, let's say, educate a patient on preventative practices, identify what the patient *could* be facing because of their lifestyle, or anything else that would otherwise help the patient proactively improve their HealthSpan.

And, okay, I can hear you thinking something along the lines of "Caleb, I'm not an obese grandfather with a series of medical conditions." Not yet, at least. You'd be surprised how quickly a few bad health habits can catch up with us. This is also a lesson for young people, not just those in their later years. I experience folks like Charles of all ages on a near daily basis. And I don't want you to be one of them.

Your healthcare routine depends largely on your age and situation. But do you exercise routinely? Are you evolving your vision of your own health to be appropriate for your age *while also* considering your future? Are you practicing burpees or just getting down and off the floor multiple times a day to help prevent the sometimes fatal ramifications of a sudden fall? Are you taking care of your mental health regularly? Do you have a "quarterback" healthcare provider and a larger team of health professionals whom you visit consistently? Do you not only eat healthy but keep track of what you eat and are intentional about what you put into your body? Are you balancing your business or career with your personal life and making sure to not overstress, overwork, and reach burnout? Do you practice and maintain good posture? Do you have good sleep hygiene? Are you avoiding alcohol, coffee, and soda? Are you doing light stretching daily to maintain flexibility? If you do all of these things, then why are you even reading this book? You're probably fine. Go read Trevor's WealthSpan side of the book and focus on the health of your finances.

It is far more likely, however, that you are in a situation where your lifestyle and habits of mind are causing you to neglect one or more crucial aspects of your HealthSpan. Like the capital in your financial plan (and Trevor can attest to this), your daily health habits—or lack thereof—will compound into the future.

Right now, you might think your bad sleep hygiene is fine. But these choices are actively shrinking your longevity. You might not be regularly going to the doctor—and the doctor may be going out of their way to tell you not to come—because you don't have an active, ongoing problem. These choices *will* cripple your sense of confidence, happiness, fulfillment, purpose, and overall health.

START NOW, NEVER STOP

The human body starts maturing at twenty, not forty or fifty like some people say. Yet we tend to not feel the ramifications of things until we are "older." I remember my family giving my teenage self a hard time all the time: "If you keep eating sugar this way, you'll really struggle to lose weight when you're older." I would think, "Whatever." Then I got older—like around thirty—and I was still eating sugar and still stayed in pretty good shape! For a long time I liked to internally tell myself, "They were wrong!" But then I was in my late thirties and early forties, and clearly they were right! I guess I was a little late to the game, but they weren't kidding...it's tough to lose weight now. Now it took work and required change. The type of changes that would set the stage for that transformation back to a healthier lifestyle and weight with my daily habits.

Things don't happen all at once when we're older. The truth is that our bodies actually start aging when we're still feeling great. The fact that I loaded my body with a bunch of garbage in my twenties has contributed to the later onset of my weight-control challenges. I could have pushed out my metabolism farther if I had been working on my HealthSpan earlier.

Not only are the consequences of our actions delayed, but we also need to think about the *balance* of actions we take to stay healthy. For example, even when I was in "great shape" in my twenties through activities like rock climbing, I was too hyperfocused on specific movements. My passion for rock climbing was making me "healthy" in an unbalanced way. I developed a very strong chest and muscles in the front of my body. My back, by necessity, was loose for the flexibility required to move from hold to hold. Over time, my posture became ape-like. And now I have to go out of my way to train my body to hold a better, healthier posture to combat the fact that I've put myself at higher risk for back issues—issues that I caused myself.

There are so many factors contributing to our HealthSpan, and we need to start now regardless of where we are. And by "start now," I don't mean wake up tomorrow and implement the perfect healthcare routine. There are many incremental steps we have to take first.

The first is a mindset step. We have to give ourselves space and permission to recognize our future, what we want from our future, and how to adjust our daily health habits accordingly to fit that future. We need to recognize that proactive mental health options, like therapy, are not just for crazy people. We have to realize that stretching is not just for old people. Nutrition is not just for those with celiac disease or dietary restrictions.

If you want to invest in yourself, you will need to harness a proactive approach.

BE PROACTIVE

The healthcare industry, in general, has become a siloed mess of specialists. Doctors are, in fact, discouraged from offering advice outside of their specialty.

I remember a patient who, in the middle of their orthopedic consultation, interrupted our discussion of her elbow pain to talk to myself and my attending about the pain in her ear. "Let me tell you everything I know about the ear," the attending physician began. "It has three bones in it. And none of those bones are ones that I have anything to do with. So you need to talk to your family doctor or to an ENT about that." This physician, of course, knew *way* more about the ear than that. But he had found a polite way to fend off the question because he was not trying to be the all-knowing source of medical information for this patient. He had additional patients to see, he had additional surgery to try to schedule, and he needed to keep moving. Plus the ear was not his specialty, and it was probably best that he not spend a bunch of time consulting on this ear issue when he could potentially lead the patient in the wrong direction!

In our society, we operate in a system that doesn't really encourage us to operate outside of our "lane." There can be legal issues to giving patient advice that is outside the scope of our own practice. Consultations are focused and specific. A specialist is paid to address the problem. The job is to identify the problem and treat it. In this way the specialist helps the patient. But it is largely about interventions, less about consulting and coaching.

For example, as an orthopedic surgeon, I am a human construction worker. In some ways, I am a hammer that is looking for a nail. Specifically in my case, these ailments (nails) that I am looking to fix are shoulders, elbows, hips, knees, and some occasional wrists and ankles. In my personal practice, I am rewarded financially most when I repair one of these structures. Consultations, coaching, and education are part of the job; however, the financial reward for those activities pales in comparison to the surgeries that I can perform. Have you ever been to a surgeon's office and felt rushed, and that they hardly heard you talk, but that they got to the point and discussed a potential intervention or procedure, and that you were then sent on your way? This is why!

While this may seem somewhat restrictive, the specialization of the healthcare industry *can* be advantageous to us as well. With these highly trained and specialized individuals, you can create a team of professionals that combine specialists and generalists—like a functional doctor—to keep your holistic understanding of your own health situation crystal clear. You need to balance your team just like you need to balance your health. Basically, we have created the need for a bigger team, but each teammate is way more talented than the prior generation!

Converting old habits into new ones is hard. It takes months, sometimes longer. The mindset issue is the first, perhaps hardest issue we face. Unless you were a high school athlete that learned how to be a gym rat with proper technique, chances are you don't know how to properly work out—and working out with bad technique can create *more* problems rather than prevent them. Leaning on the support of a team of professionals is imperative to helping you change your habits. This includes a personal trainer. Trust me, the money is worth it.

Let me be part of your support team. Let me help you identify the people that you need to be talking to. Let me help you recognize if the team you have chosen is the type of team that actually does have your best interest in mind! It's possible that they sound great but that they're leaving out some very important parts! I've seen firsthand the rat race of the medical field that doesn't optimize preventative and proactive work for people's HealthSpan. I hustled through that rat race myself. Now, I'm ready to share what I've learned with you.

What's tough is that maintaining our HealthSpan requires our time and money. Special doctors cost more. Organic food and quality meat costs more. Whenever I leave the grocery store, fight off my inherent cheapness, and leave with an organic vegetable, I know I'm building a strong habit of mind.

The healthy habits you'll learn in this book are extensive. After going over what makes up our HealthSpan, we'll begin with that all-important mindset shift. And while that is a tough hurdle to overcome, it won't be the only one.

In Chapter 3, we'll shift our focus to starting where we are right now by inventorying our current health situation *and* taking stock of our health goals. With that information known, we can form the foundation of the next steps of our unique health routine meant to maximize our individual HealthSpan.

From there, we'll learn what we can do to protect the most important assets of our health. But protection isn't the only thing; that's why we'll explore what we can do to preventatively and proactively improve our longevity.

After being inundated with new knowledge, we can't be expected to be capable of knowing or implementing *every* strategy required on our own. That's why we need a HealthSpan Longevity Team. In Chapter 6, we'll go over who could be on this team, how to vet them, who the leader of the team could be, and why they are necessary.

Finally, we talk about maintaining our health as we enter and thrive in our twilight years. Included in that is thinking about your expectations for your retirement and your body.

WHAT DOES "UNSPLODE" YOUR HEALTHSPAN MEAN?

We are all primed for our health to explode out of our control and for one of our tomorrows to be our last. To push that "explosion" of tomorrow out farther, we should do everything we can to, as my son would say, "unsplode" it today. Get to it first—or do the preventative work to maximize the longevity of your life and fitness now instead of when it's too late. To *unsplode* is to reverse or cancel the negative actions or state that we could be in if we don't take action now. It's about creating a health plan that allows us to live the life we want today *and* tomorrow.

In the end, and in order to live a fulfilled life, you have to take care of your own HealthSpan first and foremost. You have to commit to yourself first. You have to realize that you are of less help to your family and community if you are not at your best! Consider it like the oxygen masks on a plane. How effective are you going to be in helping your family if you're unconscious? The instructions clearly state that first you have to put your own mask on. First you have to make sure you are ok! First you have to make sure that you understand the principles and process. And then you can focus on those around you. We have to do the same with our health.

Taking time for ourselves is a sacrifice. It does take away from other parts of your life. But you will be better for it. You will be more effective because of it. You will be more productive because of it. And your relationships will have the potential for added growth and satisfaction if you prioritize it. Keep in mind the wonderful quote from *The Princess Bride*, where Count Rugen so rightly said, "If you haven't got your health, you haven't got anything."

This needs to be applied to your life in consideration of your HealthSpan in several ways: health, nutrition, exercise, work balance, longevity, investments, goals, family, friends, mental health, clarity, and so many more! But please, let's be clear. The goal of this book is not to say you need to throw your hypertension pills in the toilet or fire your primary doctor because there are alternative or preventative approaches. The goal is to recognize your current health status, give you the tools to build a health roadmap, think about your next steps, and change your daily habits to increase your chances of living a long, fulfilled life. For example, a good question to ask your primary doctor might be "What can I do naturally to not have to take these pills?" Sometimes, you have to be the one to ask proactive questions so you can get the answers you need.

You won't get healthy by drinking one protein shake or by going just to a physical therapist or athletic trainer. You'll start on the pathway to better health if you are able to use this book as a gateway to transform complex variables into simple action steps that can build on each other.

Something's got to change in your health routine, and you know it. But there needs to be a balance in your life to make memorable experiences. You'll need your health, *and* you'll need the financial tools to pay for it. As you move throughout the chapters in "Unsplode Your HealthSpan," there will be corresponding chapters related to your

WealthSpan—a financial longevity carefully designed to let you afford a fulfilled life today *and* tomorrow—in this book's complementary part, "Unsplode Your WealthSpan."

Since the chapters correspond, you've got options on how you want to read—once through *or* corresponding chapter by corresponding chapter. It's a Choose Your Own Adventure.

Don't wait until some special day to start. Don't wait until New Year's to get a gym membership that goes unused. Begin today. Tomorrow could be the day that your health DOES explode. And at that point your opportunity to *unsplode* it first has passed! You'll have missed it! Choose to *unsplode* today. Don't wait until tomorrow. Do not forget that "the pathway to hell is paved with good intentions." None of us intend to blow it. None of us intend to make a mockery of our lives or our health or our careers. But some of us will. Some of it will be because we delayed or because we didn't have the proper tools. But luckily some of us will take the warning seriously and will make the changes. Some of us will start today and will look back from a future date and be forever glad that we did not wait.

Trevor and I are finally, after a decade of work, challenging some norms in the health and finance industries. With any luck, you'll gain insight to make changes for your own betterment.

Start now. Tomorrow is today.

CHAPTER 1

HEALTHSPAN: FINDING LONGEVITY IN YOUR PHYSICAL AND MENTAL WELL-BEING

"The future depends on what you do today."

—MAHATMA GANDHI

You need a new health mindset.

That mindset should combine two primary ideas: (1) that you are only promised today to maintain presence and joy in the moment, and (2) that you can use your todays to increase the chances that your tomorrow will come. In other words, you need to purposefully plan your future without compromising today.

People, in general, aren't primed to have this sort of balanced mindset. When we are young, we want to experience everything right now, all at once. When I was in high school, I put together a spreadsheet with everything listed out. Exercise, friend hangouts, church, family dinner, school, and work all populated this meticulous schedule, color-coded and complete. I was busy all the time. In fact, there were more hours of activities on the schedule than there were in the actual week.

So what did I do? Did I recognize the problem and choose to simplify my life and minimize the problems so that I could enjoy my life and my relationships and my time and my situation? OF COURSE I DIDN'T! I put my head down, and I ground it out! I got too busy to see Trevor. I got too busy to see family. I barely made time to sleep. And I didn't go to the gym unless it was when a friend convinced me to get outside to burn off steam rock climbing or skiing or mountain biking. And if those people didn't push me, then I'd probably never have even left the cover of a rooftop!

I looked at the problem and said: *Well crap, I had better get going, or I'm never going to make it!* I didn't realize that I had the option to say "no" to some things! I didn't comprehend the idea that I could always go a little slower. I figured that if I wanted to reach my goals and dreams, then the only way was going to be to fight and fight and fight.

As a kid, to get around the issue of there not being enough time, I would cut back on my sleep. The consequences of that didn't seem too bad. I was always in a hurry and mildly tired. But I was a kid, so I could take it—I thought.

In college, I continued to be frustrated by this grind. I studied the issue, and I wanted to help others identify lifestyle habits that they probably didn't view as a health problem, so I wrote a paper in one of my English classes about this concept of being overbusy and about industrial acceleration and sleep hygiene. It was titled "Slow Down America, We Need More Sleep." In it, I pointed to the decades of evolving US culture and economics and the effect that has had on the entire global economy and culture. Our society has rewarded the 24/7 work cycle and has rewarded hyper-presence and constant availability. Stores opening 24/7 and businesses being pressured to remain open on weekends in order to survive and the effect this has on all of us. It was insightful for me to study these issues, and as I combined those findings with what I learned after I entered medical school, I began to see it even more clearly.

As I gained general knowledge about longevity and health, I started to realize that despite all of the things that I had studied and learned, that I still wasn't making the healthiest choices. If I continued down the road I was taking with poor sleep hygiene, I would have taken many years off my life. Why did it take medical school for me to learn that? Why wasn't that common knowledge?

If you're not embedded in that constant work cycle and burned out yourself, you've at least heard of it. Nonstop work and availability—remember when email and cell phones were supposed to improve our lives?—has increasingly damaged important aspects of health. Constant work has destroyed our sleep hygiene, socialization with friends and family, and our sense of self-worth and purpose, to name a few.

As I look back, my premedical advisor had been an excellent resource to me. I shared with him my concerns, my findings for my English paper, and we discussed the situation that I was putting myself in. Then he revealed to me that I needed to practice what I preached. "Caleb, what is your hurry? What is your rush? Take time to smell the roses," he said. I had heard that phrase before, but it never meant anything to me. Of course roses smell good. Of course I can smell them. But how powerful is that statement if you actually take a step back and think about it?

That was my first wake-up call, and unfortunately I have had many since! It appears that I have needed every one of them! Because over a long period of time, I didn't use any of these wake-up calls to make any real changes! There is probably never going to be an "Aha" moment. There will probably never be a movie ending that suddenly changes our life forever based on one fantastic moment. The likelihood is that we will have moments that inspire change, and then we will fall back into our old habits. Because this is a continuous process. This is a continuous fix. One with ups and downs and with turns and obstacles. We will likely never "get there," but we can aim in the right direction, and we can never give up. That is the goal.

On one of my more profound wake-up calls, it felt like it all exploded. I joined this crazy person to run a five-hour, mud-filled obstacle course. This crazy person happens to be my cousin and co-author Trevor, whom you have already met in this book. And you should know that Trevor has been more mindful about his health for many more years than I have. He's an animal. And on this occasion he cruised his way through the race without even reaching a heart rate of 100. And then there was me. I could barely force myself through it. I was miserable. I had to run multiple penalty laps for parts of the race that I simply couldn't complete. Afterward, I was debilitatingly sore for weeks. I was not healthy! My habits were terrible. My balance was a mess. Something needed to change. It was time to *unsplode*!

I finally got my mindset right and began to turn things around. "The way to get started was to quit talking and begin doing," Walt Disney famously said. So it was my turn to do the same. And now, it's your turn.

Here's the good news. Being here right now, just holding this book (or listening to it) is a sign that you've made a similar recognition and have begun the process of changing your mindset. Something needs to change, and you are the only one empowered to do it.

MIND OVER MATTER

A person who has developed a solid HealthSpan started that work by recognizing that they could do better. From that mindful starting place arises the drive to change. From that drive to change comes a plan. And from that plan comes execution and, eventually, true change.

So mindset is where we'll begin.

In my experience, *most* people live in a brain that thinks it has a twenty-year-old body. In the wintertime, my office is filled with older dudes with hip, shoulder, and back problems after taking a three-foot-fall off a ladder while attempting to install the Christmas lights. "I'm eighty! I can still put up my own Christmas lights," the thinking goes. Then we fall off the latter and incur a series of potentially horrific injuries.

TREVOR'S INTERJECTION

You didn't think I was going to let Caleb have all the fun, did you? You might have noticed how his interjections helped demonstrate how purposeful and lasting health and wealth are interrelated. Having both in balance creates a fulfilled life. So you'll see me do the same throughout his HealthSpan side.

As a wealth manager, many of my clients are up there, in terms of age. That fact might lessen some of your surprise when I say this: I've had several clients die specifically from falling off ladders. It's a big enough percentage of the total clients I've had over my lifetime to stand out.

What Caleb is getting at here, in terms of the average person walking around with a health-deteriorating mindset that they can do anything, is something I have directly experienced multiple times. Don't overlook the significance of this point.

Caleb himself has had to surgically fix hundreds of hip fractures. And when you reach the age of sixty-five, 30 percent of people with a hip fracture will die within a year. Maybe that risk isn't worth putting up the Christmas lights this year. Delegate that to your adult child or neighborhood teenager, as long as you have umbrella insurance, of course.

Falling is actually really destructive for adults. We did it so much as kids, so we think we can get back on that bike. But should we? Are we ready? Can we handle what happens if it goes poorly? When a fall does come around, so do the significantly increased chances of something bad happening. What could we do to reduce that possibility? What could we do to manage the damage of a fall? How often do you actually get on the ground? How often do you practice going to the ground and getting back up? What type of prep work or training have you done for it? Have you heard of a burpee? You could prevent some of the problems associated with falling if you do some occasional burpees!

Honestly, I adopt a "I can do anything" mentality. I'll think irrational things like "I can install my backyard retaining wall myself. How hard could it be?!" Then, several back-pain-induced sleepless nights later, I regret everything and wished I would've just hired professionals.

It's a mindset issue. We think we are capable, but we are probably much less than capable. (Or we think we are healthy, but we likely aren't.)

The hard truth is that, unless you are in your early twenties, your body is already in decline. Everything has already hit its potential max. The gap between what you think you are capable of and what you can actually do will only widen. And as time goes on, closing that gap by making gains and growth only becomes more difficult.

Mindset is so important I'll devote the entire next chapter to the topic. But it's only when you acknowledge this gap and see the need to close it that you'll have taken a mindset step in the right direction toward lengthening your HealthSpan.

WHAT IS HEALTHSPAN?

"HealthSpan" is a word that combines *health* and *lifespan.* It is the recognition that your overall health, longevity, and sense of purpose and fulfillment requires that you take control of your physical and mental well-being.

Your current HealthSpan is how wide or narrow that aforementioned gap is—that gap between what you think you can do and what you can actually do. The wider the gap, the shorter your HealthSpan and the worse your overall health. The narrower that gap, the more control you've exerted and smaller the odds of your health breaking down. It's the safety of your choices, both in preventing yourself from doing dumb things that will harm you but also in doing the proactive things that will strengthen your body and mind's natural systems.

Only then, with an active, healthy mindset, can you exert yourself in such a manner that contributes to your purpose, values, dreams, and future.

Here's another way to think about HealthSpan. You need to be the insurance company of your well-being—but focused on the opposite thing. Let me unpack that, and a small warning for cynicism, but stick with me. Insurance companies are very, very driven. It just so happens that they are driven by money. It's really expensive for surgery, for example, and the insurance companies themselves will have targets of what they want to hit—in terms of how many of a specific kind of surgery they want to pay for. They see their target, and they work backward.

In order to hit their targets, they carefully design the requirements in such a way to make it harder for folks who might need the surgery to actually afford to get it. These abundant and complex and often contradictory rules are carefully structured. They are preventing more surgeries and the monetary ramifications of having to pay for more.

It turns out that methodical and goal-oriented approaches like this work.

So if you were to be like an insurance company but with an opposing goal, we need to think about our own health like an insurance company thinks about money. In other words, do the work now to prevent the surgery from happening later.

When you *unsplode* the degradation of the human body, you'll keep your health in balance and be confident in your future. Throughout the book, we'll emphasize that our HealthSpan is made up of two intermingling parts: our mental and physical health. They need to be in balance. Without one, you can't enjoy the other. To fully understand our HealthSpan and the nonnegotiables associated with them, let's take a closer look at conveyances of both our mental and physical health.

MENTAL HEALTH NONNEGOTIABLES

First of all, what is mental health? To me, it has to do with our ability to take time every day to enjoy our lives. It means living our life based on our own values and not somebody else's. Finally, strong mental health is about taking accountability of the people in our lives.

But there are some nuances, so let's break mental health down into categories.

THE ROLE OF NEUROTRANSMITTERS

Many mental health conditions like depression, anxiety, ADHD, and others can be traced back to the root cause of an imbalance in neurotransmitters facilitating the communication between neurons. These neurotransmitters are also influential in other conditions as we age such as Parkinson's disease. These neurotransmitters are vital for healthy connections and communications—or are responsible for unhealthy misfires—and have a direct influence over our mood, emotions, and cognitive function. There are a few key chemicals at play here that I'll cover briefly. Serotonin regulates your mood. Dopamine signals pleasure. Oxytocin is crucial for social bonding and emotional regulation. And norepinephrine dictates your stress response, alertness, and attention.

Here's where things get interesting. Our daily habits shape and reinforce the body's ability to both create and utilize these signaling factors, and we need these to build healthy neural connections in our brains and to stabilize our body's functional systems. Having sufficient quantities of these neurotransmitters, and the proper use of them, is vital to our mental health, cognitive function, and satisfaction in life. And balance is key for this to work. By that I mean balance of production and also balance of utilization of these crucial components of our systems.

Each chemical at play—serotonin, dopamine, oxytocin, and norepinephrine—becomes more deficient (the brain produces less AND our ability to use what we have is inhibited) when you experience chronic stress, have poor nutrition, don't get enough sleep, or have a substance use disorder. So a person might think that they're walking around depressed and receive a pill to help combat that specific issue. However, it might actually be the case that the underlying issue is something different entirely.

Supplementing more of this neurotransmitter may provide some benefit; however, the problem is also that the body is not using this transmitter properly and that the balance between the other systems is off. If we supplement but don't address some of the other factors that are influencing the problem, such as reducing stress and improving sleep, we may actually fail at getting better and making progress. Addressing the underlying problem could lead to a much more effective solution and may even clear up this condition—or at least result in a smaller dose requirement for adequate treatment.

While I do not want to state that all mental health conditions just need to adjust their habits and their diet, I do want to say that we often chase a more simple fix (such as a pill) when our choices and daily commitments may be a much bigger part of the problem, and without addressing that component, we may end up chasing multiple medications and still not feel the improvement that we seek.

Let's break down some of the basic non-medicinal ways that we can try to create an environment for our body to have sufficient quantities of these neurotransmitters so that we can set ourselves up for the best chance of success.

Serotonin allows for improved mental stability, emotional control, and restraint. There is a space between stimulus and reaction where human beings can decide between the available options and very briefly consider the consequences before we choose our reaction. Serotonin allows us to make choices intentionally that will delay the gratification of an event, and proper levels of serotonin—combined with appropriate training—can help us to control our impulses. Low serotonin levels can lead to instability of the system and lead to volatility and emotional collapse.

Many of the targeted medications for mental health disorders are aimed at serotonin, with the intention to improve the concentration levels and improve utilization of this neurotransmitter. In the body, exposure to sunlight and aerobic exercise are necessary for adequate production of this neurotransmitter. A diet that includes turkey, nuts, and eggs is also a modifiable choice—and a series of choices can result in a new habit—to improve the availability of nutrients for creation of this neurotransmitter. Fostering good relationships will improve our sense of emotional stability and lead to a greater sense of gratitude, also improving levels of serotonin within the body. Mindfulness and meditation also stimulate production of this neurotransmitter, and production and utilization of this neurotransmitter can be improved with a dedication to such practice.

Dopamine is a large facilitator of our attention span and of our reward system regulation. This system can be thrown off-balance in a negative way by pornography, gambling, recreational drugs, social media, binge-eating, and anything that produces an artificial "high." Over time, the body's reward and pleasure systems now crave that artificial "high," which can then lead a person to have a decreased ability to experience adequate pleasure and satisfaction during real situations and real personal relationships. This can lead to dissatisfaction in our personal lives and in our relationships with family and friends. It can also get us into a lot of trouble if chasing these "highs" leads us to either personal, financial, or legal trouble.

The natural ways that the body stimulates the release of dopamine, and the key ingredients to making this neurotransmitter, come from cardio and aerobic exercise with the recommendation of thirty or more minutes of exercise three to five times per week. Adequate sleep is necessary for improved neurotransmitter production and for proper storage and filing of our daily memories and experiences. Exposure to the sun helps the body with the natural release of dopamine. And a diet including almonds and eggs can help the body store the natural building blocks and ingredients needed to create this neurotransmitter.

Oxytocin has been probably more highly discussed in relation to the bonding hormone between mother and baby during the early period of life. However, this hormone is active in all humans and has been described as a "love hormone" or as a "bonding hormone." Low levels of oxytocin lead to a decrease in interest as well as feelings of loneliness and isolation. Low levels of oxytocin are also a direct result of stress and anxiety. It is produced in the brain and is found to increase with meaningful conversation and physical touch. This hormone can be improved with performing acts of kindness, associating with pets, cuddling a loved one, and giving or receiving a hug. It can be improved with laughter and is also improved during meditation exercises and the practice of yoga.

Norepinephrine is required in the body to allow us to have the proper energy and readiness so that we can be prepared for unexpected events and surprises and to provide clarity during executive functions. When this neurotransmitter runs low, or if we are not properly utilizing this neurotransmitter, we may feel unclear and foggy. Stimulation of this neurotransmitter comes from interval training and high-intensity workouts and a recommended twenty to thirty minutes of such exercise two to three times per week.

Another stimulation tactic for this neurotransmitter is cold exposures, and we later discuss cold plunges in reference to their health benefits. Norepinephrine production is one of these benefits from cold plunges and cold exposure. A cold shower will also provide similar production of this neurotransmitter as the body ramps up production of this neurotransmitter to combat this noxious stimulus. Again sleep is crucial to adequate production and utilization of this neurotransmitter, including a diet with sufficient protein. Lastly, production of norepinephrine is improved by participating and mindfulness exercises and deep breathing exercises.

In reviewing these four components of mental health, there are some specific patterns to note. And although we discussed these factors more in a contribution to various aspects of our physical HealthSpan, here we find these contributing factors to be part of the initial building blocks of the various chemicals within our brains that allow improved productivity and satisfaction in our lives. Here is a brief recap of some of the critical components that we have choice in and control over when choosing our activities of daily life:

- A balanced dedication to physical activity, including stretching, aerobic exercise, and high-intensity exercise
- A dedication to mindfulness, meditation, deep breathing, and gratitude practice
- A dedication to close relationships, including physical touch, meaningful conversation, and acts of service
- A proper diet consisting of the proper nutrients to provide both protein and other building blocks required for production of these crucial natural chemical elements of the body and brain

So not only is exercise, mental health, a commitment to relationships, and diet critical for the overall well-being of our physical body, it is also critical for improving our mental health and emotional instability as we aim at lifestyle modifications that will contribute to the longevity of our HealthSpan.

BRAIN ACTIVITY

We've gotten this far about mental health, but now we have to acknowledge that the mental processes involved are directly underlined by the biological health of the brain. We could consider this point a physical-mental health hybrid, but keeping the brain healthy improves our overall mental and emotional well-being.

Lots of factors influence your brain activity, such as sleep and exercise. Cognitive training can influence your neuroplasticity—neuroplasticity is the brain's ability to adapt and change and learn new tasks or habits. This adaptation and ability to change is crucial for our brain's growth and for our ability to modify our situations.

When it comes to "cognitive training," that's the fancy word for keeping your brain in shape through puzzles and other activities. This could include Sudoku, meditation, gratitude exercises, and other brain-stimulating activities that build your neurotransmitters. So read a book. Take a quiz for comprehension. Learn a new language. Sign up for a continuing education class or for a home study program in a topic that interests you.

You need to figure out what's best for your age and situation. College-aged people taking advanced math classes might not benefit from Sudoku, whereas a retiree whose major event of the day is sipping their morning coffee might. That stressed-out college student might, instead, benefit from meditation to create a soothing counterpoint to their otherwise abundant mental load.

Don't overdo it. Don't underdo it. Find a balance. Overactivity and underconnectivity are linked to anxiety, stress, and depression.

STRESS MANAGEMENT

Did you know that stress is actually a really important tool? We need it for survival. Our loinclothed caveman ancestors used it to run away from predators like tigers and cheetahs.

In the modern work office, though, there are no tigers in the room—at least, not the fatal kind. Yet the stress being put on the body might as well be the same as if we're getting chased by a tiger. Most people now trigger their stress response during everyday situations at work or on a date. "If they don't think I'm cute, it's going to be the end of the world!" We've adapted the stress response to fire so that we can put our best foot forward in a number of low-stakes social and professional situations. Accrued over time, the modern human is using their stress response in a manner that generates chronic anxiety, depression, other mental health conditions, and oftentimes inflammation.

You need to put this stress response to sleep or at least use it in a balanced way where you can turn it on as needed, allowing you to stay present. Additionally, a stressed-out state negatively affects the immune system, heart, and gut health, and even increases cancer progression.

There are many small ways you can start finding balance. They include deep breathing, progressive muscle relaxation (tensing and relaxing different muscle groups), listening to calming music, getting more sleep, eating better, exercising regularly, and reducing your caffeine and alcohol intake.

There are also cognitive techniques that help us manage stress, such as identifying and avoiding stressors, challenging negative thoughts, implementing coping mechanisms, and putting ourselves in more relaxing environments. This is where you could benefit from putting vacations, friend and family time, personal time, hobby time, or time freedom (where it's dealer's choice on how you spend your time) on your schedule.

Use these tools to take a focused look at yourself. Reset using these tools to regenerate productivity, motivation, and your sense of purpose.

SLEEP MANAGEMENT

I once worked with an athlete that had a team of medical professionals around him. In a joint meeting with many of these professionals, he made a gruff complaint about minor groin pain (it wasn't his biggest issue) as we were treating his sidelining injuries. His physical therapist quickly jumped in, "If you don't start getting better sleep, that nor any of it is going to get better." It came as a bit of a surprise for this guy. He hadn't considered how his lack of sleep was affecting his state of mind, changing his gait, and resequencing how his brain was firing off his muscles (in an injury-prone way), and how, overall, it was interrupting his healing process.

A nonnegotiable for a strong HealthSpan is establishing a consistent and appropriate sleep schedule, which includes going to bed and waking up at the same time every day. Naps are fine, but don't make them overly long. Everybody needs a different amount of sleep, so find the total amount of hours that seems to maximize your mental health. For some, that can be as little as six hours or as many as nine.

The environment is crucial, too. You don't want to be falling asleep to screens. Avoid bright and loud environments. Cool the room down. Use blackout curtains where possible. And ensure your bed and pillows are tailored to your body's needs. To help transition you off your device (or if you *must* read it before bed for whatever reason), here's a trick: set your phone to a red screen. It won't spike dopamine like a blue or white light will.

Wind down using a routine, such as reading a book or listening, journaling, mindfulness meditation, or deep breathing. If you're a parent of young kids, take a look at how they approach winding down. Are you modeling good behavior for how to do this properly? If you aren't teaching them, then who is?

PHYSICAL HEALTH NONNEGOTIABLES

You should be proactively strengthening your physical health through a series of nonnegotiables. This is as true for the healthy person as it is for the person who already has two knee replacements and is working to achieve what many in their position can't. That's what Greg Paul did in 2016, when he became the first person with two artificial knees to summit Mt. Everest.

If you're twenty and feeling as healthy as an ox, middle-aged and feeling joint pain from walking up or down the stairs, or facing some sort of major health condition, there are always benefits to certain health nonnegotiables. Here are a few.

NUTRITION

Eat like you want to live. Eat like you care what you are feeding. One of my most influential teachers of my medical training used to bring his breakfast to our work space and state, "It's time to feed the machine." And then he would dig into his well-balanced and intentional meal. If we truly look at our body as a prime piece of equipment, and if we value it for the miraculous structure that it is, then do we want to put garbage in it? Or do we want to put race engine fuel in it? How you treat your body is a direct reflection of your understanding of the type of machine that you see yourself as!

If you want to live healthy, eat healthy. Besides a sedentary lifestyle, bad nutrition is the biggest contributor to a shorter HealthSpan. Junk food is like junk bonds—high risk, low return, and lots of hidden costs. A clean, nutrient-rich diet is the equivalent of blue-chip investments in the body.

A good diet is about balance. Balance a variety of fruits, vegetables, healthy fats, and lean proteins while avoiding processed or highly processed foods, added sugar, trans fats, excessive sodium, or other ingredients known to cause serious health risks. Processed foods and sugar inflame the body silently—just like unnecessary fees erode wealth behind the scenes. You don't notice them...until you do.

TREVOR'S INTERJECTION

It's me, again—the WealthSpan guy. Despite being a wealth manager, my biggest outside-of-work passion is nutrition and health. The photo of myself I chose for this book might not show it, but some of the other ones did. All kidding aside, Caleb knows his stuff, and so do I.

Here's some nutritional advice I live by. Grocery stores tend to organize their products by separating the healthy lean meats, vegetables, and fruits from the processed foods. Make it a habit to shop for foods outside of the aisles—those meat and produce sections. Avoid the aisles that stack all the processed foods with startlingly long shelf lives.

When it comes to healthy fats and oils, try to avoid cooking with vegetable oil or seed oils. They tend to be higher in acidity and contribute to inflammation. Less acidic oils include avocado oil, olive oil, coconut oil, and beef tallow.

We're a bit at a disadvantage when it comes to adopting and maintaining a healthy diet. More often than not, the most delicious food is often the cheapest, fastest to get, and the worst for us. I won't name names, but many processed food companies have labs and teams of scientists whose goal is to make the food taste better and be more addictive.

Cultivating good nutrition often means sacrificing what we like most (such as cookies) while making time to research, acquire, and cook organic ingredients. Once you find some recipes that you like, consider bulk batching and meal planning so that you can make a bunch of food at once and eat it slowly over time.

Keep portion sizes limited, as larger portions can increase risks associated with heart disease, blood pressure, and some cancers. I don't mention weight gain here because research suggests that weight gain is associated with total caloric intake over time. So currently, the thinking is that there is very little difference, weight-gain-wise, if you eat a specific amount in a day all at once compared to that same amount broken up into smaller quantities multiple times throughout the day.

EXERCISE AND MOBILITY

Muscle strength and flexibility are major nonnegotiable factors for our longevity. Every workout, walk, or weight lifted is a deposit. Skipping movement is like skipping savings—you may not feel it now, but the balance will be zero when you need it most.

The baseline is whether or not you can step down from a curb. If you can't do that, you might be in trouble. If you can, it's time to work backward from there to add strength and flexibility to your core workout routines.

For muscle strength, you need to keep the muscle groups strong that are associated with your desired hormonal balance. For me, an aging man, I need to do the work to keep my cortisol and testosterone levels what they should be. That means I'll need to build muscle in my proximal trunk (core), upper arms, quads, and hamstrings. These will regulate those hormones as well as my insulin balance and production.

While muscles let you move your body with strength, they also need to be flexible enough to make the range of motions required to perform actions. Flexibility reduces muscle soreness, improves our performance, reduces risk of injury, and adds longevity to our joints, among other things.

Poor flexibility can lead to muscle imbalances, throwing off the supporting structures like one beam knocking the whole house down. But it can also lead to poor posture, which itself can cause hypertension, circulation issues, and a number of other health maladies.

By going to yoga or working with a physical therapist or athletic trainer on a routine, flexibility can improve with regular static and dynamic stretches. LeBron James is famous for popularizing flexibility, yoga, Pilates, and mobility work to increase the longevity of his HealthSpan. His results speak for themselves.

Alternatively, you might reach out to an athletic trainer (ATC) or strength and conditioning coach (CSCS), or another physical-medicine-based specialty. Whoever it is, be committed to the process. Focus on muscle groups that matter most to your situation. If you have had knee surgeries, your stretches will likely be targeting your upper and lower leg muscles. You may not necessarily be doing a lot of arm stretches.

PREHABILITATION AND REHABILITATION

If you expect to need surgery, which is almost inevitable for anybody who lives past the age of sixty, the success of that surgery increases if you carefully prehabilitate—or do the exercises necessary to prepare for the surgery.

What does "success" in a surgery mean? A surgeon can fix a joint, but the successful outcome of that will mean that the patient can successfully use it. In other words, and what many people don't realize, the success of a surgery is largely dependent on the patient and if they are properly prehabilitating.

Prehabilitation is not always possible. But when it is, it's a nonnegotiable.

When I see patients after their surgery, I always tell them the same thing: "*I* fixed it. Now *you've* got to heal it." The surgical repair work is only part of the work. And you can put your trust in yourself or in sheer luck to finish the rest of the job! One of the most important parts of having strong physical health is doing the rehabilitation work required after a surgery or other injurious event. That's a habit of mind thing. If you stop doing your exercises, your issues are on you. A patient once told me, when recalling an injury years prior, that she was surprised that it took her eight months to return to sports activities. In that same breath, she off-handedly mentioned that she *never* did her post-injury physical therapy. I told her that the extended length shouldn't have been a surprise and was directly linked to the (lack of) rehabilitation work she put in.

Outcomes (or outputs) are dependent on our inputs.

BE PURPOSEFUL ABOUT YOUR HEALTH

Even if you have millions of dollars in your retirement account, it will not matter if you retired with a truncated HealthSpan fraught with debilitating physical injury or mental health issues. You will have exploded your health, and your opportunity to *unsplode* it will have been missed. If a life in your career has left you depressed, you won't suddenly get better when you retire. If you worked your body to the bone and now have all sorts of joint issues, you won't magically transition away from that to enjoy your twilight years.

And if you're younger, you are laying the path toward your future life today without even knowing it. Keep that in mind. Tomorrow is today.

Commit to change now by unsploding and purposefully planning your HealthSpan to cultivate success and longevity. Combine that with Trevor's strategies to maximize your WealthSpan on the other side of this book, and that's a recipe for a long life filled with joy and purpose.

You have enough time in your day. You have what it takes to address what you can control about your health. You don't lack. You have the choice to be proactive and prioritize what your day consists of. In the end, you choose to be too busy and unfocused or controlled and focused. If you think you don't have what it takes, or if you think you do not have enough time, then you've got a mindset issue.

I want to point out to you that this type of thinking is not easy. Absorbing our own faults, accepting the blame, and internalizing the problems that we have in our own lives is not easy. Just like living a life with purpose and with clarity is not always easy. But it is worth it! You will have ups; you will have downs. You need to forgive your past self. You are here reading this book now; you are learning. You are learning and developing tools that you previously might not have had. You are making decisions and changes that go against what you previously might have done. All of these are fantastic steps in the right direction. I encourage you to approach them with grace. Grace for yourself. The future is bright and will be worth it if you choose to take it.

The all-important mindset is what we'll focus on in the next chapter.

CHAPTER 2

THE NEW PURPOSEFUL MINDSET OF HEALTH: HOW TO RETHINK THE WAY YOU APPROACH WELL-BEING

"I have always been in the right place at the right time. Of course, I steered myself there."

—BOB HOPE

Aspirations and goals are only achieved if you do two things: (1) you have put yourself on the path to achieve them. Things aren't given to you. They don't magically happen. Stop making excuses. And (2) you have to adopt the mindset that your goals are achievable.

Part of my success in medicine has been based on these principles. I'll give you an example. It involves somebody that many sports fans have heard of: Dr. James Andrews. He is the surgical extraordinaire. He saved the career of Hall of Famer Roger Clemens. He's also performed surgery on Michael Jordan, Bo Jackson, Drew Brees, and countless other iconic athletes. Famously, half the players involved in Super Bowl XLIV—on both the Saints and the Colts—had been operated on by Dr. Andrews.

He is an icon in the sports medicine industry. A pioneer. *The* sports physician.

Okay, the background has been established. Now let's get to the story. It was my dream to work with him, so I applied for his training program. A few phases into the selection process, I found myself sitting in a conference room with Dr. Andrews and twelve other finalists.

Each of us was given the opportunity to ask him one question. One of the finalists asked him this question: "Who do you want to take your place when you retire?" He sat thoughtfully. Then he turned the question back on us, asking us each to reply. As we went around the room, the names of famous sports medicine surgeons were coming out of the mouths of each applicant. The names dropped were from well-known NFL and MLB teams, covering the top surgeons from both coasts. It seemed to become a competition to see who knew the most about the big-name people in the industry and their specific talents, and who could "wow" the rest of us with their reasoning for why this doc or that doc should be the next top doc.

Then the question came to me. I was one of the last to answer. I knew what I wanted to say and quickly assessed if my planned response would come off as bold or arrogant. But how many other chances would I get? So I took my shot. "Me." And the room was quiet. Everybody looked at me with puzzled faces and with surprise at the unexpected and incredibly brave answer. I can imagine that they were all assuming that this was the exact moment in time that I had destroyed every possible change of being selected for the program.

I continued, "I should be the person to take over for you, Dr. Andrews." The room remained quiet because they now had confirmation that I did indeed say that I should be the next in line! "And that's because I want to spend this year learning directly from you and to round out my education to become a surgeon that has an elite-level education, confidence, and set of skills that makes a lasting contribution to the profession." Keep in mind, I wasn't even a fully certified physician yet! And I definitely didn't have any guarantee that I was going to have a spot at any additional specialty training programs upon graduation yet.

And the truth is that nobody was going to give those things to me. If I wanted it, I needed to name what I wanted and believe in my ability to get there and to go for it. Dr. Andrews gave me a pretty smart look, and with his index finger pointed in my direction and with his giant national championship ring glistening in the light, he nodded his head at me while saying, "I like that answer."

The rest of the day was pretty lonely! I don't think any of the other candidates said a word to me. I had taken my stand, and I got absolutely no acknowledgement from any of them for the rest of the weekend. But guess what? I was granted the honor to work with him the following year. And the difference that has made in my career has been fantastic!

My mindset made the difference, helped me stand out, and gave me the tools to put myself on the pathway that I wanted. I steered myself into my situation.

If you are reading these words, it's because you are interested in unsploding your HealthSpan. And if you want something, there is a difficult first step that must be taken. You need to rethink your approach to your well-being and, starting from what you *can* control, adopt a mindset that anything is possible for you, and you will *unsplode.*

NEWTON'S FIRST LAW

Bodies at rest remain at rest. Bodies in motion remain in motion. That's Newton's famous first law of physics, and maybe the most important.

In the health world, many people stay at rest (and don't get started) because of analysis paralysis. It's easy for us to get so analytical about our health—to make too many plans or read too many books or indulge every impulsive need to check our phone during a moment of our free time to doomscroll until we find an article with the latest health trend we want to learn about. We stay stuck and motionless, just swiping and reading, and the action never comes.

What matters most is that you move. Get your body in motion intentionally. In the book *Atomic Habits*, James Clear argues that to achieve a goal or complete a task, you need to break it down to the smallest initial step. Taking that first small step is where you make the biggest change and the biggest difference. For example, you don't tell yourself, "I am going to go on a jog for twenty minutes at an eight-minute-mile pace at exactly 6:30 tomorrow morning." Instead, you set the alarm clock for 6:30, and the goal should be to put on your running shoes. And if you get up and take that initial step, then what is going to happen? YOU ARE GOING TO GO RUNNING!

If you lace up your running shoes, the likely next movement in that inertia is to step out the door. From there, your body's motion will carry you down your porch, onto the sidewalk, and before you know it, you're on a jog or on a high-paced walk. Both work. And you will have been successful! You will have gone on a jog. But you won't have made the goal to jog; you will have made the goal to put on your running shoes, and your inertia carries you the rest of the way.

Until we build a healthy habit of motion, complacency is the easier path.

That complacency that keeps our bodies from moving is the same one we use to stay in our dead-end, health-injurious pathways (jobs, routines, diets, habits, ruts). You might be in the middle of a career that has little promotional prospects, you no longer enjoy it, or something else that is sowing the seeds of burnout, and you're thinking to yourself, "I'm gonna stick it out because I'm already halfway to retirement." That creates "middle of the week thinking," where you are working for the weekend. Don't wish your week away. With enough repetition, you'll find yourself in "middle of life" thinking, where you were simply working for retirement and an age where your body will likely be significantly less mobile and strong as compared to your midlife.

The inertia has been set. Changing it feels daunting, but consider that this type of person is committing to unhappiness, an unsatisfied life, and an unhealthy life. Maybe this person needs an entirely new career, or maybe they need to approach it in a different way to find purpose and meaning in their life. Either way, that change has to start somewhere, and that first step will follow Newton's first law of motion.

Reframe your priorities and make your life work for you now. Find a way to refocus yourself around having experiences, joy, and physical fitness. Be intentional about seeking them out. Manifest what you want. Decide your trajectory and then get moving!

If you're in the middle of writing a work email and your kid says, "Come sit with me," don't reply, "Okay. One second, honey." Go sit with them and enjoy that moment. If a child is begging for your attention, they are telling you that you are more family-poor than family-rich. And hopefully that or a similar experience triggers you to acknowledge that truth and reframe your mindset.

If you're writing a series of work emails and are putting off your physical therapy exercises, stop writing your emails. Pause, stretch that body out, strengthen what you need to strengthen for a very small portion of your day, and return to your work. Balance health and wealth so that one doesn't dominate the other. Then make that a habit. You'll be surprised how much more productive you will be when you reset your mind and body.

Work is meant to be used as a tool to enjoy the world, to produce and provide for the people that you love, and to give you the financial means to live your life, not *become* your life and suffocate the real experiences or body that bring about joy.

Speaking of your body, have you ever thought about its purpose—other than keeping you alive, of course. Think of it as an asset; it's the vehicle by which you get to experience the joys brought on by your balanced HealthSpan and WealthSpan. It's your machine! Treat it like the hotrod it is. Take care of it. Wash it regularly. Polish the tires—I'll let you decide what that means. Doing so will keep your engine humming and help ensure it stays on the road as long as possible.

When you approach your body or your work in a way that misaligns with the above understanding, you stand to lose your joy. That loss of joy will create a significantly negative impact on your HealthSpan.

TREVOR'S INTERJECTION

HealthSpan and WealthSpan need to be in balance. Caleb is pointing out that when we emphasize one too much, the other suffers. I've lived that. Although my profession is in wealth management, my primary hobby is living a healthy lifestyle. Without success in one, I doubt I'd have success in the other.

People that focus too much on work but then lose their joy and social connections might be asset-rich but tend to be experience- and family-poor. Don't forget that finances are simply a tool to use to live your life. Nothing more, and nothing less.

Unsploding your HealthSpan and WealthSpan means that you need to start thinking about other "rich" versus "poor" categories related to your health. Are you endurance-poor? Stretching-poor? Nutrition-poor? Mood-poor? Cardiovascular-poor? Strength-poor? Sleep-poor?

Then extend this to your mental health, too. Are you time-freedom-poor? Vacation-poor? Goal-setting-poor? Mindfulness-poor? Relationship-poor?

With a simple trick like this—applying financial terms like "asset-poor" or "asset-rich" in a different context—and applying it to your health can be an effective way to change your mindset and rethink your approach to your health. That can be part of the initial inertia, that first actionable step that puts you on a new path to a healthy lifestyle filled with purpose and meaning.

Obviously, there has to be a balance. You can't abandon your job and watch movies with your kid all day. Focusing all on HealthSpan on not on WealthSpan will explode your life. The same is true with social and romantic relationships and even our approach to our physical health—there needs to be a balance. It doesn't have to be a kid constantly asking to be with you. Maybe your head constantly hurts because you have tension in the back of your neck. *That* chronic experience is trying to tell you something about being health-poor.

Make a motion toward *better*. If you aren't growing, you're dying, as they say in the business world. And the same might be true when it comes to your overall health.

Here's an example of balance. Literally as I'm writing these words, I'm at a golf clinic with my kids. I'm not 100 percent at home ignoring them. I'm not 100 percent playing golf and ignoring my work responsibilities. I'm being intentional about spending time with them, and now that they have broken away to work with an instructor, I am balancing that free time with them with work time. My priorities are balanced—it's not one or the other but a place for space to exist for both. And I can fluctuate between them as I see fit. I can honestly tell myself that I am adequately engaged in both. The key is to place value on both and to find a way to make room for both. To find balance.

Be intentional about your time and how you're balancing health and wealth. When the weekend comes around, I don't lounge around and live a sedentary lifestyle. I invest in my health. I'll make a point to meet up with Trevor so that we can both run a Spartan Race. When I'm on the plane and on my way to improve my health, I get some work done by knocking out some writing for this book or finishing up clinical paperwork. Finances and health in balance.

CALEB'S INTERJECTION

That's right! I'm interjecting myself here. I just wanted to note that running the most recent Spartan Race with Trevor is a memory I'll hold on to forever. And despite Trevor's desperate plea to keep this a secret, I want to make sure that this was known to all! You see, near the end of the race, Trevor "accidentally" skipped the final hill climb and made his way to the finish line. He got his finisher medal and grabbed himself a banana and a protein shake. Do you realize what this means? Well let me sum it up for you...he cheated! I beat him! He doesn't want to admit it, and clearly the race results do not prove it. But if you see him, ask him about it. And don't let him distract you with true details such as how I was huffing and puffing the whole time and how he barely broke a sweat.

Now, to be fair, Trevor took his mistake to heart and realized that I was absolutely going to hold this against him. And I vow that I will. But Trevor is by no means a quitter, because the following day he ran that part of the hill twice to make up for it. So over the three days, he did complete the full distance. But on that first mud-filled and painful day, the victory was mine!

USING YOUR PEAK YEARS

From a financial standpoint, people like to talk about your "peak years." This refers to earning data, which shows that a person's income really starts to peak through their forties and seventies, creating an earning potential that does the bulk of the work, in terms of saving for retirement.

What very few people talk about is that the "peak years" are when your body is already in decline. And because, culturally, we tend to focus on earning and our careers, this means that the average person isn't very focused on their HealthSpan when it matters most. And we are likely neglecting the changes that would positively impact the trajectory of our HealthSpan! It's not even on our minds!

We need to reframe how we think about our "peak years" to include maximizing both physical health—around age twenty is when your muscle mass, bone density, and neuroplasticity peak—and mental health—around age forty is when you start mastering emotional control, critical thinking, and stress management.

When I was twenty-two, I was still a couple of years away from medical school, but I was already hard pressed into the grind of applications and resume building and competition to look better than the other candidates. I was burning the candle at both ends and ready to sign up for summer school when a friend of mine who was nearing matriculation into medical school called me up: "We gotta take a trip," he said. "Gotta get one more good one in before I have to go away for school."

I was resistant to the idea because it felt like my career was only a mirage in front of me and that any waste of time or effort might just be the thing that made me miss out on it forever. But that was just it! My life was actually the thing that I was about to miss out on forever! I was so hard at the grind that I was blowing through my college years, with the only focus being to get to the next four-year block of school where I would just disappear from the world again in an effort to gain my education. Plus, I had a summer job to earn money on the side while trying to balance everything else.

Well, my friend persisted, and luckily he was very convincing! I put the summer on hold, and we went country hopping in Southeast Asia for six weeks. When you added up airfare, scuba diving, rock climbing, hostels, buses, trains, and food, the whole trip was less than $2,000. I wasn't a highfalutin doctor yet (look up the average doctor's student debt to understand the joke), so I was intentional about maximizing experience and minimizing expense.

In order to save money, I spent a lot of nights sleeping on a train or bus in an upright position. Thankfully, I had a young body that could do that. Now, as a man in my mid-forties, there is zero chance that my body could physically handle the demands of that trip. Today, I would need air conditioning, a nightly mindfulness meditation, custom ergonomic pillows, and orthotics on the train ride just to alleviate *some* of the pain and discomfort of sleeping in an upright position for multiple nights in a row.

Thankfully I went on that trip! And I have something memorable to speak of about my college summers. Because for several of the other summers I was in school, I was working, attending class, sleeping very little, and slaving away at my application and resume so that I could chase my career. And had he not pushed me, I might not have taken even a single summer off from that grind. But instead, I was able to use that summer, during one of my peak years, to go on a dream, once-in-a-lifetime trip. If I had waited until retirement or, better, a few years after safely establishing my medical career, my peak physical years would've already been over.

You might be older than twenty and thinking, "Crap! I've already missed the boat on my peak physical years. So what's the point of changing my mindset?" You might even be old enough to require sleep apnea aids, thyroid supplements, and heart disease medication—you don't get to leave your pillbox at home. That doesn't mean all of your opportunities are gone. There are opportunities everywhere! They are all around you! They are just different.

You have to apply this mindset shift to where you are now. Identify the opportunities and experiences you want to have that are appropriate for your age and social situation. If you are in your mid-thirties and are about to get married next year, you might want to think about organizing that once-in-a-lifetime golf trip with your buddies right now. As your social circle ages and everyone starts having kids, you might not get another opportunity until you're in your sixties.

So be mindful about what experiences you want to have relative to your HealthSpan trajectory. In each phase of our life, we face health and financial limitations to some degree. But those limitations should not block you from joy. Be flexible! Experiment! But don't sit around and do nothing!

Here's the point: you might be past some health peak, but once you get the inertia going to reshape your physical and mental health, you'll put yourself in a spot where you can generate life experiences that your current trajectory would never allow. Your window is always open; your job is to keep it from shutting and, if you are really working on your HealthSpan, opening it little by little. Having said that, the longer you wait and the older you get, the harder it will be to get back into shape. So start now. Fight for yourself and the people that care about you. Consider that being unhealthy isn't just hurting you, it's also hurting your loved ones.

A crucial sidenote here is that optimism is nonnegotiable when rethinking your approach to your health. You must believe that your window is always open. It's not only possible for you to open it but to also climb through it.

A GRATITUDE ATTITUDE

Related to optimism is being thankful for the things that we have now. With our busy lives that pull us in seemingly every direction, it's easy to never pause and be thankful.

Here's some doctorly advice for you: take your vitamin G—the *g* being for gratitude. This isn't just some hokey self-help mantra. Science has literally proven that practicing gratitude improves your mental health by reducing stress and anxiety, improving your mood and self-esteem, strengthening your resilience, keeping you more optimistic, and enhancing your empathy, compassion, and relationships in general.

But it gets better. Gratitude also has lasting effects on your physical health, too. It lowers blood pressure, improves sleep, and reduces inflammation. If I were to invent some pill that had all of these benefits, it would become a billion-dollar-a-year miracle cure that would feature on a dozen episodes of *Oprah*. But there is no pill required. You just have to practice gratitude.

Okay, "practicing gratitude" sounds simple enough. But what are some practical ways to implement gratitude exercises? Let's look:

- **Gratitude Writing:** Keep a journal or write somebody a letter, emphasizing topics that you are grateful for and that had a positive impact on your life. You can revisit your journal to return to memories of gratitude. And a letter helps foster a closer relationship with the person you send it to. If you don't have time to sit and write, talk into your phone and use speech-to-text.
- **Mindfulness Meditation:** Many mindfulness meditation apps have specific types of meditations (usually five to fifteen minutes long) geared toward specific experiences. Most have a "gratitude" meditation that will guide you through a process of feeling thankful.
- **Gratitude Walk:** The research shows that going a one short walk a day can improve your heart health, overall mood, sleep quality, and cognitive function. Why not double dip? While you're out on this walk improving your physical health, do a gratitude exercise at the same time.
- **Gratitude Box:** Use a box, jar, or container and fill it with pieces of paper of things you are grateful for. Whenever you want a pick-me-up, reach in and read a few of the notes to generate some instant gratitude. Keep adding new notes!
- **Visual Cues:** One thing I do is leave myself Post-it notes everywhere in my house of motivational and gratitude-oriented messages. These visual reminders help me keep my mental health intentionality top of mind.
- **Gratitude Affirmations:** The easiest way to practice gratitude is to give yourself affirmations. Do it verbally or with that voice inside your head. (Did you know that not everybody has a voice inside their head?!) Fill in the blank: "I am grateful for..."

These are just a few examples of what you can do. If you are excited about these and the improvements they could bring to your

HealthSpan, now is the time to start collecting more gratitude exercises on your own.

Just by practicing a little bit of gratitude, you create an inertia that eventually changes your outlook and your approach. You start living for tomorrow *and* today. You get healthier sooner. You adapt those same self-improving habits to your work life, working in a less stressful way that additionally helps you recognize your value. You start earning more because of your improved health, and when tomorrow (retirement) comes, you will be on a better pathway to achieving a comfortable retirement income.

Your transformation might lead to better job opportunities, new and better relationships, a healthier body that can sustain into retirement, and so much more. You will become more attractive—meaning you will attract more joy, excitement, and meaningful experiences into your life. When you think positively, you attract positive people. When you think negatively, you attract negative people. You might even make a positive person become negative or vice versa. What do you want to project onto the world? And who do you want to attract?

NET GAINS VS. NET LOSSES

Here's where Trevor's world of finances gives us another useful analogy when it comes to health. In health and wealth, the human brain illogically views the situation in the opposite light of the actual truth.

In the finance world, good wealth managers will talk their clients down from the cliff during market fluctuations. The common investor's instinct is to sell things off when the market goes down, but that's actually the worst time to sell. In the past, the market has always picked back up, so what seems like a loss now will actually be a net gain if the investor keeps their money in.

It's similar when it comes to our health. When our health is down, our instinct isn't to "buy in" and start getting in on the ground floor where there is potential for improvement. Instead, we "sell" by deciding any effort it would take to get back in shape is actually time away from other parts of our day. Exercises and making that healthy meal (instead of settling for the quick, poor-nutrition meal) get lower and lower on our priority list. We are prone to making the worse of the two decisions.

So what's going on here, psychologically? Our brain is misleadingly telling us, "If I take thirty minutes to exercise instead of finishing that report, I'll be *losing* salary." Eating can also be a point of difficulty for us: "If I don't eat that ice cream after every dinner, I'll be *losing* my nightly joy."

But in reality, what we are really losing by our continued imbalanced habits is our long-term health and ability to enjoy the usefulness of any salary and investment earnings we accrue. Bad habits are like taking money out of our portfolio when the market is down.

We need to think of our health the same way we think about retirement investment: if we maximize our contributions now, plan with purpose, and keep everything consistent (create and maintain an exercise routine that evolves with age), the compounding interest on that ongoing investment will give me a comfortable retirement (my body will be fit as a fiddle as it ages). You've got to change your mindset to think both in the short-term but especially the long-term. And the short-term is probably a little heavy on the input and sacrifice side as you look forward to the long-term enjoyment! But it's completely worth it!

So while there might be some short-term financial loss when prioritizing your health—on "lost" income or paying for massages, gym memberships, personal trainers, nutritionists, etc.—those short-term losses are actually net gains on your HealthSpan (and likely WealthSpan).

THE BYRON KATIE SYSTEM

I want to offer you one more practical way to start reframing your mind as part of your larger health goals. In this case it will be improving your mental health, but in doing so, you'll free up energy to spend on your physical health.

We live in a time where stress and anxiety seem like our best friends—they are always around and ready to give us a call to let us know they're there. To help you manage your stressful thoughts, you can implement the Byron Katie System to process that stress in order to let it leave your body. This system is a series of questions you need to ask yourself. Here's how it works.

THE CORE FRAMEWORK

Step 1. Is it true?

What You Do: State the stressful thought verbatim and ask yourself if it's factual.

Why It Matters: Pauses the automatic, emotional response and brings the mind into conscious scrutiny.

Step 2. Can you absolutely know that it's true?

What You Do: Go deeper—look for irrefutable proof.

Why It Matters: Highlights the uncertainty built into most of our beliefs, creating mental flexibility.

Step 3. How do you react—what happens—when you believe that thought?

What You Do: Notice emotions, body sensations, behaviors, and ripple effects on others.

Why It Matters: Makes the personal cost of the belief untenable, boosting motivation to let it go.

Step 4. Who would you be without the thought?

What You Do: Imagine yourself in the same situation minus the belief.

Why It Matters: Reveals a calmer, more creative state is possible right now—no external change required.

Step 5. Turnaround

What You Do: Flip the thought to its opposite and find at least three genuine examples of how each "turnaround" could be as true—or truer—than the original statement.

Why It Matters: Converts intellectual insight into lived experience and balances perspective.

As you move through this five-step process, journal what you experience. Reflect on that experience as part of reshaping your belief system via neuroplasticity. You'll likely have that same stressful or anxious thought again in the future, and it'll be important to take it through these steps again.

Like working out, you build muscle incrementally over time. Similarly, you have to slowly and incrementally strip away the stressful thought (the fat) before you can strengthen confidence and composure (the muscle). You'll be opening up new neural pathways that divert away from the stressful pathways, and you'll be instructing your brain to take those pathways the next time the thought occurs. Pretty soon, those stressful pathways will be indefinitely closed.

YES, YOU HAVE THE TIME

If you have time to worry about your problems or the problems of the world, then you have time to improve your health. Shift your mindset to believe that fact.

But keep in mind that you can only control what you can control. Don't let your emotional health be affected by things you can't control. That will ruin your mood and lead to physiological no-nos like inflammation.

Your mind is your leader. You are what you think. If you think you don't have time, then you'll unconsciously go out of your way to make sure you don't. If you don't think you can become physically fit, then guess what? You won't be.

If, on the other hand, you think that achieving a healthy lifestyle is possible, you'll use that inertia to keep going until you've achieved it. Make that initial step. Start small and go from there.

Your target destination, and the location from which you start, will be different from your neighbor's, your spouse's, and likely from everyone else. That's okay. Stop comparing yourself. Recognize that you are unique and have unique health needs. Taking stock of your health goals and needs, then, is a great first step. And that's where we will pick up this conversation in the next chapter.

CHAPTER 3

WHAT'S THE PROGNOSIS? TAKING STOCK OF YOUR HEALTH GOALS

"Start where you are. Use what you have. Do what you can."

—ARTHUR ASHE

Most people don't have short-term or long-term health goals. And that's especially true when we still have our health. Goals are often the last thing on our mind when everything seems to be functioning properly. Calling attention to health goals is important because usually we don't recognize the decline until it is pretty far along the process.

But health goals are important at any age. As an orthopedic surgeon in private practice, I'm often contacted by various organizations to give talks or presentations or to assist with question and answer sessions about health and wellness from an orthopedic standpoint. Almost yearly, the local high school baseball teams come to talk with me about injuries and prevention and to present to the athletes my perspective on their sport, their potential for injury, and to review prevention techniques before a season begins.

At these types of meetings, it doesn't really matter what uniform or outfit that they wear; each group or team is made up of three general personalities. You have the young hotshots doing everything they can to make the team and leave an impression. You have the veterans who have established a routine and likely won't be bumped by the newbies. And you've got everybody in the middle that is fighting to get as much playing time as possible. Regardless of the type, each will do anything it takes—even letting health advice go in one ear and out the other.

And in the mind of almost every baseball parent, their child is the next Roger Clemens. And they'll teach their kid to think of themselves that way (despite the fractional odds of ever making the major leagues). With this type of expectation combined with the student's ambition, the physical work that these student athletes put in to make the team is immense. And these players are almost always afraid to admit injury or pain because any sign of weakness might just cost them the edge that they have worked so hard to attain. The consequence of not making healthy choices, in their mind, might cost them their entire shot at taking things to the next level.

My role in the preseason meeting is to combat all of that pressure a little bit and to get them a little bit more conscious of the reality of injuries, how they happen, how to prevent them, and to establish short-term and long-term health goals. My goal is to help them see what is happening and to get through the season unscathed and ready for the next one.

Ultimately, the intent of my discussion was to get through to some of these kids about the fact that they haven't really even conceptualized health goals. Student athletes are so hyperfocused. They are focused on getting wins, pitch counts, workout reps, and anything that is immediate and related to the team. What they don't think about is the fact that this high school baseball season is just a small moment in time. They aren't thinking that their hyperfocus now that they can explode their future potential. Instead, they need to take care of themselves now so that they *unsplode* the HealthSpan for the rest of their lives.

When I ask them to stop and think about their long-term goals, they realize two things very quickly: (1) they have long-term goals like pitching at the next level or having an arm that worked, and (2) they hadn't spent any time thinking about their long-term goals.

What's true for these high school athletes is true for the vast majority of people out there. We have these tacit health goals. "I don't want to be overweight." "I want to maintain the use of my limbs." "I want to live a long life." Things like that. But we just keep them lingering in the back of our brains and don't actually identify specificity within them or design our HealthSpan around them.

We tend not to think of our goals until something horrible happens. When there's a middle-aged patient in my office with an obliterated ACL from playing recreational soccer and surgery is on the horizon, I start my plan for them by asking a few questions:

- What do you want to be able to do long-term?
- Are you planning on going back to that same job, or to that same sport?
- What sort of demand will your plans require? What muscle strength will it require? What flexibility will you have to overcome?

I'll give them some prompting examples like, "Do you want to play with your children?" or "Do you plan on competing in a body building competition?" Knowing a patient's goals is crucial so that the medical team can mirror our treatment to help the patient achieve their goals.

My guess is that you have some idea of your health goals and that you are interested in making yourself fitter to increase your HealthSpan. You've shifted your mindset to know that you are capable of doing that regardless of where you are. That's the first step.

Now, you need to define the foundation from which you will build out your healthy lifestyle. That means you need to know your health goals, both short-term but especially long-term.

If you just hit the ground running without a clear direction, then your efforts won't affect much change and/or you'll be surprised that your efforts did very little (encouraging you to quit). Instead, name your *why* and use that to create a health portfolio.

THE HEALTH PORTFOLIO

Do you have a health goal? Is your health trajectory pointing you at it? Are you planning with purpose?

The answers to these questions are fundamental. You cannot truly start a tailored health routine designed to increase the longevity of your HealthSpan until you can answer "yes" to both questions. The rest of this chapter will be devoted to helping you get to a place where you can answer "yes."

To locate your health goals, you have to first identify where you're at. What are your current assets? What are they worth? Where are they headed? What's the prognosis? Determine where you are so that you can identify any gaps in your health. It's completely mirrored from Trevor's side, who encourages investors to identify gaps in their financial plan. So let's call this inventory the "health portfolio."

You insure your wealth, your house, your car. Why not insure your health with protective labs, screenings, and optimization?

There are certain aspects of our health that are important to understand and inventory—certain "asset classes," if I may. For each, it's important to assess where you are. What state is your flexibility in? Your cardio endurance? And so on. Once you understand where you are, that can help you form a health goal. For example, if you have bad gut health, you have a goal right in front of you—to improve gut health.

Having a snapshot of your current health portfolio will play a role in your unique HealthSpan plan.

MUSCLE MASS

Muscle is protective against nearly every cause of age-related decline.

Healthy muscle mass is distinguishably formed, metabolically active, supports strong bones, and improves cognitive and physical function. To throw some general numbers and groups out there, women, at various points in their life, will have healthy muscle mass if between 23 to 36 percent of their body weight is muscle mass. For me, it's between 30 and 46 percent. These numbers are influenced by age.

Factors such as inactivity, aging, chronic disease, chronic poor posture, and malnutrition can reduce muscle mass. When we aren't in a healthy range, we increase our risk of type 2 diabetes, cardiovascular disease, and bone fractures.

So, now equipped with some basic information, let's consider how taking stock of our muscle mass could relate to health goals. If you are in an unhealthy muscle mass range, do you want diabetes? Do you want cardiovascular disease? My guess is that you're thinking, "No, it's actually a goal of mine to *avoid* cardiovascular disease." And maybe you have a family history of cardiovascular disease, making you the type of person who really needs to focus on reducing risk. Ipso facto, taking stock of this one asset in your health portfolio has helped you determine a health goal—namely, to improve muscle mass.

I won't take you through this "how to make a goal" process for each asset class. My expectation is that you can now take yourself through this process.

CARDIO ENDURANCE

There are no universal "healthy" numbers when it comes to cardio endurance, like needing to be able to run a mile in under four minutes or something. Instead, you can determine if you have healthy or unhealthy cardio endurance by your general routine.

If you implement a variety of aerobic activities each week, targeting 150 minutes of moderate-intensity activities and seventy-five minutes of high-intensity aerobic activities, then you are doing great. If you are seventy-five years old, hitting those numbers might be more difficult. Regardless of where you're starting, work your way up incrementally, only adding a couple more minutes each week.

Is cardio and endurance training boring for you? Do you lose focus and struggle to maintain motivation with consistent repetitive exercise that is the make-up of many endurance and cardio programs? Have you considered mixing it up? You can still get cardiovascular and endurance training while introducing variety to your workout. Consider using high-intensity interval training (HIIT) workouts as part of your aerobic routine. They are fantastic! They provide for a lot of variety and keep things fun and interesting. Consider this transition if routine and traditional cardiovascular and endurance training do not excite you. And if you love that type of repetitive training, it would be a good idea to add some HIIT training to your routine as well!

Just be mindful of your routine in combination with your recovery. Don't overtrain to the point where you have burnout, create structural damage in your body, and can't recover easily from a workout. Listen to your body.

Without strong cardio endurance, you will increase your risk of heart disease, circulation issues, high blood pressure, or stroke. You'll also experience shortness of breath, fatigue, and decreased energy more easily. Your energy is your body's spending power to experience daily joy.

FLEXIBILITY AND AGILITY

How functional is your body to move freely and efficiently? Healthy flexibility creates a range of motion in your joints and muscles that allows freedom of movement, pain-free movement, and ease in finding correct posture. With great flexibility, you reduce your chance at injury and alleviate tightness and stiffness and the pain associated with them.

Healthy agility is your ability to change your body's position efficiently when combining speed, power, balance, and coordination. You're looking for quick reaction time, efficient changes in direction, coordinated movement, and balance. Without strong agility, you'll increase the risk of falling (which has huge implications once you reach a certain age) and otherwise increase your risks of sports and recreational injuries. The other thing here that sneaks up on us is that poor agility will compound with overcompensation, meaning your body will be overloading certain muscles and joints that, over time, will create major health issues (joint replacements, torn muscles, and more).

When your flexibility and agility aren't working together to keep your body moving, this can create major problems over time. The debility that can develop may surprise you. Have you ever heard of the step-down test? This is a simple test to see if a person can step down to street level from a curbed sidewalk. It seems simple, right? However, there are many that struggle with that activity. There are many young people that do not ever take the stairs and never perform that type of mobility and mechanics. For them, one step presents a challenge. When a person loses this ability to descend from a single step, then they have progressed to a dangerous place in terms of their HealthSpan. This is usually a sign of major upcoming health issues because it tells us that they are suffering dynamic lower limb and neuromuscular deficits.

BRAIN HEALTH

Have you ever heard of the phrase "functional alcoholic"? The idea is that a person can drink themselves to intoxication but still maintain enough function to live their life as "normal." While that may sound like a terrible compensation pattern to allow for poor health choices, how would you feel if I told you that many of us share similarities with a functional alcoholic? Many of us walk around with deficits to our cognitive health while still able to hold down our jobs, enjoy our friends, and generally live our lives. Many of these deficits are due to our own neglect and poor choices. And with these choices, slowly and surely, certain health deficits are compounding in the background.

A healthy brain is characterized by adaptable, self-aware, morally confident, open-minded, insightful, and empathetic behaviors, whereas unhealthy brain health is marked by manipulative, stubborn, obsessive, anxious, attention-seeking, or self-destructive behaviors.

While "self-destructive" is a pretty harsh-sounding term, it could be a really small, seemingly innocuous act. Maybe, because of a high-stress lifestyle, an individual needs to take the nightly edge off and fall asleep by eating a carb-heavy snack. Ultimately, this is a self-destructive act that, over time, will completely derail this person's HealthSpan.

So get to know what constitutes each of these behaviors on the micro level if you are interested in taking stock of your brain health.

GUT HEALTH

Did you know that most doctors receive less than twenty hours of nutrition education? The medical industry sees food as a secondary subject to pharmacology. Many medical curricula neglect to provide the connection and understanding of how our digestive tract contributes to our remaining systems besides its ability to absorb the food that we put into our mouths. The connection with our gut bacteria and the effect on our immunity, mood, inflammation, and chronic disease is not deeply taught.

Probiotics and treatment to maintain gut health is discussed more in terms of reestablishing attempted normal levels after pharmacologic or infectious changes within the GI tract. The goals and strategies to promote gut health to support its contribution to our body systems other than nutrient absorption is not a focus and thus is not something that very many physicians would feel comfortable discussing.

Some of the GI tract disorders that are now considered to be connected with our remaining health systems are even looked at with a jaded eye as these conditions are scrutinized by more mainstream medicine, while they are more supported by nontraditional and more holistic practitioners. This means that very few physicians are actually equipped to prescribe dietary strategies for disease reversal, metabolic health, or performance. Furthermore, doctors can miss upstream causes to conditions like nutrient deficiencies and the toxins and chronic stress associated with them. The lack of training and lack of integrated consideration of these conditions often leads to lengthy delays in appropriate diagnoses and treatments for those that present with these concerns and are seeking resolution.

The intestinal tract is located lower in the abdomen and apart from the more frequently involved and more critical heart and lung issues that we more commonly consider. As a result, not many people put much thought into their intestinal health. Heart and brain health get all the attention. However, gut health is probably just as important of a system as any other.

For example, there is this condition called "leaky gut syndrome." I'll spare you the gruesome details, but the ramifications of this are that the body's white blood cells congregate around the abdomen instead of distributing to the other necessary areas of the body. This creates a lack of these cells in these other areas, which makes it very difficult for the body to use those white blood cells to do other work, such as joint repair and immune system response.

When a person takes a lot of ibuprofen or eats certain triggering foods—tomatoes, peppers—then the gut tends to get inflamed. This can cause chemical and hormonal imbalances, which can then create anxiety and depression. Then when treatment for this anxiety and depression are discussed, it might not be a pill that is actually needed to help with the anxiety and depression, but more frequently that pill is the initial recommendation for treatment. The better approach, in many cases, would be to consider a better diet and probiotics to improve gut health, which will then encourage serotonin levels to restore back to normal and to get back to the brain.

Gut health is essential for maintaining a healthy body and preventing a host of health issues. How are you treating it? Are you stuffing it with Oreos for lunch instead of a nutritionally balanced meal? That's like putting motor oil into an EV car. So stop it.

NATURAL SLEEP REQUIREMENTS

I've touched on this already, but everybody has their own unique sleep requirements. Some people are totally fine with four hours of sleep a night (which, to me, is exhausting just to think about). But most healthy adults will need seven or eight hours a night.

You can determine your natural needs by going on vacation and committing to figure it out. (Thought I'd throw in an excuse for you to take a vacation while I was at it! You are welcome.)

To do this, I want you to pick a consistent time every night to go to bed, and I want you to wind down using some of the previously discussed techniques to prepare you for a good night's sleep. Then, I want you to sleep without an alarm clock, and I want you to wake up when you feel rested and restored. Do this for about a week without an alarm clock. Just let your body find its own time duration for adequate rest and restoration by having a consistent bed time and by allowing morning wake-up to normalize after the body has had the opportunity to stabilize and level out. Observe your natural patterns. Keep track of how you feel and how alert or fatigued you are. This adjustment will let you know how much sleep you need (and when you need to go to bed and wake up).

Don't let this test frustrate you. You might be surprised. And maybe you can make some subtle adjustments over time. But with this test, your body is telling you what you need. You might discover that your natural sleep requirements are at odds with your work and life and that the two are not compatible with one another. You'll have to decide if your health (sleep) and wealth (work) goals are in balance, and you'll have to decide what you plan to do about it.

NECESSARY CALORIE INTAKE

How many calories are you consuming daily compared to what you need?

Your calorie needs are unique to you. I have no idea who you are, so unfortunately I can't tell you what you need. That number is largely determined by your age, gender, activity level, and physiology. In general, men need between 2,000–3,000 calories per day, whereas women need 1,600–2,400. Most people consume way more than that unless they are actively counting.

People who don't exercise regularly need to eat less. People who are active need to eat more. It's said that, prior to his weight-loss "transformation" in 2025, Dwayne "The Rock" Johnson consumed up to 7,000 calories per day—mostly in cod—to combine with his workout routine in order to maintain a bulked-up body.

Not eating enough calories can lead to fatigue, a slower metabolism, hair loss, mood swings, and muscle loss. Too many calories can lead to obesity, type 2 diabetes, heart disease, and other health issues. Watch out for foods that spike insulin. Not every calorie should be treated equally. When insulin rises, fat-burning temporarily decreases.

PURPOSEFUL PLEASURE

Consider this me giving you permission—nay...demanding!—that you fill your life with joy. There is a "fun factor" to your health, if joy for the sake of joy weren't enough. Filling your life with the joy of purposeful pleasure has a number of health benefits. Positive psychological benefits include lowering your stress hormones and thus your inflammation, reducing blood pressure, boosting your mental resilience, promoting heart health, strengthening your immune system, reducing chronic pain, releasing endorphins, elevating neurotransmitters, increasing physical activity, and improving your sleep habits. It doesn't take a rocket scientist to do the math: when you add all of these things together, it turns out that pleasure increases our longevity. It increases our HealthSpan.

If I were your pleasure coach, I'd tell you to pick up at least one hobby that is based in or requires some type of physical exercise. And if you aren't able to be overly active, at least find some hobbies outdoors. Studies have shown that the mere act of getting out in nature lowers blood pressures, reduces stress, increases vitamin D levels, strengthens your bones and muscles, boosts immune function, and is great for your cardiovascular health. The green spaces of the great outdoors, it has been shown, also help reduce inflammation, which is the root cause of many chronic illnesses.

But as much as I'm emphasizing using the body, don't forget about the mind. Travel to learn. Generate some perspective and learn not to be busy. I'll never forget a recent trip I took to Japan to see an old friend. The train ride would be a couple hours, and I immediately saw it as an opportunity to stay busy and get some work done. But, to my shock, this was a "quiet train" where devices and talking were prohibited. At first I was pissed. But as I sat there and took in my beautiful surroundings, that quiet space gave me the chance to reflect and rejuvenate. I felt refreshed upon arrival; it forced me into a healthier state.

If nothing else, purposeful pleasure helps us reset. It gets us out of our habits and routines. That variety itself helps us reconnect with and strengthen dormant neural pathways. The great news is that you don't need to have a lot of free time to have fun. You can take it in small doses or big doses. Maybe it's getting coffee with a friend for a half-hour. Maybe it's a week-long vacation. The point is that it allows you an alternative route to your *why*. The purpose of your life doesn't have to be something you build toward, something that happens in the future. Take doses of that purpose now by injecting some fun. Put fuel in your tank so that you can rely on yourself. Live *now* as part of your health routine.

SCREENINGS

So much about your current health snapshot can be discerned through various tests and screenings. Many of you are used to the standard health screenings for adult cancer, cardiovascular disease, and lung conditions. Protocols exist for when—in terms of your age—each test needs to be performed and when you should return for follow-up testing. These established intervals for timing and for how long a person should wait in between tests exists to properly identify future problems are a key part of healthy screening.

But there is more. Aside from the mainstream and disease preventing/monitoring techniques, let's explore a few additional health strategizing and screening techniques that you could consider:

DNA methylation testing: This test reveals your genetic predispositions toward nutrient processing, detoxification, neurotransmitter production, and other things. It can tell you how quickly you process certain medications and substances and can even be used to help determine which medications are more likely to be of most benefit for you. Working with a medical professional, it can help you target specific supplements or lifestyle adjustments to maximize your HealthSpan.

V02 Max: This tests the amount of oxygen you use during an exercise. It gives you an idea of where you're at from a cardiovascular fitness standpoint. It can help you set training goals and make more informed decisions about how to exercise as you build a customized program to improve your HealthSpan. This test can be repeated as you progress in your program to confirm that the steps are working and that you are responding as expected. If you are not meeting the expected improvements, then the program can be adjusted.

Bloodwork: Getting your bloodwork gives you a holistic view of your overall health by checking things like organ function, inflammation levels, reaction to certain nutrients, disease, potential health risks, and anemia. This information can help shape your diet, reveal food allergies, or identify other issues that you may need to account for.

I had a friend who was feeling tired and sleepy all the time and couldn't understand why. Sleeping too much, she'd wake up fatigued and lethargic. Despite dieting, her weight was climbing and her satisfaction in life was worsening. She was showing signs of an overall major slowdown in productivity in all areas of her life. After some bloodwork, it was discovered that her thyroid was underactive. And without that stimulating hormone, her body was not operating at optimal performance. She was fighting against a chemical imbalance that no amount of focus and dedication was going to compensate for. With the right treatment, she was able to return to her normal sleep window.

Mental Profile: Getting a psychological evaluation provides a deeper understanding of your personality—that part of yourself that is unique to you. The part of you that has been developing since you were a child. Understanding those developmental influences and how they impact your life today can be critical to identifying, both professionally and personally. With this information, you can better approach self-improvement as well as strengthen your relationships. It can help you manage depression without medication. You can harness your strengths, iron out your weaknesses, and map your behavioral patterns easier so that you can be more intentional about how you use your personality to live a healthy life.

POTENTIALS

Combining the asset classes in the "health portfolio" can give you great insight to your "health potential." This potential is made up of factors such as lifestyle, genetics, and environment. Each has an impact on how healthy you can get from where you are now.

As a lifestyle choice, let's say you are a smoker or that you drink to excess on the weekends and struggle to regroup and be ready for Monday's workweek. That will negatively impact your cardiovascular, heart, and lung health. Your "health potential" will be undermined by these choices. And those choices will require additional effort. This is an example of unnecessarily unhealthy behavior. And when you are ready, there are ways that you can combat and quit those parts of your routine. So if you are finding it difficult to sustain your cardio endurance, for example, the additional factor of being a smoker will weaken your "health potential" to improve your cardio endurance. You'll have to work extra hard to try to make up for that loss. And the best choice you can make is to get rid of that factor entirely.

PUTTING IT ALL TOGETHER

Now you know how to get a clearer picture of your entire health portfolio. It lets you know the value and potential of the various asset classes that determine your HealthSpan. And further, you can now make adjustments to your allocation in each asset class based on your crystalizing goals.

If you want to be a body builder but your portfolio identifies your muscle mass as toned and your blood pressure as high, you'll know exactly what to change in your health routine to approach your goals safely (in this case, you'll have to lower your blood pressure first before building muscle).

TARGETING A GOAL

Okay, now you've done the work to understand the current snapshot of your health situation. From here, you have what you need to start brainstorming what a health goal means to you.

And brainstorming is necessary because nobody is going to help you live your life for you. You are on your own on this one. Is there an upcoming race you want to train for? If it's the Spartan Race, Trevor and I might see you there. Just make sure you keep an eye on him as I mentioned previously! If it's not a race, then do you have a hobby that requires joint and endurance needs, like playing recreational softball? Maybe, as you age, you're noticing that walking up and down the stairs is becoming painful, and you want to increase your flexibility and agility? What is your target? What are a few targets that you want to hit?

As you explore what you want for your HealthSpan tomorrow and today, I have some guiding principles that make for better goals.

QUALITATIVE AND QUANTITATIVE

Goals should be quantitative *and* qualitative. In other words, it should include some numerical elements, like "I want to walk ten golf courses this year instead of riding in the cart." It should also include a "how" or "why" to keep your purpose crystalized, like "I want to walk ten golf courses this year to maintain my joint and hip health so that I can play with my grandkids when they visit this summer."

INCREMENTAL MICRO-GOALS

Any good health goal is actually a series of smaller health goals. They are progressive goals that build on each other one step at a time. You can build them however you want, from micro to macro or the other way around.

Let's say a person instantly comes up with a larger goal, like "Despite my mobility issues, I want to walk my daughter down the aisle next year without the assistance of my cane that I have been dependent on for the past five years." Right now, it's hard for this person to walk without significant joint and hip pain because of a sedentary lifestyle and arthritis from the effects of a life well-lived. Working with a physical therapist, strength coach, athletic trainer, and other medical professionals can get this person moving in the right direction to reach that goal. They can set micro-goals of transforming their mechanics one component at a time over the course of the year. Then they could add muscle mass to support their bodily structure. Those smaller goals will have even smaller goals tied into them. As each one is achieved, they should naturally lead to pain-free steps and meet the larger goal.

ACHIEVABLE BUT CHALLENGING

Goals need to be achievable and challenging. But they can't be so achievable that it kills motivation. And they can't be impossible because then you'll never feel good about your lack of progress, and you'll quit. You can't reverse a disease overnight. Just like you can't reverse your weight issues or your mental health or your flabby biceps overnight! Impossible goals, like easy goals, are motivational killers.

When you combine an achievable goal and a challenging goal, that's a sweet spot of discomfort where growth and change are possible. It's the right balance to create motivation and keep the momentum going.

CHECKBOX GOALS VS. HABIT GOALS

In an ideal world, you are creating a goal that has no permanent end. One that will continue to push you. Because when there is a "destination," it is often just a checkbox, meaning that when you reach that goal, you'll put a checkbox on it and revert back to the way you were prior to working toward the goal.

If you give yourself a goal to lose twenty pounds, you stand a good chance of reaching it. But what happens when you check that box? There'll be nowhere to go from there. The food in the pantry might start looking extra yummy, and there is no incentive to keep the weight off. Instead, the goal should be something like "maintain [appropriate healthy weight target] as my standard weekly weight."

Replace "checkbox" goals with habitual goals. If you need the dopamine rush of checking a box, then create subgoals beneath your habitual goals that you can check off, but make sure that the larger goal is continuous. A goal needs to be written to encourage consistent improvement to health that requires something more than temporarily changed behavior. Instead, accomplishing a habitual goal will transform you. That new health routine will just become your normal routine—your habit.

PUTTING IT ALL TOGETHER

Health goals provide a purpose. And having that purpose can help you *unsplode* your HealthSpan. How do you want to use your physical and mental capacity to live a joyful and fulfilled life? When you know where you're at today with your health *and* have a clear view of your health goals, that clears the fog and sets you on a clear path toward improving your HealthSpan.

TREVOR'S INTERJECTION

In my experience managing my clients' wealth, what Caleb is discussing here has a clear correlation to your WealthSpan, too. That's why everything I do for my clients is built on the foundation of purpose. Just like with maximizing the quality of your HealthSpan, you can improve the direction of your WealthSpan by building it around your *why*. If you set a goal of taking two vacations a year while still living a comfortable retirement, that gives you information about how to start planning your finances.

Something that should excite you right now is that, in essence, we are talking about concepts that you get to use on both sides of this book. You're taking the same actionable blueprint and applying it to two different but equally important areas of your life. Your health and financial fitness are all tools—they are things you need to keep in tip-top shape in order to experience life.

So why not adjust your trajectory based on your newfound goals so that you can live the life you always wanted? Get going and start today.

Not all paths are straight. Your health goals today will not be your health goals later. They change while we are living and creating daily. Even our purpose that the goals serve will change. Without adaptation, we lose sight of our goals and motivation, and ultimately, we stop seeking to improve our HealthSpan.

But with strongly made health goals, we can almost guarantee that we'll work toward a lifestyle of meaning, purpose, autonomy, and connection. When we are healthier, so are other parts of our lives. When we live with purpose, we set off in the direction of those healthy habits and control our destiny. That's when we are able to foster memory dividends and experience a return on this investment (ROI) through our personal time, vacation time, mini-retirements, sabbaticals, and other instruments of balancing our HealthSpan and WealthSpan.

PUT ME IN, COACH!

We've gone over quite a bit of stuff. Let's acknowledge that to help you identify your health prognosis and, to some degree, your goals, you'll likely need some sort of medical team or coach to help you. A thorough evaluation to your HealthSpan will require a physician for lab work, a nutritionist, a physical therapist or athletic trainer to test flexibility, and so on and so on.

Don't worry. I'll cover what your ideal medical team might look like—a group I call the HealthSpan Longevity Team—in a future chapter.

WORK BACKWARD

Don't leave your health behind by not imagining your future. Bring your future to the here and now.

When we have a larger goal in mind, one that is farther away than we thought it should be (recall those high school baseball players), we allow ourselves time for true habit-building changes to occur. We allow an evolution of our plans and approaches. Just like we might now know our future career or family situation, we probably do not know exactly what our fitness goals and our health situation will be! So set some overarching, long-term goals and get started making smaller steps to getting your life in alignment with them.

A crucial step in your HealthSpan-lengthening journey is to identify that end goal and work backward. From that end point, what are all of the secondary goals that are required to successfully achieve the larger goal? What are the tertiary goals? The micro-goals from there? What is your purpose? Plan for that. Keep building out those goals until they become an adjusted daily routine of health improvement and maintenance.

No matter how old you are or your situation, there is a unique plan that will improve your HealthSpan. It has been proven that there is not a single age group bracket that will not benefit positively from a weight training program. So don't let your age or your situation be the factor that stops you. Work with it! You can't change it. So get going! Create a vision and chip away. Just remember, you'll never be able to reach your goals if you can't be honest with yourself about where you are.

Once you are honest with yourself and acknowledge your current situation, and once our plan is in place, how can you protect it? How can you protect your new knowledge and your new mindset? How can you protect these new assets? We'll try to answer these questions next.

CHAPTER 4

ASSET PROTECTION: SAFEGUARDING YOUR OVERALL HEALTH

"Be proactive, not reactive."

—KEN POIROT

Have you ever heard of Rick and Dick Hoyt? They were better known as Team Hoyt.

It's a touching, tragic, and inspiring story. Dick's son, Rick, was born with cerebral palsy. He couldn't do much of anything. He couldn't feed himself, wash his hands, or communicate. He was trapped inside his body. Universities worked with Rick to develop systems that could help him regain some function and eventually this led to the invention of a head-controlled computer that allowed Rick to communicate.

The first thing he asked his dad was to help him participate in a charity race that was raising money for a paralyzed classmate. Dick would be his legs, pushing Rick in a wheelchair through the race. They ran the race together.

Over time, the pair continued to race for charity and did all sorts of events, which included swimming, biking, and jumping. All told, from 1977–2014, the two completed over 1,100 total marathons, triathlons, bike tours, and other events.

Their story is part of the canon of cultural events that demarginalizes people with disabilities and instead positions them as individuals who, like anybody else, can accomplish what they set out to do. Rick overcame perceived limitations, and Dick had to make himself strong enough to become a marathon runner.

A devoted father, Dick trained his body for events and then some. He had to push, bike, swim, and exert enough force to move two people. In a way, this drove Dick to a fitness level he wouldn't have achieved otherwise.

As Dick advanced in age, his risk for various health events increased. During a marathon in 2003, he felt a little weird. But he continued on and finished the event. Afterward, he went to the hospital out of an abundance of caution.

After analyzing him, they quickly realized that he suffered a major heart attack. They rushed him into surgery and placed three emergency stents. It was a successful operation, but the doctors admitted they were baffled by the entire thing. Based on their data and the seriousness of the heart attack, Dick should have been dead. He withstood the "widowmaker," which is a blockage or complete disruption of blood supply of the left anterior descending artery, for you nerds. For the rest of you, that's the main artery that supplies blood to the front and bottom of the heart, and such a blockage is usually fatal.

Thankfully, his abundance of exercise had allowed him to have a significant amount of additional blood supply to his heart. Basically, he had built extra blood vessels. More branches were created in response to the demand that he placed on his heart, which actually provided him with additional support to the heart when this main artery was blocked. Had he not been so active with exercise, this blockage would have killed him.

Dick not only survived but continued racing with his son for another decade. This is an example of a human being who invested so heavily in his physical health that, when it came time for life to throw him a curveball, his HealthSpan work actually helped him protect that asset.

His health goal to bond with his son saved his life. Probably in more ways than one.

Dick passed away in 2021 at the age of 80, well after retiring from racing life and in an advanced age thanks, in part, to his protective and proactive work regarding his HealthSpan.

When it comes to our own health, how do we want to protect it? And how aggressively will you pursue it? Do we want our body to react to major health events in the state it is now, or do we want to take the proactive steps necessary to maximize our body's strength and thereby increase the odds that our bodies will protect what we have?

The question answers itself.

EXECUTING ON GOALS

Dick Hoyt formed health goals, executed them, and, by doing so, *unsploded* his HealthSpan for a long, fulfilled life.

In the last chapter, you spent quite a bit of time assessing your current HealthSpan and building new health goals. Now it's time to execute on your goals. While your health goals will be unique to you, what I'll do in this chapter is to offer a variety of strategies that could apply to you—like a buffet you get to pick and choose from.

Being proactive about executing your goals is *the* best way to protect your health. And nobody is going to do it for you. We live in a culture—and frankly with a healthcare system—that doesn't emphasize taking care of our bodies. It's more reactive based—we go to the doctor when something goes wrong (sometimes, when something is really, really wrong) rather than to plan how to maintain health.

It was about five years ago, when I was in my late thirties, when I scheduled an appointment with my primary care physician and asked him what lab work I would need to get a pulse on my overall health. I also told him that I'd be committing to see him once a year. His response opened my eyes. "I mean, you can come in if you want to," he started. "I know you're a busy guy, so you could take a year off and come every other year." He elaborated that since I was physically fine overall, not on any consistent medication, and didn't have any other ongoing medical issues, I probably didn't need to come in.

While, on the face of it, this is reasonable medical advice, notice that the approach and attitude is more "fix it after it breaks" rather than "let's keep this engine humming." He gave me some little tid bits of advice, such as making sure I was getting some exercise and trying to keep my weight manageable. But there was definitely no additional input for proactive measures that I could be taking. Supplements to try, preventative measures to take, therapies, meditations, holistic approaches, or new information coming down the pipeline weren't addressed. I need to point out that I didn't ask him about any of these things. I did not ask what was new. I did not ask what alternative medicine tactics I could attempt. I did not ask for a list of supplements that might help me prevent aging and stay active for longer.

He did not offer. I did not ask. The opportunity to be proactive thus did not exist.

There's a resistance in the industry to help "healthy" people maintain and improve their health. Healthy people do not need doctors, right? And there can also be a tendency, on the part of individuals, to neglect their health in times of peace. Just like I did when I did not even bring up options or questions.

TREVOR'S INTERJECTION

This is a good time to remind you that the majority of the financial industry also lacks the proactive attitude. It's a similar laissez-faire attitude of kicking the can down the road, only reacting when something horrible happens. "You've got an illness; *now* let's prescribe you something." "Your portfolio took an unexpected dip; *now* let's look to diversify."

When we aren't being intentional and purposeful with our health and wealth plans, we might as well be ticking time bombs with an unseen number inside of us not only ticking down but ticking much faster than it has to. One day, something will explode—a significant health issue will arise or a major and unforeseen expense will come your way, or both—and you won't have done the purposeful planning to either prevent it from happening or mitigate the damage.

What our theories on WealthSpan and HealthSpan aim to achieve is to unsplode that process so that, starting right now, you are living a healthier, more meaningful, and purpose-driven life—both financially and healthily.

When reading Trevor's thoughts on financial asset protection, he's done such a good job educating us on diversification, insurance, and other strategies. From a medical standpoint, the best protective investment you can make in your health is proactively executing your health goals on your own (and ideally with the guidance of a team). You'll be giving yourself a robust insurance policy—a primary and umbrella policy all rolled into one where you are covering the health of your body but also what might not be "covered" when you run into a catastrophic "market fluctuation" like Dick Hoyt ran into with his heart attack.

What we have to understand is that we are the authors and signers of this insurance policy, one we execute with a daily walk outside, balanced nutrition, and any other steps that apply to our specific goals and routines and needs.

BURNOUT ISN'T A BADGE

But let's recognize that there are hurdles we have to overcome in order to start executing on our goals. The average person doesn't exactly have the time to devote hours each day to exercising, prepping and cooking meals, and staying on top of all of their health needs. Why is that?

There's something about American work culture right now. Dubbed "hustle culture," there is an emphasis on utilizing almost every second of our free time for work and earning income. Not only are people getting side gigs, it seems like their side gigs have side gigs. It's almost like burnout is a badge of honor. "Yeah, I've got the awesome remote job that I devote my weekends to," a friend told me, as if they are completely unaware that they are giving up important time they should be spending on experiences that make life worth living.

No profession is really safe, either. Doctors are facing burnout just as much as teachers, construction workers, or anybody else. The American worker faces exhaustion, emotional drain, being spread too thin (which leads to invasive thoughts of ineffectiveness), pressure to overwork, and a general lack of supportive workplace environments.

Both Trevor and I know burnout well, and our stories are part of the reason why we decided to write this book. He went to work for organizations for many years. I worked in a busy private practice office for many years after finally graduating, which required constant hustle. Prior to that, I was in residency trying to get my next shot, and before that in medical school trying to get a chance, and before that in college trying to beef up my resume and MCAT scores. It was constant hustle after constant hustle!

In situations like this, where you're the newbie answering to "the man," you get your butt kicked every day. Over time, our careers exploded (but not in a good way). You're taking work home with you. You're working on the weekends. You're never seeing your family. There are members of the old guard, taking it easy now, who just look at you like "Tough luck, kid. This is how it works." But is that really the case? Is there an option for better balance and for improved satisfaction with life and careers?

I don't think that "burnout" should be the norm! In no career should that be "the norm." Because of that burnout, we see the newer generation giving up on the old, traditional ways of education and dedication to work. We're seeing a very strong shift in the interest in hard work and in career investment. The new generation is looking at new ways to get what they want because they're seeking for better reasoning on why it has to be that way! Part of me hopes they figure it out because I'm going to need their help when I'm old and they're in charge!

But for now, for those of us who know this feeling, what do we do next? If you are like Trevor and I, we're now trying to *unsplode* the damage from all that hustle that we've already lived through.

Ultimately, burnout is having a rampant and negative impact on our mental and physical health. The stress, anxiety, and depression associated with burnout culture increases our inflammation, thus making us more susceptible to chronic diseases.

Keep in mind, burnout doesn't have to be occupational. Those with toddlers in the house know the pain of sleepless nights, spending half your day trying to prevent a kid from choking as they put *literally everything* in their mouth.

If you want to protect your health and give yourself the freedom to execute your HealthSpan goals, you need to evaluate how you fit into the hustle culture narrative. It is ultimately your choice, and if you are choosing hustle culture, you will be sacrificing health, happiness, fulfillment, and purpose. You'll be all wealth, no health. You'll "explode" instead of *unsplode*. But if you balance your health and wealth instead, you'll give yourself an opportunity to execute your health goals.

Obviously, burnout will come in phases. College and early-career phases tend to be more work at first. Established folks can cruise a little bit more. What balance means to you will depend on what phase of life you're in. For those who are grinding their way through an internship or residency, that means you'll have to be much more intentional about finding ways to take care of yourself. It's a constant evolution and reevaluation process. You have to plan for it your whole life.

Be vocal against detractors in their various forms. For example, the medical field is making some progress in fighting burnout for physicians. Some hospitals are setting hour limitations and penalties for failure to comply. Yet places like these are sometimes met with ridicule or dissatisfaction from mentors who treat it as a weakness of incoming generations.

Don't let anybody normalize the narrative that you have to work every minute of your life until you're dead. That's a prolific American narrative, and we need to break it.

Make your health the badge of honor, not your burnout.

THE HEALTH PYRAMID

There are certain aspects to health protection that are foundational. Others are high-level, and very specific to a person's situation. And there is another category that is between the two, a mid-tier layer of health protection that many people could benefit from. Using base, mid-, and top-tier health strategies, let's build a new health pyramid. With this pyramid, you can approach your HealthSpan by planning with purpose.

BASE LAYER

The base layer of the health pyramid is going to be about all of us and what we put into our bodies and minds. Who are we keeping in contact with to protect our mental health? And we need to eat to stay alive, so nutrition isn't something that a person can avoid. That means, each and every day, we are making choices about our food intake. That's our foundational health choice.

Vitamins and Supplements

The first thing to keep in mind is that, historically, vitamins and supplements have been poorly regulated. That's important because it's an industry that brings in $150 billion (with a *b*) a year.

Everywhere you look, somebody is selling some sort of miracle supplement to cure some sort of ailment, with an asterisk, of course. Follow that asterisk around the label and you'll eventually run across the phrase "These statements have not been evaluated by the FDA." Translation: "This is probably a bottle of bullshit!" Okay, that's a little harsh; lots of supplements and vitamins do important work for a lot of people, but my point stands. There is a lot of snake oil in this industry that has no medical verifiability.

That creates a lot of misinformation and conflicting information about what is healthy and what's not. And most of the advertising you'll see isn't necessarily geared toward making you healthy. Instead, they fear-bait you ("Your tap water will kill you unless you supplement it with *this*") or hero-bait you ("Eat *this* to look like me, an industry influencer") into buying something.

The truth of the matter is that vitamins and supplements are extremely useful, but just not in the way that many people engage with them.

When it comes to vitamins, that's easy. Just get a comprehensive multivitamin. Done. Anything you don't need, your body will pee out.

With supplements, that's where you can customize it to your health needs a little bit more. In the previous chapter, we talked about the need to get various screenings to see where your health is at right now. Let's say a screening indicates you are low on testosterone, then a person on your medical team could advise that you add supplements like zinc and magnesium. Or if you do the math on your food intake and find you aren't consuming enough protein, you can start testing protein supplements and find a product that works for you.

Your deficiencies will change. Your goals will also change. Your situation will change. And your balance will change. Reevaluate and target what you need as your needs evolve.

And I don't want to make this the "here's what's wrong with America" chapter, but let's face it: the most accessible and inexpensive food is usually the most toxic for our bodies. There is nothing that can compete with an instant, five-dollar pizza. And despite how good it might taste, it is in no way a replacement for a home-cooked and balanced meal!

Highly processed foods in our groceries stores are made to sit on the store shelves (or pantry shelves) longer. This longevity is not a nutritional thing. It takes time to ship and shelve products. Adults are busy and need to stock shelf-ready foods for themselves and their children, spending less time making food so that they can bring home the bacon (remember that whole "hustle culture" thing?).

The lack of time in the day to visit the market to get fresh foods and the overall disinterest in visiting the store daily are part of why the processed foods have nearly replaced fresh options in the store. In some foreign countries, local markets and open-air markets are in many locations within the city so that people can easily drop by and pick up what they need as they travel to and from work. In many cities in the United States, the "Farmer's Market" is a weekend-only option and is only frequented by the hippies and grandparents! But have you ever taken your kids to a farmer's market? They are in awe! It is beautiful! The smells of fresh-baked bread. The beauty of local grown fruits and vegetables with their vibrant colors and aromas. It's a wonderful sight to see! Yet during the week, that opportunity simply doesn't exist in many cities!

Not only are the better foods often harder to find, but there is also an intentional push to make the processed foods more appealing! There is an intentional targeting, prepared by the food industry, to play on our sensory mechanisms as we eat more of these processed foods. This is a calculated effort to encourage increased frequency and increased quantity of sales.

Have you ever heard of the "umami blast"? How about "flavor potentiators"? The umami blast is that satisfying savory taste that is built into many of the few processed foods we eat. It's chemically built. Sure, this is "nacho" and that one is "cool ranch," but they both deliver the same chemical compounds to the consumer that ensures the brain and taste buds react to engineered combinations of salt, fat, and carbs—all boosted by MSG—to trigger the brain's reward system in an addictive way. The MSG and similar ingredients act as a "flavor potentiator" that unnaturally amplifies the taste sensation up to thirty times. Many processed foods are designed to initially satisfy you, leave you unsatisfied after the taste goes away, and train the brain to continue to seek out that flavor profile.

I would also suggest that you avoid gluten and any foods that can trigger chronic inflammation, such as trans fats, refined carbs, added sugars, processed meats, and vegetable oils high in omega-6. If you're eating food that puts you in a chronic state of inflammation, what will that get you? How about prolonged damage to your immune system to make you more susceptible to disease? How about damage to healthy tissues, organs, and your DNA over time? Inflammation acts as a silent underlying cause of common, debilitating, and often fatal diseases, such as cancer, type 2 diabetes, Alzheimer's, autoimmune disorders, and heart disease. Heart disease is the leading cause of death in the United States.

Ever heard of TB12? Or the Tom Brady Diet? This elite NFL quarterback, Tom Brady, famously follows a strict nutrition practice that minimizes inflammation and maximizes recovery. Because of the results of this diet and the ability he had to continue playing a very violent game deep into his career, this diet has gained attention and a strong following. So how does he do it? He hasn't touched dairy, gluten, white sugar, or processed foods in decades. Seven Super Bowls later, he was playing at the highest level well into his forties. Despite suffering injuries and despite his age being almost double some of his competitors, he was able to play and succeed in the NFL for many years. And his calculated approach to avoiding additional inflammation has played a large part in that.

Additional quick and ready food options have other additives that would be best to avoid. Frozen and quick-ready food, which is often high in sodium, sugars, unhealthy fats, and refined and processed ingredients, may allow us the convenience of keeping the freezer stocked for our late days at work and provide an easy evening of meal prep, but they also come with a cost. The chronic health effects of these include damaging cardiovascular and metabolic health—contributing to inflammation, obesity, hypertension, fatty liver disease, high cholesterol, and, yes, heart disease.

Although I could go on, that was a long walk to say that, in most cases, protecting your HealthSpan involves avoiding processed foods entirely while eating natural foods that are, nutritionally speaking, tailored to the nutrient profile your body requires based on the screenings you took earlier.

You have got to put good fuel inside your body. For overall health but also for fat loss—something many people are interested in—it turns out that the extra weight we carry is not always caused by a lack of exercise. Some studies suggest that your weight (or lack thereof) is determined by your nutrition by a factor of 80 percent.

I have frequently heard from body builders and athletes that they do not "work out" into their physique, but that they "eat" their way into their physique. Working out is simply not enough. It's largely diet! And no amount of time in the gym or on the treadmill will compensate for filling your body with garbage!

Keep your food as fresh as possible. It will be slightly more expensive, but the health benefits are invaluable. Leafy greens, grass-fed and lean beef, cruciferous vegetables, sweet potatoes, and berries. Sometimes protein-rich foods like nuts, salmon, yogurt, can be excellent choices. Overall, fresh food contains greater amounts of essential nutrients like vitamins, minerals, antioxidants, and fiber. And by having less inflammatory properties, fresh food reduces the risk of chronic disease.

While I'm here, I should give a special shout-out to A2 milk. Compared to conventional milk, A2 provides easier protein digestion and reduced inflammation. It's also nutrient dense, packed with quality protein, calcium, vitamin D, potassium, and phosphorus. Because it is without the peptide BCM-7 (found in conventional milk), A2 milk supports lower blood pressure, lower cholesterol, and a healthier heart.

Last thing. You still might be in shock that I've advised rethinking your relationship with gluten. "What can I cook? Flour is in almost everything!" Seek ancient grains and alternative organic flours that offer superior nutritional value. Kamut flour, for example, is non-GMO, has more protein than most standard flours, is anti-inflammatory, is unmodified, has high fiber, and is easier to digest.

Long-term health in eating natural food is not just promoted through nutrition. Time must be spent thinking about and preparing this food. Guess what? You can do that with friends and family. Make it a bonding moment to cook the family dinner with the kids. Your relationship to food doesn't just need to be numbers. It can also be social, filling and strengthening any gaps in your mental health.

We talked previously about dopamine, serotonin, norepinephrine, and oxytocin. Each of these have their own chemical make-up, and some of the things that we ingest will actually promote and help with making sure we have enough based nutrients to provide improved levels of these transmitters.

We can improve our ability to form these transmitters by taking some of the same food groups into consideration. Eggs are shown to assist in the creation of both dopamine and serotonin. Almonds specifically assist with dopamine, and several members of the nut family will help with serotonin. Turkey is also a good source of the building blocks for serotonin.

In summary: eggs, nuts, and turkey. These are noted to be some of the most beneficial. If these are not foods that you like, or that you cannot eat, please do some additional digging for alternatives that may better fit your needs and wants.

Oxytocin and norepinephrine are more influenced by the activities that we fill our lives with and less influenced by the foods that we ingest. But a balanced diet nonetheless provides the basic building blocks for all of our bodies' systems. So keep in mind that focusing on that balanced diet and appropriate nutrient supplementation will help you generate the response that you seek with the remainder of the changes you are implementing.

Maintaining Healthy Relationships

Studies show that those with healthy relationships with friends and family are less at risk for physical and mental health problems. It's therefore important to protect our health by maintaining healthy relationships.

You know a relationship is healthy when it adds value to your own sense of purpose and well-being. If it is built on honesty, trust, compromise, respect, and open communication, then you are likely in a healthy relationship where there is a balance of agency. These relationships need to go both ways: sometimes you need, and sometimes you can give. Make sure that these people in your life are also able to do both for you and that you are willing to do both for them. If you can't, or if they can't, or if you aren't willing, then you need to give some careful consideration to the value of this relationship and to your commitment to it and to what it is providing for you.

When you have a relationship that doesn't fall into this category and is instead taking part of you away or somehow contributing to an imbalance in your health, you need to detach yourself from that individual. That could take time and courage, and perhaps even some outside help. But you need to stand up for your own needs first. And you need to fill those placeholders in your life with people that you enjoy caring for and that also have the capacity to be there for you.

If you have made the decision that such a person in your life exists, breaking the tie may be very challenging! Some people will happily walk away from you. Some people will walk away more violently. And then there may also be some people that refuse to walk away—that attempt to turn this situation on you. They attempt to convince you to change your mind or even manipulate you. This may involve blaming. This may involve shaming you, guilt tripping you, or even threatening you.

If this is the case, you probably have an abundance of evidence that this person was not the type of person that we are talking about! And that this person needs to go. This may require outside help, especially if this becomes frightening. Unfortunately, many of us have this type of person in our lives. There is a helpful tool for dealing with that: though their actions toward you might hurt, and might stir up the desire to backpedal on your decision, you need to keep moving forward.

Next, try to stand your ground while remaining very neutral to their threats or retaliations. This process is called "gray rocking". When dealing with an unhealthy relationship and/or emotionally volatile person, the last thing you want to do is to engage and fight! If you are able to stay neutral and unresponsive to their emotional volatility or manipulation, then you are headed in the right direction. This tactic creates a temporary emotional protection that allows you to de-escalate conflict, regain control over yourself, and build a path to going forward in your life and to cutting off contact with them. And this reaction has probably convinced you that you have made the right choice!

Keep in mind, this "gray rocking" technique is not for all of your relationships, and it is not a long-term solution to all of your friend and family issues. It should only be used as part of a detachment mechanism for the people in your life that try to blame and manipulate you for moving forward in a healthy direction when they would rather hold you back.

If you are considering gray rocking with a more violent or abusive person, then you will need a different approach and likely professional help to determine how to proceed. The last thing we would want is for your situation to escalate, moving from suffering their unhealthy behavior toward suffering from their abuse.

Make sure that your support team and close family and friends are aware of your plans and approach and that, if needed, you bring someone with you or seek out some professional advice prior to giving this a go on your own. Please be safe!

MIDDLE LAYER

The middle layer still concerns everybody, but these activity-based concepts aren't things that we think about in our daily lives—not like the way we think about our next meal constantly. Once we've put the right nutrients in our bodies, we should be energized enough to tackle that thing that's a little bit more difficult and that we love to avoid: exercise.

Stretching and Flexibility

One time, as an early teenager when my family was picking up my sister from a gymnastics class, I watched this gray-haired old-man coach get the attention of the crowd. He then proceeded to climb his way up a thirty-foot rope with nothing but his arms. Just arms all the way up (no legs or feet assisting the ascension). Then, at the top, he hung from the ceiling with one arm while pointing at the crowd and said, "Age is an attitude, not a condition." The room was silent and filled with open-jawed, "holy crap that's impressive" faces. Including mine. Even at the peak of my rock climbing days I don't know if I'd have been able to one-arm pull-up my way to the top of that rope the way that he did! And I certainly couldn't do it now. And now I'm still only about half the age of that guy!

Flexibility is the perfect example of something that has to be prioritized by everyone but is essentially not on our radar. Instead, many of us sit in a hunched, horrible position all day while we write that work email. Over time, those of us in this group will get stiff backs, stiff hamstrings, stiff quads, stiff shoulders, and curse themselves to a life of limited mobility.

If you've ever been around a baby, you've probably seen one reach down, grab their little foot, and bring it all the way up to their mouths.

It's cute, but it's also kind of amazing. They are so bendy! Just the thought of trying to get my foot anywhere above my stomach from a standing position makes my back and hip hurt.

We don't have to be as flexible as a baby, but we should be seeking to improve our flexibility. And that will be a daily journey if you actually want to put a dent in it. That means intentionally tackling it, adding dedicated flexibility work to our routine. That means doing any functional training of any kind—walking, running, cycling—and then following it up with intentional stretches. Only this will help improve flexibility.

Body Fat Percentage

Although it may become more difficult to control as we get older, our body fat percentage is always modifiable. There should never be a time in your life where you're saying to yourself, "Well, it's too late." Sometimes people will say, "I don't know why I'm overweight." But there are no exceptions to the rules, in terms of balancing intake and activity.

What is considered a healthy body fat percentage for your body will be unique to you. Consult with a medical professional to determine that number. Factors will include your age, gender, and activity level. People who aren't active *can* have a higher "healthy" number compared to an athlete. And in some cases, people have too little body fat and need to work to increase it. Being too fit and potentially not eating enough can lead to alternate issues! I've had friends who, in the peak of their fitness, were actually told that they were suffering from anorexia! Calories in and calories out have boundaries on both sides! So make sure that you are being careful with the extremes to which you push your fitness and diet. Your body fat percentage can be a good indicator of this balance.

Once you've determined that number, find the right balance of food intake and exercise/activity to start moving the needle in the right direction.

Cardiovascular Health

Heart disease is the leading cause of death in America across gender and ethnic background. It is, to say the least, a problem. Improving your cardiovascular health will help keep stents, strokes, and blood clots out of your heart.

Continuous exercise is the prescribed protection here. Work incrementally, meaning only exercise to your tolerance and, over time, try to build up that tolerance. The higher your tolerance, the more your HealthSpan is protected. Ride bikes, jog, and swim laps in the pool. Anything to get that heart rate up. And build from where you are. Intensity (speed) or time. The body is a huge muscle, and as you work it, you must also work to challenge it in new ways. Exercise, rest, and mix it up so that you keep adapting and keep improving.

Diet plays a huge role in this, too. It probably trumps exercise. The fattier and sugarier your meals, the more brittle and clogged your blood vessels will become. Right now that garbage food tastes delicious, but by the time you are sixty, it might cause a health event that, if it doesn't kill you, might just prevent you from using an arm, leg, or portion of your face for the rest of your life.

TREVOR'S INTERJECTION

Although I'm a wealth manager, one of my primary hobbies is health and fitness. I might be one of the "gym rats" that Caleb mentioned in a previous paragraph, so cardiovascular health is an important topic to me. When it comes to nutrition, I follow the 80/20 rule, which says that 80 percent of our cardiovascular health is actually determined by what we eat. But in terms of long-term health, studies show that your nutrition is *the* most important thing. Movement and training is the second most important thing. And sleep and stress management is third, but still very much important.

So if it has such a big impact, what should we be doing? There are some key strategies, but this is a topic worth exploring in more detail. One is keeping your muscles strong; this leads to longevity. Another thing is to consider your nutrition. I prefer a caveman diet or macro balance that incorporates meat proteins, healthy oils, vegetables that are lectin-free to mitigate inflammation, a variety of (different colors of) fruits (mostly berries—all other fruits are high in sugar), and good carbs such as rice or sweet potatoes. Look up the caveman diet, the Mediterranean diet, and the DASH diet, all of which are shown to contribute to a healthy heart. Stay away from sugar and absolutely no processed foods.

As part of the last chapter and the screening process, you should have some idea of your heart health right now, as well as your family history. Tailor your cardiovascular health to that particular snapshot. If nobody has ever had blood sugar issues, then perhaps that's not where you need to focus your attention. But if all of them end up with dementia or fragility fractures, then that would be an excellent place to start! You are unique, so don't treat yourself like a star-shaped cookie, straight out of the star-shaped cookie-cutter mold. Be you. Let that unique part of you help guide you toward what is most important for your individual HealthSpan.

TOP LAYER

In the top layer, we've moved beyond universal health protections and will now focus on things that mostly concern specific groups...namely folks that are transitioning between their middle age to retirement age.

Inflammation

Most people don't have inflammation problems until they are in their middle ages or right near retirement age. This is when joints start to hurt, arthritis may appear, we lose our appetite, experience bloating or abdominal pain, and things like that.

When you're in your thirties or forties, you can do a lot of protective work to diminish the consequences of chronic inflammation. An anti-inflammatory diet might be one of those, and it can emphasize certain supplements like turmeric. Staying hydrated, staying smoke-free, and exercising regularly are other ways to stave off inflammation.

If unaddressed, inflammation can create an untold number of serious health conditions.

Cellular Structure

The integrity of our cell structure is constantly changing. The young person's mind is plastic and moldable, and so too is the rest of their body. In my medical training, we joked that children are like salamanders. Parts get broken, and they just grow back! Kids heal things that adults couldn't even dream of healing! Their ability to compensate and recover is incredible. They bounce back like you wouldn't believe. But that ability does not carry with us forever.

As we age, everything's structural strength gradually breaks down. Mitochondrial function loss can contribute to lower energy, fatigue, quicker aging, and disease. Our blood vessels become more fragile. They tear and break easier. This is why older people bruise so easily. And those same bruises turn into strokes and aneurysms (or at least more so than happens in younger people).

This is a top-layer protection because it doesn't need to be addressed until you hit a certain age (probably your fifties). There are many ways to protect your cellular structure through strengthening strategies, and I encourage you to do your own deep dive. Some include the intake of antioxidants, phospholipids, phytochemicals, and anti-inflammatory spices. Beyond nutrient intake, it may not surprise you that aerobic training, resistance training, HIIT exercises, and brisk walking all promote strong cells. And talk to a dietician; some supplements can also serve the body well in this area and can be tailored to match your genetics and metabolic testing. What you need will likely not be what I need or what Trevor needs. You've got to do the testing and have the insight to fill your own tank.

Bone Strength

This is a top-layer issue because it will affect only a specific category: older adults. With kids, bones break, but (in the absence of disease) they repair themselves really well. When adults break bones, the healing times get longer, and the rates of success also go down. There are a lot of additional treatments that an adult might have to do in order to heal an injury that a kid just moves right past. For adults, there are a lot of subcategories you might fall into that will determine the best course of action for *how* you can maintain or improve your bone strength.

First is gender. Women are much more at risk of osteoporosis, a condition where a weakness of the bones makes an individual more susceptible to fracture. This risk factor for these fractures has to do with decreased bone density compared to men. While this can be due to many environmental and developmental factors, it is also hormonal. Estrogen is the primary source for bone health in women, and it declines quickly after menopause. And the effect on bones can vary between women, but overall this leads to a diminished density of bones, which can lead to fractures.

Another factor is age. When a person turns sixty-five, the risk of osteoporosis increases significantly. Peak bone mass occurs between the ages of twenty-five and thirty. So, after that, density is in decline. At forty, it declines even faster. You can't stop the timing, but you can certainly do your best to stop the severity! Or at least slow it.

In terms of protective, proactive action, a person can maintain strength in their bones with a diet rich in calcium, vitamin D, and protein. They need to implement an exercise routine that includes jumping and maybe even includes falling down! Believe it or not there are therapy techniques that focus on how to fall and how to get back up! These exercises stimulate the bones. Weight training, too, tells the bones to stay strong.

One of the standard health screens as we age is a DEXA scan, which is performed to measure bone density and assess for fracture risk based on the person's density compared to younger persons. This then calculates a risk for injury and is used to determine treatment strategies as we age. If you're not in a category that actually warrants medication treatment, then focus on the other steps to keep your numbers healthy! Get educated on the additional steps you might need to take in order to maintain or improve the results of your next test.

REGENERATIVE MEDICINE

In the realm of alternative medicine, we often place shame or judgement on the burgeoning of new ideas and techniques. It's good to be cautious; don't get me wrong. But that doesn't mean we can't also have an open mind. Let's look at some common forms of regenerative therapy.

LIGHT THERAPY

Using light therapy can help stimulate the cells, promote tissue repair, and bring balance to our lives that are now more commonly found full of indoor work and covered travel. Some of us leave our home by way of our covered garage and drive to work in sunglasses and park in the covered garage at work and work indoors until the end of the work day without even leaving the office for lunch and then reverse the travel routine only to again find ourselves indoors for the rest of the night until we repeat the process. Where did the sun go? Where are we getting our vitamin D?

Exposure to light provides many benefits to our physical bodies and emotional state. Seasonal affective disorder is a condition where the longer winter darkness plays on the mental state of an individual, leading to a state of depression and lack of motivation. Experimentation has been done regarding various wavelengths of light to determine the medical uses of these wavelengths, and this light therapy is now being incorporated into alarm clocks, inflammation treatments, and longevity treatments. This therapy can be even combined with biologic therapies such as stem cell therapy to trigger cell activity and restore function. The mitochondrial stimulation provides energy for cells, which promote tissue repair and anti-inflammation. Keeping cell systems maximized can help prevent issues later.

So whether you make effort to bask in the "morning twilight" to expose yourself to the morning dose of natural red light wavelengths, or if you choose red light therapy within the comfort of your own home, there is no mistaking the fact that we can quite literally live our lives in fear of the sun, or we can embrace the sun and light and the benefits of both and use them to maximize our physical bodies and promote more satisfaction in our lives.

STEM CELL TREATMENTS

Stem cells are basically the grandparents of all of our cells. They have "potential" to become (differentiate into) other types of cells. So, in essence, these are blank cells that can become almost any other type of cell. Because of this potential for change, and because of the effect that this can bring to our bodily systems, these cell lines are studied and manipulated and injected, inhaled, or administered to promote healing and to augment disease.

The continuous study of these cell lines has created much buzz in the medical world as we attempt to harness this power and use these "potential" cells to the benefit of patients. At present, these cell lines are used for inflammatory treatments, disease modification, immune system modification, regeneration, and many other avenues of medicine. While many of these uses remain controversial, and while regulations of these therapies remain in constant flux, it is important to educate yourself regarding the progress of these potential treatments and to not fall for the click-bait, too-good-to-be-true claims that some will make regarding the use and success of these treatments. Keep in mind the phrase "If it sounds too good to be true, it probably is."

Because the phrase "stem cells" often covers the opposing sides of FDA-approved treatments as well as the unproven, unregulated, and often dangerous procedures, practitioners and insurance companies prefer to call these "stem cell treatments" or "biologic treatment" or, simply, just "regenerative treatment."

GENE THERAPY

The goal with gene therapy is to modify genes to correct genetic defects, create disease modifications in order to alter disease, to improve cell function, and to restore equilibrium within the body. Some diseases can be cured by using virus-bound genetic codes, and the future of genetic therapy presents a wonderful world of opportunity.

But this is a very complex system, and we are talking about a human body with over thirty trillion cells, each cell with genetic code, which consists of approximately three billion pairs of coding material. That is a total of 9e+22 if you're a math nerd. Or ninety sextillion. Or 90,000,000,000,000,000,000,000. That is a total of twenty-two zeroes. That is a TON of coding material!

So if you think that genetic therapy is complicated, then you are probably underestimating what that statement actually means. But there is hope. And scientists continue to work on this with research and exploration. So if you have a family that is genetically predisposed to certain conditions or diseases, you can see how success in this line of therapy could be so impactful.

SAUNAS

Using a sauna introduces moist or dry heat to the body, which can be very good for improving vascular function, reducing inflammation, boosting the immune system, and providing stress relief. Notice that all of those benefits are also often associated with exercise, but instead you get to sit in a relaxing and meditative state. Count me in!

Sitting in a sauna can increase a standard heart rate to 120–150 beats per minute, dilating blood vessels and improving circulation. With frequent use, it improves the strength of the interior lining of your blood vessels (which reduces the risk of cardiovascular conditions), reduces your blood pressure, and increases your vascular elasticity.

Whether in a high-humidity environment or a dry environment, saunas cause changes in the skin, muscle tissue, and lungs—adaptations from excessive heat that you are training your body to tolerate. Much like working out, this practice extends what your body is capable of and allows faster recovery and regeneration.

Various studies have linked consistent sauna bathing—four to seven sessions per week—with around a 40 percent reduction in all-cause mortality, including reduced risk of cardiovascular disease, neurocognitive diseases, and stroke.

COLD PLUNGES

Cold plunges work in a very similar way to saunas, in that they are exposing the body to extreme conditions. But they do have different aims. Here, the goal is a constriction response to the nervous and circulatory systems to reduce inflammation, soothe sore muscles, and boost alertness. By limiting blood flow to limbs, it pushes your blood toward important organs to reduce swelling. This also accelerates muscle recovery by promoting fresh, oxygenated blood circulation to the muscles after the body warms back up. This creates a faster regeneration to stack your gains.

From a neurotransmitter point of view, a cold plunge triggers norepinephrine and dopamine. The first is crucial for boosting your mood and metabolism. As far as dopamine, cold plunges are known to multiply your dopamine output by two or three times. Because of the extreme cold, your body flags it as a stressor, triggering new amounts of dopamine as a stress response to improve your focus, alertness, and mood for hours after the cold plunge. You move from a sympathetic activation into a parasympathetic recovery.

Although the research is somewhat limited, it suggests that cold plunges help improve our perception of our own well-being (sometimes changing our interiority can help us change our exteriority), stress regulation, quality of sleep, and fatigue.

Here's something to keep in mind. Although cold plunges are great for regenerating our mood and sense of self, they could possibly interfere with our muscle-building aspirations. Frequent cold plunges, especially after training, constrict the blood flow that promotes muscle building.

PEPTIDES

Peptides are biological messengers. At their core, peptides are protein chains that influence the body's metabolic pathways. Your body produces thousands a day, regulating cells, tissues, and organs. When they are working optimally, they repair damage, increase recovery, promote your metabolism, make your immune responses more resilient, and balance your hormones.

As we age, it's natural for some peptide signals to turn off. We lose the ability to amplify, restore, and optimize signaling pathways. So what if it were possible to regenerate or maintain these signals? Doing so can help you turn specific signals on that have perhaps gone away with age.

That's where peptide replacement therapy—sometimes called hormone replacement therapy—comes in. These treatments use amino acids in an effort to stimulate your natural peptide signals. For that reason, don't think of this as the direct replacement of hormones so much as the natural regeneration of them. Peptide replacement therapy, in the limited research, seems to be more efficient when there are other HealthSpan habits already in place, such as maintaining good sleep patterns and practicing good nutrition.

CHOOSE YOURSELF

Protecting your HealthSpan starts with unapologetically choosing yourself.

Your health is a priceless commodity. Illness and disease can rob us of it. But so can procrastination and a lack of health investment. Like any asset, if you don't take the necessary steps for it to grow in or maintain its value, then you will probably lose it.

Some will use this chapter to do the work now to build protections. Some will be forced to take their health more seriously to do damage control and prevent further setbacks. Some will be backed into a corner and fighting to maintain a health they are quickly losing. In any case—rehabilitative or strengthening or both—your HealthSpan requires that you take aggressive action to protect yourself.

Rededicate yourself for you. Plan with purpose. You have that opportunity in front of you. We have given you some additional insight and some additional tools. And as we've said before, unfortunately our medical industry is largely based on pathology (injury or damage) and on the fixing or repair of that pathology. It is less geared toward prevention and improvement for those of us who aren't quite damaged yet. This means *it will be on you* to be proactive.

What we've discussed here is very basic protection that is accessible to most people. There is, however, another layer we might call more preventative—a set of health choices we can make using a little bit more of our time, effort, and money.

CHAPTER 5

PREVENTATIVE CARE: HOW TO KEEP YOUR OVERALL HEALTH MAXIMIZED

"Take care of your body. It's the only place you have to live."

—JIM ROHN

Most doctors are not trained to prevent health problems. Sure, they know the basics of the good things that everybody should be doing, but they aren't catering their practices for coaching and education and for the prevention of illness and disease. Remember, they make their money on disease! They need disease to keep happening! And so do the pharmaceutical companies. The system needs disease! So most medical doctors are trained to *treat* health problems, not so much to prevent them or avoid them. In medical school there is so much to learn that the building blocks of prevention and longevity and supplementation were not the primary material to learn. With the focus on physiology, pathology, and treatment, prevention was somewhat left for other providers to focus on.

To add to the complexity of your healthcare team, doctors in training are tested very early on to assess the broad aspects of medicine as they learned to have a general understanding of the human body, but as they progress in training, they compartmentalize their focus of study, and the overall broad understanding begins to dwindle and fade. The focus becomes the specialization and the expertise of their desired niche in the medical world, and their focus on that portion of medicine becomes the primary focus. Thus, the updates and cutting-edge, broad understanding of medicine gets lost.

Doctors are highly specialized. Each specialist is like a specialty tool in the toolbox. Some are hammers designed to hit their unique nails, and some are wrenches designed to tighten a bolt! But just like you wouldn't take a hammer to cut a PVC pipe for your lawn project, you wouldn't take a wrench to paint your wall. I don't want to proclaim that having specialists is a problem, because having improved expertise is not necessarily a problem; it's even a good thing. But what it means for you is that you have to know the "language" of healthcare in order to speak to a provider that will best fit your needs and in order to navigate to the people that can best help you.

You can't ask an orthopedic surgeon like me about diet tips to improve your libido in the middle of your surgery consultation. I might give you my half-baked opinion for what I've heard works, which might be an unhelpful meathead response cloaked in doctor terms. But there is certainly a better person for that discussion, and I'd love to encourage you to seek out the better and more helpful information that you would find during a conversation with that person instead of with me!

And if you do want to pick the brains of your providers about these alternate treatments and about these additional opportunities, please don't be offended if you're met with some resistance or if these providers simply don't know. Also, please be respectful of their time, because the face of medicine continues to push these providers to see more patients and provide more care per hour just so that they can keep paying their staff and so that they can keep the lights on.

Doctors today have to do more busy work and see more patients than ever before, and I don't want to get a bunch of phone calls from my colleagues that I've encouraged the nation to make their job more difficult. But this is our system. Learn how to navigate it to succeed within it.

Think about it. When was the last time you heard of a doctor that delivered babies, removed thyroid glands, assessed somebody's range of motion, reviewed an MRI, interpreted blood sugar results, performed a colonoscopy, put a cast on a broken wrist, and checked somebody's vision all in the same day? Outside of fictitious doctors on *Grey's Anatomy*, they simply don't exist.

Some patients assume that going to medical school means any doctor knows every single thing that could ever happen to the human body and how to prevent, maintain, and correct all diseases. Doctors definitely go to school for a really long time, but no individual doctor can do that sort of holistic preventative work.

In fact, I have a little bit of a story for you. A family friend of mine—a woman in her mid-seventies, let's call her Sally—had a freak-chance diagnosis of type 1 diabetes. Prior to experiencing symptoms, she had never had any blood sugar issues her entire life, had a healthy diet, had a lean 110-pound frame on a five-foot body, and there was never an indication of any problem throughout her life.

A few weeks before the diagnosis happened, she was feeling really dizzy and decided to go to the ER. She had been feeling slight dizziness and even incremental weight loss for months (she was now under one hundred pounds). But that day, her dizziness hit a breaking point.

After some tests, the ER doctor noted that her blood sugar had crashed. Slightly confused, he nonetheless told her she may be experiencing some prediabetic (type 2) symptoms and needed to raise her blood sugar. This wasn't his area of expertise—he was used to high-trauma situations. So he gave her snacks readily available at the hospital, which included refined and added sugar. (Giving a diabetic refined sugar is a big no-no.) Then, he quoted her the incorrect "high" and "low" blood sugar levels to monitor at home and released her.

He reassured her that, since he believed it was type 2 (where the pancreas is still capable of making insulin for the body), she would be fine. Well, she actually had type 1, and she was making *no* insulin. Had she not followed up with her primary to get further information or if she had continued to use the incorrect blood sugar numbers he gave her, she could have easily died.

The primary was equally befuddled but was able to correct the high/low monitoring range. A week later, that led to a referral to the endocrinologist—one of the most prominent endocrinologists in the state—who was able to determine what was going on and that it was a much more serious type 1 variety. Her endocrinologist, who had practiced for decades at that point, stated that she (the patient) was the oldest new case of type 1 diabetes they had ever seen by a decade. The previous "oldest case" was in their sixties.

It can be frustrating and can potentially delay necessary healthcare to have to see multiple physicians. But in today's modern world of constant research, education, and evolution, it is not possible for one person to have all the answers.

The moral of the story? Singular doctors don't know everything. A secondary moral is to not wait months to see a doctor if you are experiencing dizziness and weight loss.

But hold on. It gets *even* worse when it comes to the medical industry. In order to maximize your HealthSpan as you engage with the healthcare industry, you'll have to do due diligence that nobody really teaches you—probably because a lot of it is outside our health insurance network.

What might that due diligence look like? Maybe it means seeing a preventative specialist you've never heard of, like a naturopath. Maybe it's realizing your primary provider has their own specialties that could detract from how they provide care to you. For example, if you are in your thirties and the only primary care doctor available in your area is largely taking care of a Medicare population, they'll be really savvy with treating high blood pressure and diabetes but probably not have an aggressive mindset to help with the comparatively minor health concerns of somebody approaching their middle age. This doctor is going to be much more like "You're fine. See you next year. Or maybe even skip a few."

The typical and standard preventative care that exists in the insurance-covered medical industry is the proven age-based and gender-based testing and screenings that have been researched and calculated to be both cost-effective and to be appropriately timed for the proper population. It is averages and numbers and statistics. And I'm talking about colonoscopies, pap smears, mammograms, prostate screenings, bone density testing, and so forth.

And if you're trying to push for testing outside of those boundaries, you are likely going to receive a "denial letter." Because the insurance is typically going to follow the rules of these screenings, and if you're trying to do more than the standard, then they're going to push back. So the next step is to complete the testing that you can obtain and meet with the right people to discuss how to use it.

Some of the data will be easy to interpret. Other data will require more expertise. Identifying the proper individuals is your next task. Medical professionals in this space are all around you, most likely. So which ones are we talking about? And where can you find them? And who is going to help you interpret that information or give you guidance based on the results you now have?

WHO WORKS IN PREVENTATIVE MEDICINE?

There are so many ways you can stay on top of things and get involved in the preventative maximization of your HealthSpan.

Longevity and prevention strategies are becoming very popular. These services are being offered more and more by chiropractors, nurse practitioners, hormone clinics, naturopathic doctors, geriatricians, and concierge doctors who specialize in functional and integrative medicine.

So, longevity doctors do exist. And the training for these individuals continues to evolve and improve. You just need to know where to find them, discover what they do, and realize that anything in life worth chasing is going to cost you something. In this case, it'll be money because most of these folks can't provide longevity services without cash payments. Nonetheless, let's go over each and the basic preventative services they can provide to you.

Many, but not all, providers who work in preventive care can fall outside a traditional healthcare system. In other words, they might not be covered by insurance. Some of the following practitioners may cost you money, but what they offer is well worth it. Lastly, the ordering in this following list is intentional. We will move through practitioners whose work is embedded in preventative care and proceed toward those who are more associated with traditional medicine.

I chose this ordering because it's best to take care of yourself and your preventative health naturally and before you end up in the traditional healthcare system. There's an epidemic in our country right now that people wait until they go down the road of traditional medicine—with prescriptions, surgery, and the side effects of those choices—instead of letting the human body take care of itself. Flip the way you think about it. Prevent instead of treat.

NUTRITIONISTS

Historically, the nutritionist has been known to be a hospital assistant. You know, the person who gets called in to coach the newly diagnosed patient with pamphlets or one-sheets with example menus and pictures of food, offering relatively general information such as "eat less salt."

But nutritionists can be much more than this "coaching session in response to an illness" narrative. There are professional nutritionists who run regular clinics—called registered dietitians. On the other end of the spectrum, you might also see that your local or boutique gym has their own nutritionist on staff. These professionals are good for telling you what foods to stay away from, what foods to eat, how to create portion control, and gain an understanding of how the types of food you intake can affect your specific and overall health. They can tailor their work to you, looking at your health history or testing your response to different foods and their absorption potential.

When people fail to maintain good long-term nutrition habits, serious health issues could be brewing internally that you should otherwise be going out of your way to prevent. Those include but are not limited to obesity, type 2 diabetes, heart disease, fatigue, a weakened immune system, cognitive decline, digestive issues, hair loss, metabolic slowdown, anxiety, depression, organ damage, and muscle loss. I had to stop myself, but that list could be much longer. Suffice it to say that working with a nutritionist can prevent a lot of issues most people face.

STRENGTH AND CONDITIONING COACH, PERSONAL TRAINER, AND ATHLETIC TRAINER

There are a set of professionals whose goal is to train their client in functional bodily prevention and optimization. Although they each have minor differences, they are the strength and conditioning coach, the personal trainer, and the athletic trainer. Generally, these folks are looking to improve your fitness, strength, conditioning, and flexibility. The end result of all of that work is that the overall well-being these coaches and trainers drive you toward will make you more resilient to chronic conditions and diseases.

Personal trainers work for the general population to tackle a range of issues, including weight loss, improved fitness, muscle tone, injury prevention, flexibility, strength training, and cardiovascular training. By creating targeted and progressive workout plans, improving your overall health through their programs can help prevent chronic conditions, maintain healthy habits, alleviate stress and anxiety, and prevent sedentary-related diseases.

Strength and conditioning coaches usually require a certification and, at minimum, a bachelor's degree in exercise science, although it's becoming more common for the threshold to be a master's degree.

This person will design and implement training programs targeted to your specific needs, ensuring that a focus on reducing the risk of injury and building muscle are core values. A little more advanced, they usually serve those who are still participating in athletics. Athletic trainers are very similar, in that they focus on injury prevention work with athletes. They also require similar educational requirements.

CHIROPRACTOR

Chiropractors are sometimes known to be bone crackers. Someone has a hurt back or neck, and they go see the chiropractor to get a "snap, crackle, and pop" to leave feeling better. However, many chiropractors are very progressive in their approach to medicine, and many of the technologies that become mainstream in medicine begin their trial phases with chiropractors before becoming mainstream. They approach their assessments holistically and may dive deeper into your nutrient and supplement history, potentially discussing options to promote improvements in those areas of your habits. They may also make recommendations to promote healthy aging and improvement to vital areas of your health like flexibility, joint function, and pain reduction.

Although typically focused on the spine, the chiropractor will build a foundation of identifying any deficiencies, root causes to already existing issues, and provide basic feedback and lifestyle recommendations that you can take with you as you seek out other preventative doctors. They can diagnose and treat problems of the muscles, joints, and nervous system, too. By restoring proper movement patterns, you can reduce any mechanical stress on the body that may lead to problems later. Having a well-trained chiropractor in your corner can be a very vital tool in the team approach to your HealthSpan.

HORMONE CLINIC

Hormone specialists are essentially hyper-specific practitioners (physicians, PAs, or nurse practitioners) that go out of their way to examine your hormone levels and educate you on any lifestyle changes that could be tailored to your diagnostics.

Hormones are the body's chemical messengers that regulate your energy levels, metabolism, mood, sleep, sexual function, muscle mass, weight, and aging. Specific hormones could include testosterone, estrogen, progesterone, thyroid hormones, cortisol, and insulin.

The way they screen and test is usually slightly more advanced than regular bloodwork. Having a practitioner that you trust is crucial because the appropriate understanding of these hormones and the potential complications of adjusting them must be carefully monitored. You do not just want to whimsically start adding hormones without considering the effects, consequences, and side effects.

While adjusting those hormone levels and balances, many of these practitioners also will create protocols and longevity goals relating to your physical and mental health. I know many of these practitioners that will fire you from their practice if you prove to not follow the remaining treatment objectives. This holistic approach is incredibly beneficial because you do not want to just take a hormone supplement or replacement and assume that this medication change will magically cure you. This is a sustained and complex approach to *unsplode* your HealthSpan.

The preventative steps that they'll address to help you extend your lifespan include nutrition, exercise, stress management, and sleep hygiene. Depending on location, clinics such as these may also partner with musculoskeletal specialists, some of which will take a keen interest in your musculoskeletal longevity, including your muscle mass, flexibility, tendon condition, and other fitness criteria.

NATUROPATHS

Also looking at a holistic snapshot of your current health, naturopaths focus more on genetic and environmental factors that could negatively impact your health down the road. Another way to put that is they support the body's natural ability to heal using holistic prevention. That includes looking at your entire health history (and getting as much information about your family's health history as possible) to determine what possible triggers or factors may be trending in your family, and how you might modify them or alter them as you aim to prevent illness in your own life and as you aim to maximize your own longevity. Tools they use include nutrition plans, herbal medicine and supplements, lifestyle counseling, stress management, and sometimes peptide therapies.

They combine these tools to discover root causes, strengthen overall well-being, stop symptoms, and prevent disease. Instead of putting patients on multiple prescriptions—like conventional medicine—that could create negative polypharmaceutical effects, naturopaths look for natural solutions.

TREVOR'S INTERJECTION

Here is an example of the consequences of this dichotomy—of the polypharmaceutical approach of conventional medicine versus the holistic and natural approach of naturopaths. This is something I just experienced with, let's say, a client. And what happened to him was astonishing.

He went to the doctor experiencing shortness of breath. After bloodwork, his conventional medical provider looked at the results in a reactive way through prescription medication. Seeing that my client's blood pressure numbers were high, this conventional physician suggested lisinopril, a blood pressure medication. This was despite the fact that he was a diabetic and the lisinopril might create negative polypharmaceutical effects—as these medications are known to do when mixed. Further, lisinopril is known to have various side effects, including dizziness, headache, and fatigue—not ideal things to have to deal with.

Not excited about what the conventional doctor had to say, he went to a naturopath. They identified some root causes, including diet and stress, and assigned him a new diet, some targeted herbal supplements (like fish oil), and some lifestyle changes. My client went for the naturopath's advice, and his blood pressure came down. Rather than simply manipulating a number with a drug, the naturopath identified and remedied bad habits and deficiencies.

Because of this natural approach, it's not unusual for professionals in traditional medicine to, sometimes falsely, claim that naturopaths are fringe experts or somehow undercut their expertise.

Their preventative and early intervention tactics focus on reducing inflammation, regenerative therapies, detoxing, and tailored supplement and lifestyle needs. If you approach a consultation with a naturopath, please be open-minded and consider the approach and recommendations as sincere offers to help you in your journey to your best HealthSpan. Some recommendations may seem to come out of left field (or possibly just seem straight up weird), and you have the choice to listen and incorporate, or to opt out. But these practitioners stay in business for a reason, and the considerations for treatment that they suggest are based on experience.

NURSE PRACTITIONER

You're going to pick up on a theme here because nurse practitioners also approach their patients with a holistic approach—they aren't an orthopedic surgeon like me who, despite how much I may enjoy talking to you and hearing about your day, really wants you to give me the details about your knees, shoulders, elbows, and other joints. Nurse practitioners, on the other hand, are, well, nurses. They have more face time with patients and exhibit that empathy in their style, focusing a person's overall well-being instead of treating a specific pathology. A nurse practitioner will consider the factors contributing to the problem and its future prevention, not just the problem itself.

Through screening examinations and bloodwork, a nurse practitioner can identify deficiencies in various parts of your health. Because of their training, this nurse practitioner could help you avoid a chronic condition or disease by means of making modifications based on the screenings performed. Maybe it's not a problem now, but they can help you develop support systems that will help prevent a problem in the future.

They can also work up pathologies that you may experience, prescribe medication, and follow up on the success of treatment. This can be especially important if your test results reveal hormonal imbalances.

CONCIERGE DOCTOR

These are a gold mine. I have never met a patient that utilizes a concierge doctor that ever wants to go back to scheduling appointments, limited visit times, and limited access.

A concierge doctor is a primary care physician, internal medicine specialist, geriatrician, pediatrician, or other specialist that has decided to retain a set number of clients and to stop accepting new clients after a predetermined number is reached. The cost to be under the care of this physician is a monthly membership fee instead of insurance payments. This "membership" now gives you direct access to this practitioner's services, same-day appointments, longer appointments, and around-the-clock communication options. By keeping a smaller pool of patients on a monthly fee model to float their practice, these doctors can give their patients more time, do more thorough evaluations, and address additional mechanisms for preventative care.

Most patients under the care of a concierge doctor will still have primary health insurance to cover emergencies, major medical issues, medications, screenings, lab work, and things that are outside the scope of their business model.

As far as primary doctors go, this model is a fantastic option for discussion and incorporation of a preventative approach compared to the rest of the industry's reactive approach. And as far as costs, the more the market demands these sorts of doctors, the more we can expect their price to go down. (Currently, the majority of concierge doctors are found in affluent areas. But with the additional demand, we are seeing more diversification and more access to them.)

GERIATRICIAN

These doctors specialize in the aging process and how to maintain and maximize health as we age. For that reason, they specialize in the care of older adults, usually retirement age or older. So if you're on the younger side, you can skip down to the next section. But if they apply to you, then geriatricians, almost by definition, are focused on improving a patient's HealthSpan.

Because their niche is the much broader "age" and not just one part of the body, like the foot and podiatrists, their approach has to be broad, too. That means they do things holistically—there's that word again. They'll provide these services by combining screenings and lifestyle counseling. They'll manage multiple things at a time, with an expertise to manage a variety of simultaneous issues that could include osteoporosis, heart disease, diabetes, medications, dementia, chronic conditions, and more. Their goal is to extend your longevity and help you keep your independence, functionality, and purpose as long as possible.

PUTTING IT ALL TOGETHER

You see! Even though I put the fear of god in you about the over-specialization of the healthcare industry, you *do* have preventative options. The only bad news is that usually patients have to pay out of pocket for these options. Again, remember how the medical industry caters to the treatment of disease? Well, we are not trying to treat disease but rather do all that we can to prevent and avoid disease! The success of these preventative techniques, tactics, and the education required to weaponize you with the best approach to win this recurring battle will be best approached with the team members that we have discussed. The key will be that you remain willing to share your honest situation with these team members and that you remain willing to make the sacrifices that are recommended to you in conjunction with this approach. Making that decision today and beginning the hunt TODAY is the best approach to this treatment program.

MAKE PREVENTATIVE HEALTH A NONNEGOTIABLE

If you are serious about unsploding and maximizing your HealthSpan, doing preventative work now is a nonnegotiable. The same way people save for their retirement funds, we need to proactively "save" now for our future health in order to build up our retirement well-being.

If you're in retirement age, you already know this. If you're not quite there yet, think about your future for a moment. You *will* have to get surgeries. You *will* have to manage some sort of chronic condition or disease, like diabetes, arthritis, kidney disease, cardiovascular disease, something else, and/or a combination of things. This is not a question of if; it's a question of when.

Let's be honest, we really do not have any control over the potential problems that our body may encounter. I laugh when I see a video short or a claim from a practitioner that claims that if you use his bath salt and soak your feet every day, then he can prevent you from ever visiting a hospital again. What a bunch of garbage! So why do we buy into that crap?

It's because we are gullible. It's because we all wish the pathway was easier. We all wish there was only one step that would work and that this singular step would make everything else easier. But I hate to break it to you...it won't. We are talking about the human body. We are talking about the most complex device ever built. A machine that can regenerate and heal, a machine that can grow and adapt, a machine that can be repaired and that can mature and that can process food and air and can withstand temperature changes and battle illness and that can come out on top even when the most severe odds are against it.

This machine does this by constant cell replication and cell division and copying and creating. And despite how amazing this is, and how accurate it usually is, we have no idea when a mistake in this copying and coding may occur. And one seemingly simple mistake in that process could lead to catastrophic effects. Suddenly this could be cancer. Suddenly this could be organ failure. Suddenly this could be memory loss and a loss of bodily control.

So what do we have control over? What can we manipulate for our favor? The truth is we only have control over how we invest our time and in the investments that we make to keep this machine in as best shape as possible and to invest in our approach to live in harmony with it. You don't want to be in retirement spending all of your time managing your health. Or you don't want to be that healthy retired person who thinks they don't need to go to the doctor regularly only to have that plan backfire. I know people who are visiting doctors four days a week to manage their many conditions. Instead, do the preventative work now to maximize your HealthSpan to meet your future health goals.

If you only read Trevor's side of the book and retire with millions in your account but never read my side, you'll be imbalanced. You'll still explode instead of *unsploding.* You won't get to live a life of purpose and fulfillment because your constraints will be in your health. It's not uncommon to talk to a retired person and they reveal that their weekly schedule is filled with and based on the various doctors appointments they have to attend in order to manage their many chronic issues. Instead of the vacations that they wished they would be taking and that they thought would make up all of their schedule in retirement, they are nursing a dying body and trying to hold on to hope that they can still take those trips and accomplish those goals. In essence, they're playing catch up on the medical conditions they neglected for years.

This could be a mindset issue that you need to fix. You are not invincible. Yet many people think they are.

About a year ago, I challenged my dad to take better care of himself after I realized that he was becoming very forgetful and seemed to be losing his edge and his memory. He was forgetting people's names and was forgetting various tasks and responsibilities. Even the names of my own children. He talked about how he thinks of the kids often and how he hopes the best for them, and then as he continued to talk, I realized that he couldn't even recall their names. This was concerning to me. I told him to get it checked out, to get an MRI, to ask for testing, and to see if there's something going on that he could work on and make this better. I followed up with him for a while and tried to encourage follow-through on my recommendations, and eventually I got busy and didn't check in for a while until a more recent conversation when this topic came back up again.

He never did make the calls. He never did get things worked up. He never had an evaluation and never instituted treatment and never made any progress on it. And he was worse! He now reported that he was struggling at work; he continued to have difficulties with his memory. He was struggling financially because of some decisions. He clearly did not have a good grasp on his finances, and some of the choices he had made were a direct result of the progressive memory issues that remained unaddressed. He needed real help, but he did not like the help that I offered, and I felt crippled as to how I could make this easier or better for him.

But unfortunately, despite our best efforts, we simply cannot light the fire for another person. If you have that fire, then run with it. If you can inspire others to have that fire, then embrace them on your journey. But if you can't get someone else to have that fire, then love them anyway and be grateful that you have a capacity. Trying to convince another person to take on this challenge might just drain you and might destroy your relationship with that person in the process.

Anyway, I do hope that he makes progress, and I continue to seek ways to help him, but I have taken a back seat in the way of pushing him, and I strive to be careful in the interactions we have because I do not want him to feel like I'm disappointed in him.

Moral of the story...don't delay! Get moving! Make that investment as soon as possible so that we start earning health dividends and let them compound in our favor over time. Investing in your health will require time. It will require some adjustment of your priorities. It's a tough thing to do and can be a lot to deal with. It's so easy to neglect our health, especially when things seem to be sailing along smoothly. But make time for it. Plan on it taking some additional time at the onset.

And plan on it requiring some time throughout the year. It might take you three hours this week to get out of work, drive to the doctor's office, sit in the office for an hour because they're running behind, meet with them for fifteen minutes, then leave. Perhaps you recognize this sacrifice and don't feel like you can handle it. It might not sound fun. But fun isn't the intent here. Longevity is the intent. And good things in your life will require sacrifice. And this investment has to be made; otherwise, we'll lose out on our health portfolio.

So embrace that investment, and embrace the evolution of your HealthSpan because, from year to year, the investment will change. It will demand more out of you as you age, but by initiating that process earlier you will have better success in the future. The future of maximizing your HealthSpan as you age will require adaptation. It will require additional rest periods, longer warm-ups, post-exercise care, and changing nutrition. Let this process excite you, and let your maximization of HealthSpan be a challenge that motivates you.

PRACTICAL PREVENTATIVE STRATEGIES

We've talked about what's at stake. We've talked about preventative healthcare professionals. But what can you do? Let's go over some simple strategies you can implement to prevent symptoms from happening, going from most to least important.

NUTRITION

I don't want to be overly repetitive in this book, but I do want to point out that your nutrition might be *the* most important behavioral choice you make for your health, in terms of preventing health issues in the future. Return to what I had to said about nutrition in Chapter 4 to revisit the crucial principles.

FITNESS ROUTINE

No matter what age, a fitness routine is critical to preventing and reducing the likelihood of chronic conditions and diseases, like cardiovascular disease, diabetes, cancer, and arthritis. It also boosts mental and emotional health by using the body's natural systems to reduce stress while improving confidence and cognition. And any fitness routine should include getting a lot of sunlight and spending time outdoors.

With that said, *how* you go about using a fitness routine to prevent chronic illness depends on what age you are. Let's go over the various life phases or age brackets and how our fitness routine should be approached. I'm not going to give you specific exercises to try but instead talk about overall goals and what you can prevent. Talk to somebody on your HealthSpan Longevity Team to come up with the specific exercises in your routine.

Children

Early routines for children should be focused on the enjoyment of movement, play, stimulation, and balance. Kids are initially preprogrammed to enjoy activity and running, and their energy levels seem to be endless! That is until they hold still for two minutes and fall asleep because they've depleted all their stores and need a recharge. My son Boss has so cleverly coined the term "out of batteries" when his younger brother Canyon sits on a couch or in his car seat and falls asleep. These kids play hard and crash hard.

Kids need permission to run and a safe place to explore and discover. Otherwise most of the programming for their fitness is already inside them! The goal of parenting is largely just to let them embrace it and to not squash it with screens and TV and apps and electronics. If we can just get them outside and get them playing in a hands-on fashion, then they'll do the rest.

Usually kids have very little problem maintaining a strong heart and overall weight because their bodies are just primed for activity. However, we do have a childhood obesity issue in the United States. If a child is becoming obese, it is highly likely that this is an external problem like eating too many (highly processed) calories combined with general malnourishment (getting too much of certain nutrients and not enough of others) and a sedentary lifestyle.

Prevent and combat the long-term effects of childhood obesity by letting children play outside daily. Jumping, running, and crashing around as a kid is crucial for strengthening bones, stretching and building muscles, and cardiovascular health.

Late childhood and into the teenage years, these kids begin to need some additional attention. This is the time when their bodies are changing, and they begin to experience progression toward their adult frames and sizes. We grow in spurts during our young years, but preteens and teenagers tend to tolerate this rapid bone growth differently and may require some additional coaching and intervention. Muscles, at that stage, are hanging on for dear life. The bones don't wait. And as these bones progress, the muscles and tendons may experience pain, and you might even see your child begin to limp or experience pain in their extremities. The introduction to stretching and a focus on flexibility will be at an all-time high. Adding a flexibility routine and aftercare to their sporting practices will be important, as their body will have new areas of inflammation due to the growth and the response to their rapidly changing body.

Teenagers and Early Adults

This is the prime time to build muscle. People this age tend not to need warm-ups—they can just jump off the couch and go from zero to sixty.

All of this endless energy is being combined for the first time with a hormonal sense of self—or a desire to build out their aesthetic based on their growing sense of identity. For a lot of teenagers, that means hitting the gym and trying to bench press way more than the next guy. I have to tell my patients all the time that the human body was meant to walk briskly on two legs, not to walk on its hands, and not to bench press 300 pounds. Sure this will make them look fantastic, and their beach body will be at its peak, but there is wear and tear brewing that might just complicate their HealthSpan later in their life. The shoulders weren't meant for that load, and without a careful approach to that type of activity, injury could occur, and internal damage may lead to the progression of instability or arthritis. In some cases this can lead to a thirty-five or forty-year-old shoulder acting more like a sixty or seventy-year-old shoulder. When endless energy meets a dangerous goal, dangerous things tend to happen.

For this age group, the fitness routine needs to be balanced and not overly focused or targeting specialized goals that will do long-term damage to the body. Strive to balance your workout regimen and implement the nutritional information that we have discussed so that you can build the best foundation for taking your body into the remaining decades of your life in as healthy and balanced of a way as possible.

Late Thirties to Early Forties

If you're in this age bracket and not warming up or stretching before and after a workout, you're doing it wrong. That's especially true for men. Men more frequently still feel like they can compete with the younger crowd and want to jump right in and prove it. This is where disaster can strike. This is the age group where muscle tears and tendon ruptures are more common. Especially the quadriceps, biceps, patellar tendon, Achilles, hamstring, and others. We've all seen this happen. For me, knowing the physiology behind these injuries, it sends a harrowing chill up my spine when I'm at an event and I see an athlete trying to give it their all only to pull up and limp to the sideline or fall to the ground and require help off the field.

Regardless of *who* experiences that sudden rupture, it can be a surprise because they still feel healthy enough overall. Just on the other side of youth, they still carry youthful habits, like jumping off the couch and going straight into a resistance training activity without a warm-up. Old habits die hard.

Not committing to the warm-up and the cooldown could create degenerative and blood supply issues in the forties.

To prevent those things from happening, this group has to invest in exercises that target predisposed and predictable tendon inflammation. Good stretching, warm-ups and cooldowns, icing, and frequent exercise can do this. A commitment to muscle and tendon care is crucial for this age group, and this commitment must continue into the remaining years of your life. So develop it now and stay committed to it, because it's a part of you forever!

Fifties and Sixties

At this age, almost no matter what the pain is, the first thing your doctor will do is tell you to go see a physical therapist for an exercise program to target and improve the ailment that you have. And let me tell you, people HATE being told that they need to exercise through their pain! But this is a real fix. This works. The reason why is because these people have skipped the necessary step of learning a proper routine and, subsequently, have failed to maintain the routine they should have been using into their later years. And it feels counterintuitive to patients: "My joint hurts. Moving it around more will make it hurt worse, right?" Wrong. But that initial perspective is understandable. We need to put obstacles in front of us because it teaches us how to overcome them.

It was like the five-foot hay bail at the Spartan Race I did with Trevor. Who practices jumping over hay bails? I certainly never jump over things like those. Trevor jumped over it with ease, and there I was, stuck. And there was nobody behind me, so I was the only one getting stuck, and I couldn't even ask anybody else for a boost. It wasn't something I had been practicing and acclimating myself to. The moral of that story is make sure you train if your cousin talks you into doing a tough race. Okay, the moral is actually to practice with the obstacles you can expect to face. And to intentionally make those obstacles a challenge that will push you so that you constantly focus on improvement and gains.

As we age, our muscle mass decreases. We can combat this with the appropriate exercise protocols, but overall muscle mass decreases with age, and this decrease then shifts the demand and the load to our joints. Joints for this age group are undergoing the most stress upon impact. Building muscle mass can complement the joints to better tolerate this load, and "teaching" the body how to move makes joint movement—and the overall fitness routine—more achievable. Many programs are available to focus on the activity demands and challenges that an older generation begins to face, and through this practice these demands can become easier and less daunting.

Seventies and Beyond

At this stage, the fitness routine must adapt to include lifestyle hacks and maintenance activities to keep you independent and not give up your freedoms and flexibility. Strength gains can continue to be made, as our body responds to strength training indefinitely, but it is also mandatory to include dedicated rest. Our recovery times are lengthening, and a focus on recovery and repair will be at its peak. Most everything else should stay the same; the goal is to balance endurance exercise, flexibility, and strength training.

Proper resting will prevent overuse issues, like muscle strains and pain. It will keep your energy levels high enough to continue and complete the fitness routine. That recovery time becomes essential for keeping your body motivated to keep working both in the immediate and long-term. You'll help fight chronic fatigue and encourage better exercise technique. Getting good sleep, working to manage the quality of your sleep, perhaps finding time for a nap, and promoting time for muscle and fitness repair will keep you in balance and will keep you prepared for a continuous effort to the remaining goals in your life.

Plus, you've earned it! Take a load off. Use that rest period to enjoy time with family, read a good book, and keep your brain active and continue learning. Keep expanding your opportunities and use your fitness time to explore social activities and sports that keep your mind and body engaged. These activities can stimulate the brain and can keep your social network intact, contributing to your satisfaction in life and to your overall sense of accomplishment and joy.

BODY COMPOSITION: GLYCEMIC INDEX

Sometimes abbreviated as GI, glycemic index measures how much and how quickly a type of food will raise your blood sugar. Foods are given a score from 0 to 100. The higher the score, the harder that food is going to hammer you, in terms of spiking your blood sugar and slowing your body down.

That slow down occurs because foods with a high GI score—soda, white rice, potatoes, bananas, cookies and pastries—will cause acute triggers inside your body. The body uses its systemic responses to equalize these acute spikes. This will cause a release of chemicals and immune system reactions that are aimed at trying to restore homeostasis. Processed and (refined) sugary foods will have much higher GI scores than natural foods. Your response to these types of foods may differ from others. Glucose monitors now can alert you to the spikes that your own body experiences in response to these various foods. You may find that your personal reaction to these ratings may actually differ from the predicted values that are reported on food containers. Learning how you respond to these foods will help you realize the way your own metabolism is reacting to the foods that you choose.

You can prevent a lot of the inflammation and negative long-term health effects by eating foods with low GI scores, and if you're using a monitor, you can also adapt to the foods that specifically trigger your own personal systemic responses. That improves heart health, promotes weight loss, and otherwise benefits your overall well being. The one trick with GI scores is that they represent one serving. You might come across a sugary treat with a low GI score, but the serving size associated with that is like one-sixteenth of a full cookie (or something). That one additional step of math—or the lack thereof—can lead to people spiking their blood sugar dangerously when they otherwise think they are eating something "healthy."

SLEEP HYGIENE

Sleep affects every system of health. You name it. Can't quite get over that cold? Interrupted sleep is dragging down your immune system. Is that pulled muscle still causing you pain months later? Bad sleep is slowing down (or stopping) the repair process. Is your memory suffering? Lack of sleep may be compromising your brain's ability to store memories properly. Hormones out of whack? Inconsistent circadian rhythms could be telling your body to produce an imbalance.

The role of deep sleep is integral to our mental and physical health. It directly affects our lifespan.

Get good sleep each night, which should be a fixed amount like we discussed earlier. "Good sleep" is usually fostered by low-stimulation activities like reading a book right before bed. Mid-day naps can help, too. Noise isn't a big issue with sleep disruption, so you can utilize a sound machine to help you fall asleep.

What gets in the way of a good night's sleep are temperature, hyperstimulation, and light. You want to be cooler rather than warmer. Avoid hyperstimulation tasks that otherwise seem mindless—phone scrolling or screen time of any kind. You want to especially avoid blue light; consider special glasses that filter out blue light. And make sure you're in a dark environment. Think about investing in some blackout curtains. If you have to use a nightlight to make your way over to the bathroom, consider getting one with a red light. Those disrupt sleep the least.

TREVOR'S INTERJECTION

Maybe it's because I'm a man of my age, but I know a lot of people with a common sleep hygiene problem they don't even realize is having a profoundly negative impact on their HealthSpan: sleep apnea. If you are getting plenty of hours of sleep but never feel rested, then this is a very common disruption of sleep. And doctors used to save their sleep apnea diagnoses for obese or old people. But now we know that it's an extremely common problem, even in younger people and without the complication of obesity.

For context, sleep apnea is an obstruction in the airway that can cause mid-sleep airway collapse, leading to disrupted sleep, congestion within the cardiovascular system, starvation of the brain for oxygen, and death. It's a structural issue, really. Our habits—smoking and improper eating—are actually reshaping our throats and airways over time to create these obstructions and malfunctions. Maintaining a healthy diet, sleep schedule, and sleeping on your side are all ways to prevent this physiological change. If this sounds like you, please get it assessed. The treatment for this condition isn't cute (unless you like the idea of wearing a snorkel to bed), but it can save your life.

STRESS MANAGEMENT

Stress is a killer. How? Chronic stress keeps the body in a fight-or-flight response, filling the body with cortisol and adrenaline—an exposure that can cause high blood pressure, artery buildup, heart disease, diabetes, obesity, immune suppression, burnout, memory impairment, and chronic pain. More than three-quarters of Americans say that their prolonged stress has a negative impact on their health. So managing that stress can become a profound preventative strategy.

Managing our stress will look different for everybody. For example, regular exercise is known to reduce stress—walking, dancing, yoga, etc. Yet not everybody might be capable of these physical activities. Other techniques include deep breathing, meditation, and mindfulness exercises. Along with massage therapy, these exercises trigger the body's relaxation response, lowering the heart rate and blood pressure while no longer promoting the release of fight-or-flight hormones.

Lifestyle and behavioral adjustments can also be important to reducing stress. That might mean eating well, sleeping well, eliminating certain toxins like alcohol, learning to say "no," connecting with friends or social groups, and shifting your perspective from negative to positive.

ALLERGY TESTS AND TREATMENTS

Do you have certain foods that seem to give you an upset stomach? Are there certain foods that will make you spend a little bit more time in the bathroom? Are you tired right before lunch? Right after lunch? Do you wake up tired? Do you get unexplainable rashes?

You might want to consider the fact that what you're putting into your body can cause a number of health issues. You might have an allergy or, better stated, an "intolerance." When unaddressed, it's like a form of physical abuse that you're putting your body through.

What's even more confusing is that you can develop an allergy at any time. Take me, for example. I grew up with cats in my home. I grew up with allergies that I blamed on the seasonal pollen and the local weeds and trees. After moving out to attend college, I returned home only to realize that I felt terrible. I sneezed and itched and coughed and swelled up in the face. Was I allergic to my own cat? When did this happen? Growing up and living with these pets had at least provided some type of tolerance to the dander. But I was living with this constant inoculation! The effect of this constant stimulation and my body trying to cope was undoubtedly causing chronic inflammation in my skin and air ways. I was living with a constant internal struggle within my own immune system! An allergy test later confirmed it.

What this also told me was that I was living with some sort of "tolerated" baseline inflammation while I lived at home. Essentially, my body found an equilibrium but was needlessly suffering during my prime growing years. Years of inflammation that no doubt had a negative impact on my HealthSpan.

By taking the steps to stop and prevent your allergic reactions, you'll be doing more than fixing those symptoms. Chronic allergic inflammation can also harm our gut, the lining of our cells, and predispose us to other problems down the road. With the proper evaluation of your own personal allergy profile, you can eliminate those immune system triggers and work to decrease your systemic inflammation and promote better system functions.

BIOHACKING

Biohacking is all about individualism in approaching health. It's a counter point to traditional medicine treating everybody the same (such as taking them through the same series of treatments) using averages and odds. Biohacking takes the perspective that what's true for the group is not always true for the individual.

TREVOR'S INTERJECTION

It's no secret that structured protocols exist in medicine because it's the cheapest and directed by insurance. The same thing was true of the financial industry when I worked for larger organizations. "First we'll try this. If that doesn't work, then we'll try that." It's not geared toward what's best for the individual.

I'm a health nut, too. And one thing I've learned is that it's just natural for aging people to have more glucose intolerance or higher cholesterol. But instead of doing the work to prevent symptoms or conditions, it seems like the industry is fine with just prescribing everybody over a certain age with metformin to deal with their prediabetes or diabetes symptoms. The drug makers are fine with it, too. It normalizes unhealthiness the same way that cookie-cutter retirement plans normalize working your life away (instead of enjoying it now) for a retirement that your body might not be healthy enough to enjoy.

Many patients feel frustrated when they receive traditional recommendations and protocols when they believe their issues fall outside of the norm. These patients want to be treated uniquely because they feel unique. This more personalized approach may assist in confirming that they are a candidate for the standard treatment or if they are actually in need of a more targeted therapy. Biohacking assesses and targets very specific things with the idea of regaining control over your body and preventing symptoms.

What's unique about biohacking is it's mostly do-it-yourself. Collecting data will be on you. People like to use smartwatches and Fitbits to do this. Maybe you send your DNA to a laboratory that sends you the results. But this data analysis allows you to create your diet, set sleep patterns; find your exercise routine, set targets, and reach targets based on your needs. There are many forms of biohacking. Here's a brief list:

- Nutritional biohacking through diet adjustment or taking supplements
- Tech-based biohacking through using wearables or apps to track data
- Lifestyle biohacking through cold exposure, light therapy, meditation, thermal saunas, and breathwork
- Genetic biohacking through genetic testing and a catered medication approach based on the test findings, implantable tech, or gene editing (often controversial)

Many of these "hacks" are well proven and come with more guaranteed success and balance. Other portions of these "hacks" are still under development and may not be exactly what you are looking for at this point. Enter this world with some caution. There are holistic biohacking groups, and there are really specific groups of biohacking—like those genetic folks who focus on body augmentation. It'll be up to you to see if there is something useful in here as you look for preventative techniques.

CAFFEINE INTAKE

Once I worked with an anesthesiologist who told me a wake-up call story about caffeine. A patient they had was a seventeen-year-old kid who consumed three or four energy drinks a day (so the kid reported, but what is reported is usually an undersell). This kid had to fast for fourteen hours prior to surgery, which also meant no caffeine. Once in the operating room, while this anesthesiologist was attempting to maintain control of this young man's breathing and heart rate, he found that the body of this young man was starving for stimulation and that without aggressive stimulation, the body was actually crashing (giving up).

Patients are often placed to sleep during surgery to mediate and control the pain of the actual surgical intervention (incisions, dissection, and repairs), and the anesthesiologist had to press the surgeon to get going ASAP. The patient made it, thankfully. And the surgery was successful. But this anesthesiologist had some stern words with this boy's family and with him in the recovery room, as this was a completely unexpected and absolutely unnecessary scenario. And if this young man chooses to keep up this behavior and continue to feed this addiction, then at some point it is highly likely that his body will actually give up and his life cut short.

This story isn't meant to get you to quit caffeine. Instead, be cognizant of your tolerance. How fast do you break down without it? Do you feel sick to your stomach without it? Do you get headaches when you withdraw the typical dose? Do you fall asleep during the day without it? If you lose normal function, you likely have a caffeine problem that you can prevent by weaning off. Caffeine is fine, but dependence is not good.

And it might not be a total amount of caffeine consumed. You also need to consider time of day. Some people can drink caffeine at any point of their day (even late at night) and have zero issues falling asleep. Maybe they don't have the best sleep, which they need to test for, but it's a sign that they are tolerant. Some of these energy drinks carry 300 mg of caffeine. And there are people that drink them without any concern, while other people have one twelve-ounce can of soda (maybe 35–50 mg of caffeine) in the early evening and stay awake all night. So if this addiction sounds like you, you need to make adjustments to prevent symptoms and maintain normal function.

THE POWER OF PREVENTION

Taking time to improve your health through prevention is necessary to a HealthSpan that promotes a long and fulfilling life. Just like you might with your finances—I'm looking at you, Trevor, and your amazing ideas for WealthSpan—plan with purpose now to maximize your health later.

I'm reminded of a study I read about a group of factory workers. It was a relatively brutal environment where workplace injuries were common enough that the executive team wanted to address it.

Intuition says that if you bring your crew into work and then tell them not to work for thirty minutes, the company would be losing money, right? Well, they wanted to see. One group of workers was asked to—in full gear—spend the first thirty minutes of the day doing a series of targeted exercises to warm up their shoulders, hips, back, and other areas they'd be using throughout the day. They used bands, light weights, and just good old stretching. Can you guess what happened? The injury rate plummeted to nearly zero and production output skyrocketed. And the workers reported higher levels of joy and sense of purpose on the job.

What seemed like a "loss" of productivity at the beginning of the day was actually a huge gain. That same principle is true with preventive health. It seems like a loss that an older person with achy joints has to move them in the morning and feel that pain, but in the long run, it reduces their pain and prevents injury.

Be like those factory workers. Figure out what preventative actions you can take to maximize your HealthSpan. There is no predetermined formula for your needs. You are unique. Use the concepts from this and previous chapters to evaluate where you are and how you can tailor your next actionable steps based on your goals and options.

It can be difficult to go alone, which is why *everything* you do for your overall well-being (not just preventative stuff) can be enhanced by working in conjunction with professionals who are sitting on your side of the table. It's time to recruit a team of specialists, what I call the HealthSpan Longevity Team.

CHAPTER 6

THE HEALTHSPAN LONGEVITY TEAM: A NEW KIND OF COLLABORATION WITH HEALTH EXPERTS

"Coming together is beginning. Keeping together is progress. Working together is a success."

—HENRY FORD

If I asked you what Walt Disney was famous for, what would you say? Theme parks? Animated films? Mickey Mouse?

Any answer to this question will likely overlook Disney's true genius. What most don't know is that Walt never drew a single cel of animation or designed a single building in his parks. Disney's real super power was vetting and recognizing talent so that he could leverage other people to get him to where he wanted to go. He was essentially the idea-making head coach that recruited the best talent and created the best team. Later, he was praised for the creation and success of the entire operation while never actually having to personally step onto the field! Recognizing talent and finding a way to use it is key as you create your ideal team for dialing in your HealthSpan.

There's the famous story that, one Friday, Disney excitedly shared the idea of Disneyland to his close friend, an artist named Herb Ryman. Disney mentioned that his brother, Roy, was going to meet with financiers about funding the park in just three days, that upcoming Monday. At the end of the Disney's spiel, Ryman replied, "That sounds like a great idea. Where is the mock-up? I'd love to see it." Disney answered: "You're going to make it."

Shocked, Ryman knew that Disney needed to provide Roy with something to show the financiers. So they holed up in a hotel room for the forty-eight-hour weekend, and Ryman began designing what Disney verbally described. By Sunday night, they were done, and Disneyland would shortly thereafter become a reality. Ryman's artistry was tapped to realize Disney's dream.

Here's the thing. We've been talking quite a bit about *your* dream—a life of fulfillment and purpose experienced today and tomorrow through maximizing your HealthSpan and WealthSpan. Like Disney, you're going to have to tap into talented people to help you realize that dream.

When we narrow this discussion down to our HealthSpan, we can start identifying really specific people that might be the right choices to help us achieve our health goals. That team will vary depending on your unique situation. But regardless of who is on the team, they'll operate under the central goal of increasing the longevity of your HealthSpan. So that's why I'm calling them the HealthSpan Longevity Team. They'll help you plan with purpose.

THE HEALTHSPAN LONGEVITY TEAM

The onus is really on you to make this team, just like it's on you to *unsplode* your HealthSpan. I can only lead a horse to water, but I can't make it drink. (You're the horse in that analogy.) You'll have to find and vet people. Sometimes you'll find a gem; sometimes you'll find a dud. As you better understand your individual dream, you can use it to choose these people as you build this team individually and on your own. This chapter is meant to be a general resource with some guiding principles. Who could be on your team? Let's start building out a potential roster!

THE NEW HEALTH MANAGER

You need to have a quarterback on your team, somebody who understands your dream, who believes in it, and who leads the charge and collaborates with the rest of the team to keep your holistic situation in view. They are a longevity specialist, a person whose screenings and recommendations promote preventative and protective health measures (not just the treatment of symptoms).

They'll have the tools (or the access to tools) that create the data points necessary to help you set your HealthSpan goals and put them into action. Usually, urgent care and primary care providers are very busy in the treatment of illnesses and management that their ability to serve your preventative management and longevity is limited. And this type of provider may not have the capacity to give you the time needed for this approach and may recommend additional providers or refer you out to some other specialist.

Who this person is depends on your location and what's available. It could be your primary care provider if, after speaking with them, they are open to working with you on your HealthSpan goals, if they have the tools necessary, and if they are available for longevity consultations. It could be a naturopath. It could be a concierge doctor. Maybe it's a nurse practitioner. It just depends on which of these folks is willing to invest in you the way you want to be invested in.

What's becoming more and more common are longevity clinics that put one of each specialist on staff. They'll have a chiropractor, a naturopath, and relationships with many of the other various provider types to ensure their patients have access to a pre-built team. You'd likely see a longevity specialist at that clinic—the clinic's version of a primary provider—more frequently who would then work with you and refer you to in-house specialists as needed.

Don't be scared away if the provider isn't a DO or MD. In most cases, they'll have a robust experience that can provide you with excellent healthcare. What you need to look for to confirm that experience is how the clinic goes about training its staff. It's okay to inquire about those systems—you're the paying customer, after all.

Ideally, a DO or MD will be sitting with you at the first consultation and occasionally following up as you continue working with the PAs or nurse practitioners or other providers at a given clinic. They can be very good in their role because of on-the-job training. This kind of setup will tell you that *all* of the providers are working in coordination with the DO/MD. Keep in mind that, in general, osteopathic physicians (DOs) approach medical care with a more holistic mentality and have additional training that can be more associated with preventive medicine. That being said, not every osteopathic physician utilizes that training, and this is another point of vetting out your HealthSpan team!

FUNCTIONAL MEDICAL PROFESSIONAL

This isn't a specific physician, per se. Think of a functional medical professional as a physician that has additional training for fitness, wellness, lifestyle, and rehabilitation. It could be a primary doctor with a background in sports medicine. It could be an osteopathic physician that utilizes OMT, an approach that can be preventative.

Not only does this physician function in a specific role to treat pathology, they also have a background that allows them to help educate a patient on how to keep systems functioning well. Consider this as one of your team members that has a keen interest in movement and wellness; they have both a medical background as well as fitness interest.

DIETICIAN AND NUTRITIONIST

These folks will coach you on your diet and food intake. They'll usually start with a workup panel to evaluate your intake. From there, they can see if certain foods are triggering your immune system or another part of your body and need to be brought under control.

These folks are really important for helping combat underlying problems that may one day explode into a serious condition or disease that can't be cured with a simple change to the diet alone.

For a fun plus, you could find a nutritionist who is also a chef. You could sample their food, learn how to make healthy meals, and take their recipes home with you to continue practicing good dietary habits.

And this team member might not even be a person. There are a lot of great, fresh, and nutritious options out there for premade meals. Do your due diligence when researching and selecting the right avenue for approaching your nutrition needs and dietary choices.

MUSCULOSKELETAL SPECIALIST

Orthopedic doctors will target your nerve, bone, joint, and muscle health. They evaluate your flexibility and recognize any mobility restraints (or the onset of them) to help you prevent or reverse movement issues.

Not only can they treat chronic conditions, they can also help you prevent further damage. The best among them will understand the ramifications of social factors on patient behavior—an aspect of medicine called psychosocial.

This specialist can also assist you in interpreting both X-rays and MRIs as you gain a deeper understanding of your musculoskeletal system. Preventative and wellness scans to evaluate your body are becoming more and more common, and cash-pay evaluations are becoming more widely advertised. I frequently tell my patients that it is wise to defer advanced imaging until you are prepared to deal with the bad news that it might present, because sometimes we have damage to our musculoskeletal system that we are dealing with perfectly until someone points it out. And now that it's been pointed out, we can't get that fact out of our head, and the non-painful part becomes permanently painful! So please approach this portion of your whole-body evaluation with care, and coordinate these interpretations with a specialist that you trust.

They can easily refer you to additional surgical specialists if needed for conditions that are found that may fall outside their scope of practice. Tapping into this network of surgeons who specialize in similar but different aspects of the same field can be invaluable in maximizing your team approach to your musculoskeletal system. In their own way, they are trained to see the patient as an individual with individual musculoskeletal needs.

HORMONE DOCTORS

Although hormone doctors are under some scrutiny right now, it can't be ignored that humans are living longer than ever and that one consequence of that is the rapid degeneration of our hormonal production as we reach certain highs in our age.

And while age is a major contributor to the degeneration of hormone production, the other one is far more sinister, easier to access, and silently decreases our HealthSpan and longevity. It's processed food. By inducing chronic inflammation, creating nutrient deficiencies, triggering insulin resistance from high sugar and trans fat, and introducing endocrine-disrupting chemicals (EDCs) like plastics from packaging, processed foods lower and degenerate hormone production. Not the least of which is lowering testosterone and fertility hormones.

Hormones dictate almost every aspect of our body's function. Imbalances and production rates create a variety of health issues that hormone doctors can assess and address. And as this specialist addresses the overall level of these hormones within your body, they will also consider your body's capacity and ability to utilize a given hormone. This can even mean supplementing your levels to well outside of the "normal" range due to the body's actual ability to utilize what is currently in circulation. This means that your lab values might actually come back as abnormal because of the compensation that is required for the body's changing ability to both produce and utilize these hormones. The most common imbalances include thyroid disorders, menopause, fertility issues, and diabetes.

Like most of the medical professionals we've covered so far, they'll be able to offer their patients specialized care geared toward longevity and protection. These doctors specialize in treating imbalances in the endocrine and hormonal systems.

CHIROPRACTOR

Being in a chiropractor's office is like listening to the sound effects of a '90s action movie starring Arnold Schwarzenegger—bone-crunches every few seconds.

The manual techniques that produce those noises are actually spine and joint readjustments that are meant to help with mobility and flow within the body's natural systems. These manipulation techniques are used to treat and/or prevent a whole bunch of conditions. They include migraines, nerve pain, back and neck pain, joint stiffness, posture issues, helping with colicky infants, and a smattering of other things. Just speaking personally, I love chiropractors for neck and back pain. It'll change your life.

PHYSICAL THERAPIST

Often educated with doctorates, physical therapists specialize in offering manual therapies (flexibility, muscle firing, swimming, etc.) to help improve mobility and technique for the purposes of preventing injury. They will give you the insight and tools to maintain your body after an injury has healed, give you pre- or postsurgical care, or work with you to correct posture and movement of the body.

Physical therapists will have their own philosophies and approaches. Some like correcting mechanics only. Some focus on strength training. Try a few out and really pick their brain about how they work to get a sense as to whether or not they'll fit with your style.

You could add a strength and condition coach or an athletic trainer. Some of these specialists already work in close coordination with a physical therapist and may be better able to provide you with the time and techniques for your preventative and longevity approach.

You may also consider joining a Pilates class, tai chi, a local fitness circuit, a HIIT group at the gym, a yoga group, or a spin class. These physical-therapist-adjacent individuals will aid your hands-on rehab, stretching, and strength efforts. Most will modify your exercises based on your needs. They can also assist you in the decision-making for which fitness regimen may be best suited for your individual needs.

PSYCHIATRIST OR THERAPIST

A lot of people think that you have to be crazy or hit rock bottom before you start talking to a psychiatrist or therapist. But that's just not the case. You don't have to be weak before enrolling in a gym, right? The gym is there to maintain and build your physical health. Think of mental health specialists similarly.

Anyway, most people are completely unaware that they are walking around with various mental or emotional issues that are causing underlying problems to their physiology. These folks help us identify and master the self through processing and other techniques designed to improve our overall well-being.

There are quite a few different approaches and philosophies that psychiatrists and therapists use. And some even have specialties like sex therapies, psychoanalysis, or cognitive behaviorism. These are just a few. But the point I'm making is that you need to find one that specializes in your needs (which may be a generalist) and to try them out first before committing. Discover their approach and philosophy and be okay with shopping them around until you find the one you like.

Keep in mind that the best colleges and professional teams incorporate a sports psychologist to the training program for their athletes. This professional meets with the team in preparation for competition, and on individual bases more frequently as needed. This is not because they are sick, but because they have the drive for maximum efficiency and a dream of perfection. So you should consider your own HealthSpan in the same way!

MASSAGE THERAPIST OR ACUPUNCTURIST

That's right! I'm giving you permission to get some massages and acupuncture. Treat yo' self! They are fun and relaxing. Bonus: they are also really good for your overall HealthSpan. In one of my favorite books, *The 5 AM Club*, in reference to suggesting a weekly massage and the concern regarding the cost of this treatment, the author then states: "You can't afford not to!"* Echoing the premise of this book, you cannot afford to postpone and delay purposeful lifestyle modification unless you want to spend your retirement in doctor's offices and hospitals.

You might have a pinched disc in your back or tightness in your lumbar area. Your shoulders could be inflamed due to the posture you take at your desk. You might be loading your legs incorrectly and suffering a bunch of knee and calf pain. While you work with a physical therapist or athletic trainer to correct that, why not get a couple of massages to help alleviate the pain?

I've had friends with fertility issues, after having gone down every medical path imaginable, find success with an acupuncturist. Acupuncture can be specialized and targeted just like massage therapy. Knee pain? Menstrual cycle imbalance? An acupuncturist will tailor their work to target what you need.

Don't tell Trevor I told you, but his IT band can get a little tight. And despite his commitment to fitness and his ability to push through

---

* Robin Sharma, *The 5AM Club: Own Your Morning. Elevate Your Life.* (HarperCollins Publishers, 2018), 257.

pain, I have seen this IT band completely debilitate him to a slow paced walk in the middle of a race! Once, between races during a long TriFecta Weekend in Cincinnati, there he was, lying on the hotel floor with needles in his leg while my brother, a physical therapist and a complete monster during an obstacle course race, worked on his IT band issue to prep him for the next day of racing. Luckily, he's got friends in good places, and by using this dry needling technique, a therapeutic treatment usually performed by physical therapists, on his IT band to relieve his pain, Trevor improved movement and blood flow while loosening up his muscle. He went on to crush the rest of the race. Dry needling can be a useful treatment for back, neck and shoulder pain, tendonitis, migraines, and muscle tightness.

OPTOMETRIST

This is your eye doctor. There's a meme that goes around every once in a while about how traditional health insurance doesn't cover everything. It will read something like, "According to my insurance, my eyes and mouth are not part of my overall health." For whatever reason (let's be honest... it's money), people usually need separate dental or vision insurance to cover those visits.

Optometrists, then, are often left off the roster. But they really shouldn't be. They can detect glaucoma, macular degeneration, cataracts, and even observe early signs of diabetes and high blood pressure. Caught early, they can work with you to prolong or prevent the onset of these conditions.

They'll also consider your family history to tailor their work to your risk factors.

DENTIST

This seems obvious, right? The health of your teeth and mouth is so vastly important that they need their own specialist.

Most of us make the point to regularly see a dentist, even if we skip a year here or there (even though we shouldn't). It's one of those things, culturally, that people just kind of accept they are going to have to spend a little money on. Maybe that's why there are bargain dental clinics on almost as many corners as there are Starbucks these days. They will have a punny name like "Brite Bite" or something. My advice is to avoid those places if you can and instead go somewhere that has verifiably reputable services.

Beyond oral hygiene, dentists provide crucial holistic services (perhaps without you knowing it). By keeping your mouth healthy, you are actually going out of your way to keep several other systems of your body healthy—doing a lot of great preventative work. You may hear your dentist talk to you about sleep, about jaw pain, headaches, breathing issues, and they can also perform an assessment for potential tissue damage and detect early cancer. The mouth is one of the most rapidly healing and renewing areas of the human body, and the potential for errors in these rapidly changing cells can lead to disease that, if left unchecked, can lead to devastating consequences. Make sure that your dentist performs that thorough evaluation and be open to the other preventative measures that they might offer.

Bad oral hygiene can increase your risk for cardiovascular disease, respiratory infections, diabetes, kidney disease, Alzheimer's, and specific forms of cancer. Why? Don't ask me. I'm an orthopedic surgeon. Just kidding. It's because the bacteria in your mouth can enter the bloodstream and find its way into other parts of your body, including the joints, retained hardware from prior surgery, and the valves of your heart.

Even if you don't develop a more serious condition, bad oral hygiene (and lack of dentist intervention) will significantly increase your inflammation, which you already know can itself have massive impacts on your bodily and mental health (like chronic stress).

GENERAL PROVIDER

And now we've come to it. With all of my efforts listing a roster of preventative and holistic specialists on your HealthSpan Longevity Team, you will nonetheless still need a relatively traditional primary or general care provider.

But again, you can get creative here. That provider does not have to be embedded in the traditional medical system. And you *can* find "traditional," insurance-covered providers who are open to doing protective, proactive, and preventative work. They are a little rarer, of course. If you can't find one that suits you, consider the option for a concierge doctor—the physician who operates on cash monthly fees instead of copays and insurance. This specialist can still recommend workups and consultations through your primary insurance but will also give you additional time due to the type of model that they create for their patients.

In any case, general care providers play a part in early detection, personalized advice, coordinating specialists, managing ongoing health needs, and identifying true pathologies.

YOUR "HEALTH" SOCIAL CIRCLE

Your team doesn't just have to consist of doctors. It's often healthy and habit-forming (and cheaper) to maintain friends and family with healthy habits.

Who you surround yourself with will have a huge impact on your health. Are you constantly visiting your mother-in-law who is putting platefuls of the most delicious but also unhealthy foods on the table all day? Or are you planning friend dates by meeting at the gym and hitting targets while you're catching up on life?

If you're around people who are health conscious and make smart choices, it's more than likely that you'll be health conscious and make smart choices, too.

TREVOR'S INTERJECTION

Caleb is the doctor and the guy with all of the knowledge, but health and fitness is a really big hobby of mine, too.

To scratch that itch, I'm sending Caleb fitness videos and articles all the time. Keeping the hobby social by connecting with my cousin Caleb works in both of our favors. I have somebody to share things with, so that gives me extra incentive to read and watch for new tips to try out myself. And for Caleb, getting my messages is like having a gym buddy alongside him for motivation, or so he tells me. Without that connection, he wouldn't be working out as regularly.

Having Caleb in the social circle of my HealthSpan Longevity Team doesn't just benefit my physical health. It's mental and emotional health, too. One of Caleb's hobbies is personal development and mastering the self. I'll call him up quite a bit, asking him for help to get through being angry or upset. He'll say, "You need to read this book." I'm like, "I'm not gonna read that book. I'm going to talk to you so you can give me the five-minute version." He does a great job of it.

But by staying connected with our social circle, we're instilling good health habits in each other. Don't tell Caleb, but it won't be long until I start sending him podcasts on financial strategies. His financial health is important to me, too.

A don't be resistant to those folks with open-mindedness and health-improving ideas. Once, I tried to help my dad with a urinary issue by getting him a "To pee or not to pee" fluid input/output journal. Rather than be open to it, he resisted and said he could simply remember how much and what types of fluids he was drinking each day. Spoiler alert: he didn't remember and prolonged his pathology.

When we don't absorb the healthy habits of those around us, we may suffer the consequences.

RELATIONSHIPS AND EXPERIENCES

Everyone in your life will contribute to your joy and pain. Some contribute more joy, and some take more joy away. For those people who don't contribute a majority of joy, you might have to be very frank with them to change the trajectory of the health of that relationship. Have an honest, open communication with them regarding the effects they are having on you and how this is unacceptable to you. Discuss the change that you will require from them and explain how you are willing to disconnect from them if they cannot collaborate and the health-improving changes you are aiming to create.

You have to be able to set that type of boundary with everyone. Friends, siblings, parents, even your partner. And while I am not suggesting that you need to cut ties with everyone in your life, you need to consider the contribution that people make in your life and how it contributes to your own happiness. And demand to be treated in a way that brings you joy. That's tough, but even our closest relationships can be unbalanced and even toxic.

Your children get a pass, at least until they are eighteen, but even they can damage your mental health and should be held to a standard and a boundary. If you do happen to lose someone while you make a stand such as this, it is okay to want them back, even hope them back. And you might get lucky, and they might eventually come back. But you have to be willing to stand up for what you deserve.

I've seen it happen so many times: HealthSpans suffering because they refuse to let go of toxic relationships, even with their children. Sometimes children struggle with substance abuse disorders. That's tragic in and of itself for these adult kids, but it also has negative side effects—often parallel to the one suffering from the disorder—on the parent. What usually happens? Despite the parent's best intentions, their actions ultimately enable the children.

It's one of those stories where they essentially only come around to use the parent as a means to an end. The parent wants to support and chooses to give the kid money and an occasional place to sleep. The parent tears themself up inside, stuck between knowing what the right thing to do is (let them go or connect them with the appropriate health professional) and their parental instincts to "help" (which unfortunately enable them). Sometimes the best thing you can do is let your kids fail or, if they have a substance use disorder, let them hit rock bottom to pick themselves back up. It isn't easy to watch! But the alternative isn't really any easier!

It's a situation where these kids bring far more pain than they do joy into my colleague's life. Each relationship is a different story, but the takeaway here is that relationships that improve our mental health give more overall joy. Find people that support you and your joy, and be open to supporting the joy of others.

Foster deep relationships as assets to your health. Science has proven that those who experience more deep relationships tend to live longer and be more successful. A good tip is to surround yourself with people who have the healthy lifestyle and habits that you want to emulate. Maybe it's a gym buddy or somebody who knows a lot about healthy nutrition. Go to the gym with them. Meal prep with them. People that inspire us by way of their own actions encourage us to pursue our own physical and mental health activities. And while you are hanging out with them, you'll also foster much-needed socialization. You are who you surround yourself with.

While you're having these experiences, design your life around moments, not milestones. Enjoy the journey instead of the destination. Don't join a recreational sports team so that you can secure the win—that's a result, not the effort. Be comfortable with losing and instead focus on the growth and opportunity of playing as the win. Go to the gym so that you can invest in yourself. And in your longevity. If you do it solely for the biceps measurements or for the six-pack, then you'll lose the joy of the journey. You'll be too hyped up about the destination that you'll miss the opportunity that the journey presents.

Be intentional about the balance within your deep relationships. Don't just give. Don't just take.

PICKING THE BEST TEAM

Okay, those are some options for your HealthSpan Longevity Team. Now, how do you pick the best people? What's the vetting process? You have to learn about them, rub elbows with them, and ask questions. This can be intimidating because when we start questioning a health provider (especially if they are a doctor), it can feel like we're challenging their authority.

But in reality, the purpose of getting to know them is to (1) see if they can provide a service that meets your needs and (2) see if their approach jives with your philosophies and goals. It's like shopping for anything else. If your car needs tires but the mechanic is telling you it needs a new windshield (and your windshield is pristine), you're going to say "thanks but no thanks" and move on until you get your car into the right garage. When it comes to longevity, there should be no compromise. You are not allowed to feel a little too sheepish to evaluate a provider. You are unapologetically looking to create your winning team! There is absolutely nothing to feel bad about here!

When it comes to longevity, nutrition, fitness, and anti-aging, this isn't something to mess with. Don't become stagnant. Learn what you can learn from a person and, if that growth stops, move on. Every person on your team is replaceable. If they don't treat you the way you think is needed, or if they aren't taking you seriously, then move on. Get another opinion. This is your life!

Access to care has never been easier—or more remote-capable—so make sure you are happy with who you choose. Take them on a trial run, set goals for the relationship, and move on if you're not getting what you expect.

Something else to consider when choosing somebody for your HealthSpan Longevity Team is how much passion and energy they bring into your life. Learning about and implementing healthcare habits can be boring. But not everybody makes it boring. Some make it fun and find ways to connect joy and purpose with the healthcare needs.

And don't add people to your roster for the sake of it. Determine who you need as you see gaps. Use your health manager and your own experiences to determine any weaknesses and deficiencies in order to identify when a new specialist might need to be added to the team.

WHY YOUR TEAM IS MORE NECESSARY THAN EVER

Don't forget, the medical system is a "crisis" system. Traditional appointments are only scheduled when something is wrong (not to prevent something from going wrong).

Change this pattern by being proactive with your team. Sure, you'll have some traditional folks on this team. But there are others you can tap to cover your protective and preventative needs.

We need that team because you cannot do everything, and you certainly can't do it all from home. You need experts and expert tools. Surround yourself with the people who have the means to help you plan with purpose, find health success, and achieve your health goals.

Goals are better when they're shared and when supported by a community. Having coaches, providers, and cheerleaders helps motivate us to push ourselves ever closer to hitting our goals. Stay inspired to stay serious about maximizing your HealthSpan.

CHAPTER 7

EXIT STRATEGY: PLANNING FOR A HEALTHY RETIREMENT

"We are what we repeatedly do. Excellence, then, is not an act but a habit."

—WILL DURANT

I'm a terrible golfer. My kids aren't, though. In fact, they're great at it.

Here's my excuse: I didn't start playing until my first year of medical school, and taking up a new hobby at the busiest time of your life is not conducive to having success at said hobby. But I love the game, and I love playing with my kids. That puts two goals smack dab in front of me: (1) I want the ability to continue to play with them, and (2) I want the challenge of incrementally improving my scores.

I want to chase those dreams until I'm dead. That's good because it gives me a time horizon—to borrow one of Trevor's fancy finance terms—to work on micro-goals within that larger goal. That way I can make my life important now *and* important later, where I plan to live today but also with the future in mind.

If my goal is to swing a golf club effectively until my body can't hold itself up anymore, that means I'll need to maintain my flexibility and joint movement while maintaining a lean muscle mass to promote mobility and bone density to support a torquing frame. Today is the day I should start incorporating those strategies, chip away at them, and nurture them. If I put off any of it, I'll be totally screwed—meaning I can expect fewer golf rounds with my kids.

Boom! With just one health goal defined, I've opened up a clear path to protective, proactive, and preventative health strategies. I have a partial health exit plan that emphasizes longevity in my HealthSpan!

Whether you know it or not (maybe you skipped the first chapter), you have health goals that, if you do not nurture starting today, your health will be too wrecked to achieve.

Let me put it another way. Unlike the schedule of your retirement nest egg, your health is scheduled to only get worse. There is no retirement from health. It's on track to decline. No ifs, ands, or buts.

So if you're not planning for your future health now, you'll be in for a rude awakening when, one day, you suddenly lose it. Let's avoid that by planning our health exit strategies.

THE IDENTITY LOSS CRISIS

We've spent a lot of time talking about how to stay fit your whole life and evolve that physical routine as you age. That's extremely important.

But what we haven't touched on as much—as it pertains to health—is how much our sense of identity acts as a foundation for our mental health. When things are going well, what helps us walk around with confidence, conviction, resilience, purpose, and joy? Our sense of identity—or a clear understanding of who we are and being able to live the lifestyle that affirms that persona.

If, on the other hand, our lifestyle does little to nothing when it comes to affirming what we believe about ourselves, our mental health will quickly deteriorate.

Here's where it's time for a wake-up call. Retirement, by definition, is a huge change in lifestyle away from one of the primary elements of our identity. From a health perspective, countless retirements will fail because the retiree didn't adequately plan for the inevitable loss of identity after they stopped working. It makes complete sense since work was such a huge part of our identity during our working years.

Just like needing to plan and create funds for the financial side of retirement, we also need to plan for and create a sense of self to thrive on the health side of retirement. If you don't, you're sitting on a bombshell ready to explode the quality of your health the day you start retirement.

TREVOR'S INTERJECTION

Any imbalance—today or tomorrow—will result in pain of some kind. You need finances. You need health. You need each acting as counterweights that keep the whole system upright and functioning properly. Without that balance, your goals stand a better chance of falling by the wayside.

You can have all the money in the world and be confined to your couch or a wheelchair hoping somebody is coming by soon to help you get to the bathroom. You can't trade your money for age or health at that point. You were already laying the groundwork in the decades prior to trade your health for money.

EXIT PLANNING VS. LIFE PLANNING

Humans are living longer than ever before.

Consider this: the industrial revolution was around one hundred years ago. Prior to that, the average global life expectancy was around thirty-five years. The number was affected by high infant and child mortality. But there was also rampant disease, a lack of abundant and complete nutrition, and decreased access to regular hygiene. With the advancement of modern medicine, humans now expect to live much longer. Within the next century, some longevity experts argue that the human body is capable of living until 150.

The concept of retirement—or stopping work around the age of sixty-five, or earlier if you plan with Trevor really well—now means that people stand the chance of having a prolonged retirement.

So the question becomes, how comfortable do you want your retirement to be? If you have extreme back pain, you'll have to consider your options. Do you want to live with the pain or get your back fused? You'll be in less pain but also likely less mobile. What kind of retirement is that, waiting all those years to not work only to be forced to choose between a painful back or immobility? Having significant health limitations in retirement will rob you of your sense of purpose and contribution.

In order to be active and healthy throughout our entire retirement, our needs are adapting. When we don't adapt, it's common for people to fail at retirement. Of course, most people think about a failed retirement in terms of running out of money. I just got an email from my brokerage firm this morning with the subject line "Living longer means planning smarter." What is often forgotten in this equation is that you'll also need to carefully think about how your health will play a role in your retirement.

This chapter is titled "Exit Strategy," which is a business phrase. The core idea of exit planning is to spend one's working life maximizing their business's value so that, on the chosen day of retirement, it can be sold to achieve financial goals and pad the financial portfolio and ensure enough money in retirement. There has to be a financial exit plan because if this person doesn't work to improve their financial situation, the number on their net worth statement can only decrease—we live in a world where everything costs money.

Let's apply the same framework to our health and see if it can shift our mindset about the total picture of a successful retirement. Think of your health like a bank account with some sort of number in there.

As you live your life, it will go down—you'll be spending it on things. Each bag of highly processed chips and can of soda will diminish that number. Gaining fat will be like credit card debt weighing you down. Each day without appropriate exercise will decrease that number. Doing a little exercise might bump the number back up a little bit. If you don't, you'll be earning high interest that, in time, will explode your HealthSpan in a way that won't be pretty.

The more you plan now to keep your health high and maximized, the more you'll be able to withdraw for retirement (the healthier you'll be). Not only that, if you start making and achieving goals for your mental and physical health today, you'll also be actively working toward living a fulfilled and purposeful life. In that sense, your health investment and exit planning is really, when you think about it, a form of life planning. It's a form of *unsploding*.

It should be obvious that you utilize *all* of the guidance in this book when planning for a healthy life. However, there are certain things that you should read between the lines (it's just one book, after all...it would be unreadably long if I put *every* strategy in here). For example, *where* you retire is going to have a major impact on your retirement health. If you're in the middle of farm country Wyoming and have cardiovascular issues, you'll likely struggle to find a cardiologist near you. If you want to maximize your HealthSpan by forming and being near a team, your health investment will need to change, in this example, by changing your location. This person is going to have to make a choice: what is more aligned with their purpose, living longer or dying in farm country?

And you should be interested in making choices like this while you're still able. If your health gets too out of control and you're not taking care of yourself, you might not be able to live where you want to. Instead, you'll be forced to live where you can get the right healthcare. You'll lose your purpose, control, and freedom. And you might lose your spouse, too. It's awful, but it happens.

Imagine something that has likely happened many times: a husband losing his health and a wife always goes to his appointments. They had married late in life and had all of these plans to explore the world together. Wanting to create new experiences together, they were highly motivated and also had a significant amount of time in front of them...so they thought. They were finalizing their financial plans and were nearly ready to set off on their adventures of retirement life, but he needed surgery.

While he was at it, he decided that he might as well double down and get the other surgeries he was putting off. Making matters worse, he had underlying health issues that slowed his recovery. And months turned into years, and as they returned for follow-up appointments, it was clear that these health issues had greatly inhibited their plans for their retirement life together—and her ability to materialize those goals and dreams.

She was upset that they were putting off plans, and her irritation with his lack of ability to chase their dreams was becoming more and more evident. Their optimism turned to arguments, and the demeanor toward each other became uncomfortable to be around. They were already well past retirement, and a few years later, he had to check into an assisted living home in order to get around-the-clock care. Not only were they not able to go on vacation, they were now living separate lives, and he had no control or freedom over where he slept or what he ate. It was tragic. He might have been able to hold on to those freedoms if he had optimized his HealthSpan earlier.

THE RETIREMENT HEALTH PURPOSE

We talked earlier about setting health goals for today and tomorrow. It's also a good idea to have a specific set of purposes devoted to your retirement. Having these carrots on sticks helps you do the work today to get there.

There is a little bit of a running joke in the orthopedic and physical therapy worlds right now about the huge uptick of pickleball injuries sending people into our offices. We like to laugh at it because reading our doctor's notes can be a little absurd: "Got tendonitis chasing a little Wiffle ball."

All joking aside, pickleball is immensely popular right now. It's one of those social phenomena that has crossed generations. It's not like music, where older people are like, "I've never heard of Mac Miller. Is that a new kind of cheeseburger?" People born in every imaginable decade are swapping pickleball strategies, comparing rackets, and arguing about where to get the best gear.

That uptick in activity is a great thing because it means that people are pursuing hobbies *and* choosing an active hobby that improves their cardiovascular health.

But for the retiree, it can also be a point of frustration. They've found a new purpose in their retirement and one that keeps both their body and mind healthy (the second due to the social community they've created). But when a person goes from zero strokes to 250 a day, that's a recipe for tendonitis. They might live right down the road from the pickleball court, and now they can't go to participate. That's frustrating in and of itself, and now add on the fact that they'll be losing the health benefits.

As we age and think about our health, it is best to cultivate *many* purposes in retirement. Maybe one is staying embedded in the pickleball community. But what happens if we lose that. Do we have other avenues to generate a sense of belonging, purpose, and fulfillment?

I have friends who are retired in a golf community. That was a major purpose guiding their health and retirement-residency choices throughout their lives. Prior to getting there, they knew that having a successful retirement meant spending their life continuing to play golf, work on their game, and do the work to maintain their core strength and flexibility. Without those, they wouldn't be able to golf five days a week. But they didn't just end there.

What if golf was no longer an option for them? Conscious of that, they also volunteer at a local food bank. It just so happens that many of the other volunteers are, like them, all retired. This gives them a social community and a sense of purpose outside of golf. But there is *a lot* of standing involved. They'll often come home complaining about sore backs and feet. They're working on it, though, making sure to incorporate light resistance training and stretching that targets those areas.

What makes their retirement successful is that they have more than one purpose, and each one contributes to their overall sense of well-being. They both have social circles, their own micro-goals, and more. By keeping more than one purpose active, they are diversifying to make sure that if there are "market fluctuations" with their health, they'll have another purpose to rely on. They are purpose-rich. *That* is smart retirement planning, when it comes to our health.

As you go to create your own retirement purposes, try to make them incorporate multiple angles of health impact. If you join a biking club, for example, you'll be maintaining your cardiovascular health, your lower extremity health, and your social and mental health. If you want to be charitable, don't just donate money. Join a board or get active within the charity so you gain both a sense of giving back *and* join a social community of like-minded individuals who are passionate about a similar cause.

Challenge your body and your mind. Mental health is just as important as your physical health. As we age, muscles atrophy quickly, but so too does the mind! Keep this asset active! Engage. This is a key to prevention of depression and forgetfulness.

FOCUS ON *YOUR* GOALS IN RETIREMENT

You have to be aware of the factors in your life that threaten your mental and physical fitness longevity. Learn to say "no" when something detracts from your overall well-being.

There are certain personality types among us that give and give and give until there's nothing left—they'll explode their health. Right now, they're giving, and they seem fine. They don't have any health issues and believe their emotional, monetary, or other forms of giving are just part of their sense of purpose and giving back. But when it's unbalanced, and they aren't putting the things back into their life that sustains them, things can go awry quickly. *Unsplode* your retirement (both financially and physically) by focusing on *your* goals.

When grandparents are taking care of their grandchildren all the time—especially to the point of exhaustion—that takes a toll on the body and mind. Not only will the stress take away from their heath, it'll also take away free time to establish a healthy routine that includes pursuing hobbies, engaging with a social circle, and doing those much-needed fitness routines. Though assisting our families may be required as an adaptation to the curveballs that life throws at us, make sure you seek balance in these changes and adaptations! Your need to set and reach your own goals should be equally as important as the need for your grandchildren to have supervision while their parents work. Chase balance. And unapologetically pursue your goals and dreams.

I'm not saying *never* take care of the grandkids. I'm saying there needs to be a balance that ensures you have time to fill your cup back up with the things you need to keep you healthy.

Speaking of imbalance, you can also focus *too much* on yourself. Another way to avoid overdoing it in retirement—and running the engine of your health too hot—is to *not* start a gray-hair project. This could be opening up a consulting firm to keep one foot in work. It could be you going hard on that car building hobby. Whatever is, don't make it your full-time thing. You'll just be back to the stressful grind that you left.

That around-the-clock productivity that you are reentering will only withdraw the value of your health faster, and you can expect a shorter retirement. And that gray-hair project then becomes something that you must get done so it will stop eating away at you. Instead, don't pick up that project in the first place! If it's going to drain you, then skip it! Seek out a more simple pleasure and fill up your dopamine reserves in a more healthy way.

Do me a favor and plan *not* to die within five years of your retirement. Instead, as you work toward your twilight years, plan to have goals and purposes that create healthy habits and positively impact your HealthSpan.

Before you get to retirement and as you start exit planning, realize that there's a strong chance that, when you're in your sixties, your children will be too busy to see you and your grandchildren might not think you're cool enough to hang out with. So don't rely on them for a social circle to maintain a healthy sense of community and purpose. You'll need to backup plan for that by coming up with targeted goals—like the pickleball or golf communities we've discussed.

Having said that, and if one of your retirement health goals is to have ongoing contact and connection with your kids, then you're going to have to foster that now as part of your exit plan. I was recently playing a round of golf with my son. The other duo in our group included a father and son—the father was a retired sports journalist that used to cover the team. As we chatted, the father indicated that although his son lived in a different state, the son made time to fly to Vegas frequently to spend time with him. When I reacted with some slight shock, the dad proudly reaffirmed, "I know! He makes time for me!" Kids just won't do that unless you've built that connection during their childhood.

Start that work early, because studies show that 90 to 95 percent of the time you spend with your kids in their lifetime occurs before they reach the age eighteen. And 75 percent of that amount will be spent with them before they hit twelve.

Time and time again I've talked to colleagues who've had regrets with their family life and not making those early connections. Orthopedic surgery is a demanding job, and it's not uncommon for prominent figures to sacrifice their family life to bolster their careers. I was recently at a lecture given by one of the big names in the field whose retirement is imminent.

For like the fourth lecture in a row, he went on a tangent about how his kids don't love him but his grandkids do. When he was elevating his career as a younger doctor, he didn't spend time with his kids. He didn't go to their baseball games, didn't drive them to their friends' birthday parties, or anything like that. He was career-focused.

Now that he's taken the foot off the gas pedal, he's going to all of his grandkids' events and, unfortunately a little too late, has realized the imbalance that he suffered earlier in his life. He's not shy about sharing the details, either. And his kids are open with him about their jealousy and resentment about his choice to now be present when they would have benefited from that connection when they were growing up. It's one of those lessons that shouldn't be learned the hard way. A solid exit plan can help you in that department.

AGING IN PLACE AND SENIOR CARE

Regardless of our age, we all like to think that we are youthful and strong and that nothing bad will ever happen to us. I hate to be the bearer of bad news, but if we're lucky enough, we will *all* get to the point where we will be decrepit and will need the assistance of others—senior care nurse, medical staff—to support us.

What's more, and with that realization in our back pocket, we need to plan for our quality of life when that occurs. And you have choices: senior care communities or aging in place.

SENIOR CARE

There are a lot of horror stories—and for good reason—about senior care. Despite that, there are actually quite a few really good options out there.

I'm only a decade away from the fifty-five-plus senior care communities near my home that, get this, have their own golf courses. While this fact is *not* easy to cope with, that sounds like my kind of place. And it sounds like I need to start trying to wrap my head around this! Search around and find the opportunities or community with the amenities that speak to you—the tennis court, the full-service bar (but drink in moderation), the game rooms, the theaters, the outdoor BBQ areas, and whatever else tickles your fancy. This is a great way to build your social circle postretirement by joining a community where the lifestyle options align with your interests.

Not all retirement communities require that you give up all of your agency. Many allow you to own your own condo or home that, while limited by the community rules, nonetheless still grant your ownership alongside access to on-site gyms, medical facilities, and other resources seniors need.

And if you know that you are genetically or environmentally predisposed to certain issues—like Alzheimer's—then you can maximize your HealthSpan now by researching a senior care community with access to quality resources to fit that need.

If you know that community living and staying connected with peers will be your preferred health-management technique in your later years, start planning for it now. Because this route can be expensive, that means you'll have to follow Trevor's advice for a successful financial retirement, too. If the cost for such a lifestyle is too much for your financial goals, there are long-term health insurance plans that can help cover the costs.

Speaking of money, that gets us back to the idea that senior care—as a concept—carries a lot of stigma. The reason is that the quality of care can drop significantly at less expensive places.

But care is care, if it's needed. And if you're broke and don't plan your finances with purpose, there are still options for you. Lots of senior care places will take in residents in exchange for that patient's social security. But they may also take elements of control away. You'll be seeing their doctors, taking their pills, and eating their food. And if you run out of assets, Medicaid will kick in, but the facility may not be as pretty as the facility that your friend gets to be in!

In the end, this system typically does a decent job of providing you the necessities; however, in the process, they also can nearly guarantee that you will be drained of all of your resources, and as a result, you will likely have next to nothing (and maybe even a bill!) to leave to your remaining family. So you need to think about what level of control you want at this stage of your life and plan accordingly.

AGING IN PLACE

If you can't stand the idea of living in a community with other seniors, then your other option is aging in place.

The benefits here are having your friends and family visit you in your own home—a place that represents *you* and the passion you've brought into this world. Although less focused on connectivity and community compared with senior care, aging in place maintains a sense of autonomy and independence for the individual.

What would happen in this situation is that the home itself would be modified based on the person's needs. If they have trouble going down stairs, a motorized stair lift will be installed. If they are overweight, they might need grab bars in the shower or wider door frames. Essentially, the environment itself will use technology to help the individual adapt to their changing health needs to maintain independent living. These modifications cost money, of course, that you'll have to plan for.

Another part of aging in place that will require money is any in-home healthcare services. Nurse and doctor visits are not free. Meal delivery is not free. On the other hand, transportation services are often provided by local transit authorities—but they are time consuming and must be scheduled in advance.

PUTTING IT ALL TOGETHER

There are tradeoffs with either option. Do you want more community, easier access to services, and less autonomy and control? Or do you want more autonomy and control, less community, and slower access to services?

These are choices you'll have to make, choices guided by the purposes and goals you set for yourself.

TOMORROW IS TODAY

We need to be aware of our goals for tomorrow to modify our today. We don't need to sacrifice our lives now to build our healthy future. Instead, invest in now to enjoy both your current and future lives.

Don't let your current external factors—work, those snacks in the pantry, stress about things yet to come, and so many other things—prevent you from doing the habitual, actionable steps required to achieve your health goals.

It requires daily work. Start today.

CONCLUSION

If there is anything you're not happy about regarding your health, your potential health, or your financial future, then what are you doing about it? How are you looking to *unsplode* the potential ticking time bomb in front of you? How are you planning with purpose in order to change things? If you take action, is it one and done? Are you going to give up quickly after your first few attempts? Or are you going to really commit? And will you develop the daily habits required to live a long, purposeful, and fulfilled life?

Over the course of this book, I've discussed a broad array of HealthSpan-improving ideas to help you identify your health goals and purpose, think about longevity opportunities that align with your purpose, and illuminate a few pathway options for your next actionable steps.

As you put this book down and begin to implement your next steps and develop new healthy habits, many external factors are going to try and steal your motivation from you. When you feel that happening, point back to your purpose.

Without a true sense of purpose and passion for fulfilling your health goals, you'll be the victim of whatever turbulence you are riding in. You'll explode your life.

Instead, look to *unsplode*. As you make those moves toward a better HealthSpan, you will have to figure out what habits you can create and consistently do to transform your well-being and your life.

SUCCESS THROUGH THE ACHIEVEMENT CONTAGION

Habits are hard to acquire. They take commitment. They take discipline. They take (re)dedication and perseverance. But you have strategies. Not the least of which is being mindful about the people you surround yourself with and the team you build.

Research has demonstrated time and time again that your friends, family, and providers influence your mental, physical, and financial health—and your overall success. This occurs through an "achievement contagion." And we have discussed a lot of "conditions" in this book, most of which are unhealthy and worth avoiding, but the achievement contagion is probably the only condition I've listed in this book that I hope you do catch. I want you to walk away with this one. I want your friends and family to catch it, too. I want you to lift each other up to a new height of HealthSpan and WealthSpan as you support and encourage each other.

Here's a great example. A dentist—or, I should say, a former dentist—was stuck in a career that wasn't going as he hoped. He noticed that many of his colleagues were semiretired and had generated alternative forms of income. By inserting himself in a circle of people he wanted to emulate, he received a natural education and motivation to achieve the same way they did—an "achievement contagion." It was more than just knowledge; he also adopted their "can-do" and "goal-oriented" mindset. By surrounding himself with this group and adopting their ideas, he found himself retiring from practicing medicine within a decade and branching his career goals into other more productive avenues as he pursued new dreams. He could fully retire right now if he wanted, but he prefers instead to help others accomplish what he did.

A key marker for your health and wealth success will require that you reevaluate the people around you. Do they add to you? Do they contribute to your well-being? Do they keep your mindset healthy and focused on purposeful achievement? Or are they taking away from you?

Inventory your life, inventory your team, inventory your own attitude and choices, and make sure that these important personal and supporting factors align with all of your longevity goals, both on the WealthSpan side and on the HealthSpan side.

THE BODY'S EVOLUTION

One of the key takeaways to internalize is a recognition that your body and mental health—and your expectations for them—will evolve over time. Preventative health in your seventies is going to be a lot different than your thirties. You'll be making withdrawals and deposits along the way that mean you are constantly changing, constantly having to reassess not just your health itself but your goals and if they are still within achievable limits.

The clock is ticking, and there are no significant renewals to our health. This life is not a video game. There is no extra life to find, no power-up, no option to "continue" after you blow it, and thus no automatic renewal of energy and power. Renewing your HealthSpan *will not happen* without an active and purposeful approach. Planning your next steps and for upcoming and unexpected changes will be your only means of prolonging the health of your heart, blood vessels, brain, lungs, liver, kidneys, nervous system, digestive system, musculoskeletal system, and many others.

Some medical advancements mean that we can get replacements or alternatives, such as knee replacements or heart valve replacements, but most of our systems do not have such options! For the ones you can replace, please keep in mind that major surgeries are quite invasive and can do as much damage as they hope to repair.

I try to remind my patients that surgical procedures are a game of odds. We hope that all patients have the optimal outcome, but if you have an 85 percent successful surgical option in front of you, what if you are part of the 15 percent? What if you don't have the success that you hope for? What if you come out of this worse? Nobody wants to be the minority regarding the odds of surgical success, but 15 percent of you will be. Are you prepared for that?

I tell my patients that if you were gambling, then those are some pretty good odds. But we're not quite talking about walking away with less cash in your pocket...we're talking about walking away with worse pain, worse function, or potentially even something more catastrophic. So don't delay your preventative choices! Nothing that I can do surgically can replace what you were born with. It might be close, but if you can keep what you came with, then that is ideal!

Prevent all that by doing the work. Discover your family history, what you're predisposed to, the unique health-affecting attributes of your environment, your own body's unique intake and output potentials, and your financial situation. Use this knowledge to make a plan of attack to keep and improve your health while you have it until it's too late and before you can no longer match the body's evolution. Shop on the outside of the grocery store, not on the inside. Get fresh food from the local farmers market. Get outside!

Control what you can control right now, forget about the bad habits of your past, and give yourself the best chance not just at surviving but at thriving.

YOU ONLY GET ONE BODY

It's never the perfect time to get started. That perfect time and perfect opportunity will simply never come. So quit waiting; just get started. Your health is finite. You began dying the moment that you were born. And everything that you do is a potential trauma to your longevity. You get two meniscus per knee. You get one occipitalis. You get two femurs. You get four rotator cuff tendons per shoulder. That's it.

When they're gone. They're gone.

You see that "Greek God" at the gym? The one that you secretly look at and wish you could replicate? Take another look. And then please consider the fact that you and that fitness nut at the gym are *not* that structurally different. The very basic building blocks of human beings are very, very similar. And it is our choice what we add to our basic building blocks.

We encourage you to seek clarity regarding the concepts that we have presented in this book. We realize that this is a lot. Let it sink in. Find a trusted friend or colleague and share this book with them. And discuss what you both think and how you can both incorporate what we have taught you and presented to you. Then formally commit yourself to be purposefully driven and to make time for yourself each day. Time for your health. Time for your wealth. Decisions that will improve the lasting power of both! These commitments cannot wait until tomorrow. *Tomorrow is today*. It is time to *unsplode* your life right now. Break it down. Clarify where you are and where you want to go. And decide who you need on your team to help you to get there.

Failing to do so will rob you of this necessary and timely change and will compromise your ability to achieve your goals. Don't approach your health through New Year's resolution intervals of three weeks on and forty-nine weeks off. But renew that commitment regularly and with purpose.

As we noted on the cover: are you ready to live a life of clarity, confidence, and purpose? If not, then we hope you have enjoyed reading our book! We appreciate your time. If so, then it's time to get started!

As we wrap this up, I want to thank you again for your interest in what we both have to say. This has been an adventure for us. And we appreciate your confidence in us, and we appreciate that you gave up some of your valuable time to take interest in what we have to say. Thank you.

We wrote this book from a profound love for life, adventure, stability, and our families. And we feel privileged to have learned a lot of lessons (some easy, some hard) along the way. And we have been excited to share what we have learned with the other fantastic humans that we get to walk this world with.

There are plenty of people out there that, despite their best efforts, are still seeking ways to restore balance to their lives. And we hope that our personal lives, experiences, failures, successes, and education can make a difference as you chase that balance.

So whether you are already in your retirement, or if you're maybe getting to these preparatory opportunities a little bit late, or maybe you're the "Greek God" that we are all staring at while we're at the gym, we hope that we can bring some positive insight and influence to your life as you create the most of your own WealthSpan and HealthSpan.

So get going. Get out there. Surround yourself with fantastic people. And go out and make your life the very best one that you can.

You've got this!

GLOSSARY

We've spent the pages of this book developing a completely new way to think about maximizing the fulfillment of your life through a balanced approach to your finances and health. Only in coordination can planning for those two things create the life of your dreams. Money helps you invest in your own health. Being healthy helps you grow your wealth. And both can be spent to live.

We've developed a unique vocabulary to talk about how you, too, can flip the script and take back control of your life. We've placed the key terms of this system here for your convenience as you continue to seek optimization.

Clarity: Having a clear, nuanced, and systematic understanding of your financial and health plan—making sure those plans are anchored in your evolving understanding of your purpose and values.

Confidence: Living your life with conviction—leading to more fulfillment—knowing that you've put a plan in place designed to scaffold and sustain the life you want.

Explode: The choices we make, large and small, that *undermine* the longevity of our health and finances. Either immediately or slowly over time, these choices accumulate to explode our lives. That is to say, our life takes a new, unexpected, and unwelcome turn that threatens living a life with purpose and fulfillment.

HealthSpan: A new way of thinking about your health that enhances your biological longevity through our unique system, one whose plan focuses on finding your wellness purpose, preventative action, ongoing healthy choices, and more. It also encourages you to keep your body and mind in use today *and* tomorrow.

Purpose: The *why* that motivates a fulfilling life. You may have many purposes, and each one will have you shape the unique-to-you financial and health plans to help you live the life you've envisioned for yourself.

Unsplode: The choices we make, large and small, that *increase* the longevity of our finances and health. By choosing to be proactive, we prevent—or *unsplode*—the negative effects of the choices that otherwise undermine our longevity.

WealthSpan: A new way of thinking about your wealth that enhances your financial longevity through our unique system, one whose plan focuses on finding your purpose, maximizing your financial opportunities, protecting your assets, and more. It also encourages you to use your money to live a fulfilling life today *and* tomorrow.

ACKNOWLEDGEMENTS

TREVOR'S ACKNOWLEDGEMENTS

To my wife, Kenalee. None of this would exist without you.

You are caring, steady, and always ready for an adventure. Your smile can change the whole tone of a day, and your humor and teasing make even the hardest moments feel lighter. You make me want to live a life with purpose—filled with travel, experiences, family, and love.

You've always given me honest pushback when I needed it most. When I was struggling in the corporate structure, knowing it wasn't allowing me to do what was best for clients, you challenged me to be true to myself. You inspired me to build a new organization rooted in purpose, truth, and doing what's right.

You sacrificed so much for our family, including stepping away from your own career as a dental hygienist to raise our kids and support our home. Through long nights, last-minute client calls, and vacations interrupted by work, you have been my constant and my strength.

You've given me the space to dream and the courage to chase those dreams. You are my balance, my grounding, and the person who continually makes me better—as a leader, a father, and a man.

This book belongs to you as much as it does to me. Thank you for loving me, supporting me, and always having my back.

I am who I am because of you. I love you.

To my incredible kids, Rylee, Jaxon, and Brody. I couldn't have written this book without you. You are my motivation, my grounding, and the reason I work to become a better man every day. You give my life purpose, and you inspire me to keep learning, growing, and showing up with everything I have. And you know me: I'm not that verbose with words. So although my paragraphs to you are shorter than Caleb's, my love is just as strong.

Rylee, at sixteen, you are the sweetest daughter a father could ask for. Your heart is enormous, your determination is unstoppable, and your quiet strength speaks louder than words. You approach everything with precision, dedication, and intelligence. There is truly nothing beyond your reach, and I admire the woman you're becoming.

Jaxon, at fifteen, you're my beach-loving, laid-back, Hawaiian-at-heart kid. You care deeply about people and how they're treated, and your humor is effortless. You make everyone laugh just by being yourself. You're incredibly determined; once you commit to something, nothing can pull you off course. You're a natural athlete with a good heart and a presence people are naturally drawn to.

And ***Brody***, at twelve, you are curiosity and joy in human form. You're always smiling, always talking, always making friends everywhere you go. You're street-smart, confident, endlessly fascinated by the world, and you're not scared of anything. Your fearless, outgoing energy fills every room you walk into, and your love of learning and adventure is contagious.

I love each of you more than words will ever express. You give me the drive to do what I do and the desire to keep becoming better—as a father, as a leader, and as a human being. This book may be part of my legacy, but you three will always be my greatest one.

To my parents, Bruce Hanson and Carolyn Hanson. Thank you for giving me a foundation that shaped every part of who I am.

Because of you, my childhood was anything but ordinary. We

lived in Dubai and Muscat, Oman, and before I was ten years old, we had traveled across four continents—Africa, Europe, Asia, and North America. Those experiences opened my eyes to the world long before I understood how rare and meaningful they were. You taught me to embrace different cultures, to seek adventure, and to live with curiosity and gratitude.

More than that, you taught me how to live with purpose. You showed me the value of hard work, of dreaming big, and of stepping into life with courage instead of hesitation. Those early lessons—the places we lived, the places we traveled, and the way you encouraged me to see the world—played a huge role in shaping this book.

Thank you for believing in me from the very beginning, for supporting every dream, and for giving me the confidence to build a life filled with meaning, purpose, and adventure. So much of who I am today is because of the values you instilled in me.

To Katie, thank you to my business partner, whom I have worked with for over fifteen years, the last twelve years side by side building a business. You've been someone I can rely on no matter what. When I'm gone, I know everything is handled. You figure things out, make things happen, and keep everything moving. While I wrote this book, you took on more—keeping the business running and making sure our clients never felt a difference. You care about clients, and it shows. You also pushed me to finish this book, and it wouldn't be what it is without you. In addition to a business partner, you're a friend and like family to me. I'm grateful for everything you've done and continue to do.

To Caleb, thank you for coming up with the concept of writing this book—wealth and health in balance. For years, you kept telling me it was a matter of time before we wrote "Rest and Invest," the first iteration of an adventure you wouldn't let die. I never imagined I'd be part of a book, let alone write one. You pushed me to do that.

You've always pushed me outside of my comfort zone. Whenever I'm with you, I end up doing something I never thought I'd do. That goes to show that you push people toward growth, toward becoming a better version of themselves. That's what you've done for me all of these years. You helped me find strengths I didn't know I had. As an amazing father, your strengths influence me in many ways. And I'm humbled by you, with the heights you've seen professionally, that you would consider me a worthy partner. The truth about you is that you're very caring and look inwardly quite easily, and you help others do the same. I've done a lot in my life, but the time I've spent with you has been some of the most interesting and fun.

You've always let me be myself around you. That has helped me stay young. You're my brother.

CALEB'S ACKNOWLEDGEMENTS

To Roman, at sixteen, you've always been a leader. You have always pushed the boundaries that life has placed in front of you. You have always sought perfection and improvement. You have also always wanted to be a generation or two older than you have to be! That desire to be one step ahead, one rung further down the line, has made you curious and subversive. I value that tenacity. I value that drive. And I value the fact that you don't let me get away with anything! I can't just tell you that this is the way that it is. I need to back it up. I need to show you why. And that is a wonderful quality. Challenge what you're told, seek to understand, and if something feels wrong, keep pushing to find out why. You make me better. You make me honest. Thank you. We are both better for it. And I encourage you to continue to seek truth and understanding. Thank you for pushing me to keep an open mind and for encouraging me to treat you like an equal as we continue to build a relationship of connectivity, trust, and collaboration. I cannot wait to watch you break down barriers as you create your future reality and as you build something out of your life that I was never bold enough to pursue. Now, if you would just let me beat you at golf now and again then, we might really be on to something!

To Kemp, at thirteen, you are a passionate and caring brute. While you can carry multiple linebackers with you as you surge toward the end zone, and while you can drill a soccer ball with such pace to strike fear into your opponents as they dive out of the way, you are also caring of others, and you wish no ill upon anyone. You are a peacemaker. And you are also a ferocious athlete. I love your passion for life. Your smile and attitude brings light and laughter to our family, and your selfless attitude is unmatched and has always been a breath of fresh air. Thank you for your commitment to service, compassion, love, and unity. Even when you are wronged by another person, you will still stand in front of them to shield them from punishment or criticism. You are quick to forgive, and you are full of love and charity. This sensibility for the feelings of others has unlocked in me a personal desire to choose higher roads, and this has unlocked new heights in my capacity for empathy toward others, even when their actions against me have caused me pain or suffering. You choose inclusion and empathy instead of neglect and revenge. Your ability to stand up for and protect others, even tormenters, is inspiring. I've never known anybody like you who truly sees the good in all people and who only wants good for all people. Thank you for continuing to inspire me to choose the higher road.

To Cosette, at ten, you are a beautiful fireball. Despite being constantly surrounded by those with XY chromosomes (your four brothers and father), you remain dainty and girly and committed to all things pink. Yet despite your undying love of romance television, and make-up, and painting nails, and creating music videos, you don't take any crap. You can hold your own, and you don't apologize for having a different opinion or for wanting something more fitting for a lady. I love that you can dish out sass without issue, and sometimes this ability is on a level better than anyone I've ever seen! I am frequently not even sure where this ability has even come from! And despite being able to get salty and to stand your ground, you are sweet and tender and still need to cuddle up and hide under a blanket when the scary part of a movie comes on. And the day following, you're back to taking the RZR off jumps, covering yourself with dust, letting your hair get tangled in the wind, and smelling like a campfire, only to brag about the "dude wipe" shower that you had to take at the end of the day in order to be just barely clean enough to climb into a sleeping bag to prepare for the next day's adventure. You are fun and beautiful and even a little bit crazy, and in my opinion that makes you one of the most fantastic women in this world. I have no doubt that you will be a treasure worth chasing as you make your mark on this world.

To Boss, at six, you are a breath of fresh air. I am not sure I have any real photos of you being serious—you are committed to being silly every time I bring out the camera. Your laugh is one of my more favorite sounds in this entire world. And when you ask me for a special favor, my heart melts, and I feel completely honored and privileged to be your dad. You and I have built some of the most incredible Minecraft creations, and even though I try to be tough when we watch movies, I have to admit that I often go to bed a little scared after you convince me to let you watch a scary show. I secretly hope that you'll ask if you can fall asleep in my bed so that I can cuddle you for a few minutes before I carry you back to your own bed, and I can't wait for you to tap my arm in the morning when you wake up, and it's still an hour before the alarm goes off so that I can have you lay down and snuggle in while we wait for the more appropriate morning starting time. I love watching you build and draw and create, and I love working with you as you learn math and reading and as you commit to your school work and learning. Walking you to school, and seeing you run to me for a giant hug when you arrive home is what I live for. And seeing you show kindness to your brother Canyon, who idolizes you in absolutely every way, is one of the most special friendships I have ever witnessed. You are simply a joy to be around. And whether we are playing games, jumping in cold pools, hiking, playing catch, doing homework, reading stories together, or just lounging around the house, being in your company is uplifting and centering, and I can't get enough of the joy and peace that you bring to my life. Thank you for your ability to calm me and for the beauty of a father-son relationship that you show me.

To Canyon, at four, you are a playful tagalong. While you can disappear in a sand box, or on a trampoline, or while you sit at your desk and draw "Among Us" or "Six-Seven" characters, you also love to be snuggled. Despite your ability to self-entertain, I love that you also want to be spoiled with attention and that you have the ability to pull me away from what oftentimes feels like never-ending work to sit with you and laugh with you and play with you. You go through five or more outfits per day as you move from army, to police, to swim suits, to track suits, and back again. I have never known a kid to fill an entire laundry basket in a single day with supposedly "dirty" clothes that have been used for, at most, five or ten minutes while indoors and while not eating. I love the magic in your eyes when I help you draw or color, and I appreciate you complimenting me on how extremely talented I am at both. The glow on your face with these seemingly simple productions melts my heart and inspires me to see the world through eyes of wonder—that value the joy and beauty of the world. At night you lay there wide awake talking to yourself, and if you see me checking in on you, I get caught up in a break-free dialogue of your interpretation on cartoons and dinosaurs and military operations. Your creative mind proceeds full-steam ahead despite your older brother falling asleep nearly instantaneously in the bed next to you, sometimes thirty minutes earlier. I love your interest in my work and my career; as you lay in your bed, fighting sleep, your imagination creates scenarios where you are injured, and it is my job to get you to the hospital and surgically fix you up. Whether you fall from a helicopter, get caught in the crossfire of a bazooka, or crash on a motorcycle, you love to be my surgical patient as I act as both the ambulance, the nurse, and the surgeon while I put you back together using make-believe power tools and metal rods and screws and rope and staples and bandages. I love your interest in being fixed and how this brings us together in relation to a profession that I have invested so much time in. I love your curiosity. And I love your imagination. This creativity of yours will take you to new heights. Never lose sight of it as you take off your training wheels and head into the adventure of life. I want to never forget the blessing of your toddler years where we had nothing but time to spend together.

To each of my beautiful children, you are my life. You are adaptable and forgiving and unique and adventurous. And I appreciate you putting up with your looney-toon father, and I appreciate you letting me be a part of your individual lives and for continuing to give me a chance despite all of the challenges that have faced our family. I wouldn't want any other group of humans, and I find myself lucky to have you in my life. Thank you for your positive influence and for the profound effect that you have had in my life.

To my parents, thank you for giving me the freedom to chase my dreams and for never ceasing to support me in any outrageous adventure I chose to pursue. I've made some crazy choices, and none of them were met with disappointment or with judgement or with "much" scolding. Whether I went on a road trip in an old beat-up van with friends that was sure to break down along the way, or if I left the country without a cell phone and an unknown return date, you always provided me a place to return to, a place for a meal, an ear to hear me out, and stories to support my crazy ideas. You have remained proud of me as I pursued a career and a family. Thank you for remaining calm and committed as I chose some rollercoasters along the way, and thank you for having my back.

To the many influential people in my life, thank you for the privilege of associating with you. Thank you for lending me your time and talents, and for helping me to gain understanding by learning from what makes you great. This group is made up of an extensive cast of characters—a list too big to put into words here. But you know who you are. You helped me during my early years of sports and public school, during my transition into college and during my preparations for medical school, during that extensive and exhausting medical training process, through the transition out of school and into the start of real life while starting my first "real job" and while striving to build my practice, and through to the present day. You are one of many people who provided me with a portion of their knowledge and education. And you have helped shape me into the person that I am today, and I wouldn't be where I am without you. Through the fond memories, through the ups and down, through the successes and disappointments, through the laughter, and through the tears, you've kept the lights on both in my business and also in my home. And frankly, you have kept the lights on inside my own heart and mind. I consider myself very lucky, and I feel grateful for the relationships that I am privileged to have and for the influential people that I have been able to rub shoulders with. Thank you for your time and for your interest in my success and for the sacrifice that you have given me. And thank you for what you continue to do for me as I evolve and grow in this pursuit of my own personal happiness and success.

To Trevor, you and your family are a home away from home. You've loved me unconditionally, let me get away with a few things along the way, and welcomed me as one of your own. Thank you for never giving up on me. Despite a fourteen-year interruption in our relationship—with careers that landed us on opposite sides of the country—you would still, without fail, bug me to figure out when we could start hanging out again. Your continual faith in me and your persistent desire to reunite our friendship is an unconditional love unique to you—something nobody else in my life has ever had and something that no other person has been so deeply committed to. And you manifested the success of that commitment! And here we are. We now get to plan and execute and create the life that we dreamed of as kids. And I owe you all the credit for staying committed to it, and for continuing to remind me of the need to make it happen. Thank you for bringing us back together—this book is a result of your efforts to stay close, and it is the perfect gift to the world as a representation of what you dream of and stand for. Thank you for keeping me close and for making this dream a reality.

ABOUT THE AUTHORS

TREVOR HANSON

I served in the United States Air Force as an F-16 mechanic, where precision, discipline, and accountability became part of who I am. I've traveled the world, and I'm also a certified scuba diving instructor—experiences that shaped how I see people, risk, and opportunity.

I've been in the financial services industry for over twenty years. I started my career as a licensed banker, where I built a strong foundation in lending, banking systems, and the broader financial picture that many advisors never fully see. Later, I worked under Greg Blood, a top-performing advisor in the Boise area. Over the course of a year and a half, he became a mentor who accelerated my growth and likely advanced my career five to ten years through the knowledge and discipline he instilled.

From there, I served as a senior vice president for a major financial firm, where I worked exclusively with high-net-worth individuals. I was consistently brought into the most complex client situations—stock options, deferred compensation, business ownership, and succession planning. Over the course of my career, I've managed and financially planned for over $1 billion in client assets, giving me real-world experience across a wide range of financial situations.

Over my career, I've worked with business owners, real estate investors, executives, private equity professionals, and multigenerational families. Through all of it, one thing became clear: people don't just need investment advice; they also need a plan. That belief became the foundation of how I built my practice and why my business grew. I've always approached relationships by looking at the entire financial picture, not just a portfolio.

Today, I'm the founder and president of ApexFlow Wealth Management and Paramount Private Wealth. I built these organizations after realizing the traditional corporate environment was becoming more restrictive, more risk-averse, and less aligned with what clients actually needed. I wanted to create something purpose-driven—where advice is tailored, decisions are intentional, and clients aren't forced into a one-size-fits-all approach. That decision changed everything.

I also created the Purposeful Planning Process, a structured approach designed to remove complexity, align financial decisions with what truly matters, and help people move from uncertainty to clarity and confidence. Wealth management is what we do, but purposeful planning is who we are.

I primarily work with business owners, executives, and families who want to delegate complexity and make confident, well-aligned decisions. Clients come to me because I simplify what feels overwhelming, challenge them to think differently, and help them move forward with clarity and confidence.

I was born in Utah, but much of my childhood was spent overseas in Dubai and Muscat, where I attended a British school and was exposed to different cultures and perspectives at a young age. Those experiences gave me a global view that continues to shape how I see people and opportunity.

Travel has always been a major part of who I am. What stands out to me most isn't the places—it's the people. I've seen individuals with very little materially who are genuinely happy, grounded, and present.

That reshaped how I think about success and what actually matters. In the United States, we tend to move fast, stay busy, and carry more stress than we realize. Seeing other ways of living reinforced my belief that true wealth isn't just financial—it's how you live your life.

I've worked through the financial crisis and multiple market cycles, which gave me real-world experience you can't learn from a textbook. It taught me how people react under pressure, how markets behave when things break, and how important it is to stay grounded in a plan.

I now live just outside Park City, where I've chosen a different pace of life. It's the kind of place where people know each other, look out for each other, and genuinely care. In a small town, you see the same faces, build real relationships, and there's a level of accountability in how you live.

The community is active, and that pushes everyone—including me—to stay fit and healthy. Every time I drive over the mountain into the valley, I can feel the shift. The stress drops, things slow down, and it brings me back to what actually matters. That balance is important to me, and it's why I've chosen to raise my kids here.

I'm also very focused on my health. I'm in the gym every day, I pay close attention to what I eat, and I prioritize long-term well-being. My goal is to live as long as possible and feel as good as possible along the way. That same philosophy carries over into how I work with clients.

Outside of work, I'm a husband and a father of three. I'm married to my beautiful wife, Kenalee, and we've been married for twenty-one years. She's my rock—my foundation and my core. She also loves traveling, and we share that passion. We're both adventurous, and when we travel, we don't sit still—we do it all.

My kids are a big part of my life. My son Brody is involved in rodeo, Jaxon is a multisport athlete, and my daughter, Rylee, has been involved in gymnastics and cheer and is finding her next path. I make it a priority to be present and involved in their lives.

I believe the biggest financial mistake people make isn't running out of money—it's never fully living the life they worked for. I've spent over two decades helping people navigate complex financial decisions. More importantly, I've seen what happens when people get it right—and when they don't.

I lead with honesty, direct questions, and genuine care. I say what needs to be said, ask what others overlook, and challenge people to think differently. I've seen a lot over the years—but I'm still coachable, still learning, and always working to get better.

I wrote this book to remove the guesswork. Too many people work hard, make good money, and still feel uncertain about their future—or never fully live the life they've built. This book is for people who want clarity, not confusion—people who want their financial decisions to align with their life.

At the end of the day, I'm not just teaching these principles—I'm living them. And my goal is to help you do the same.

CALEB'S INTERJECTION

One last interjection for the road, eh, Trevor? Just wanted to add a few things since you're too humble to do so. I would like to point out that you have become extremely successful—in the upper echelon of your field—without ever making it seem like you are a hotshot. But you are. And that speaks volumes about your success. You stay grounded and committed—a family man first. Those values, I'm not surprised, have come through in your work as you put people first.

Through it all, you've gone through the grind without complaint—even in the face of difficult family medical issues. Navigating that uncertainty, you never wavered in your purpose, attitude, and fortitude in pursuing the goals you set for yourself and the people you wanted to be close to. You're authentic, put yourself out there, and came out on top. You are a top-notch human being.

CALEB PINEGAR

Growing up in Utah, I took an early interest in all things outdoors. My friend's father was the scoutmaster, and our neighborhood was extremely involved in learning the Boy Scout way and taking regularly scheduled trips to explore the landscapes of Utah's mountain and desert regions. It was amazing. I still seek solitude and refuge in the mountains and cherish the memories of my youth exploring slot canyons, cross-country skiing, backpacking, fishing, and hiking in the wilderness of the Utah backcountry.

I was also involved in competitive sports, including soccer, baseball, hockey, and inline skating. With these sporting activities and outdoor adventures, I had the time of my life. And along this path, I experienced my fair share of injuries. Injuries that brought me to both doctor offices and hospitals, physical therapy clinics, the local orthopedic surgeon's office, and injuries that still whisper their reminders to me today! We pay for the adventures of our youth with the sounds, aches, and pains of tomorrow!

Anyway, these injuries eventually led to the recommendation for me to move away from collision sports. That's when I took an even deeper liking to the mountains and cliffs of the surrounding areas. I was surrounded by a group of friends that helped me explore more of the alternate beauties and treasures of the Beehive State. I found myself in the mountains regularly, chasing peace and adventure, but this time on a bicycle or wearing a harness and dangling from a rope.

More injuries followed and were followed by more trips to the hospital, therapist, and surgeon. Those early injuries, which seemed like a setback at the time, sparked my interest in medicine and rehabilitation. Early on, I was interested in physical therapy, and I considered a career treating patients in a PT clinic and rehabilitating injuries. Then later, I began to dream bigger; I thought that it would probably be even more fun to be the boss of that PT clinic or to be the person referring patients and clients to that clinic, perhaps a career as a family care physician or working in an emergency room.

Then I eventually found my way into some repeated trips to the operating room with that same local orthopedic surgeon, and it was at that time, thanks to these repeat encounters, that I began to challenge the idea of becoming him. Of being the one that fixes the injury and then refers the continuation of care down the chain of command until complete recovery has been achieved. As my own list of sports injuries accrued, I realized that I needed to learn that trade, and to master that skill, so that I could take this man's job.

So I set out to do just that! My collegiate degree was in exercise science with an emphasis in athletic training, where the goal of learning about injury prevention and the management of traumatic situations became a reality. I learned the key evaluation techniques, performed analyses of practice and game setting to screen for potential injury concerns, rode in ambulances with injured athletes, and helped others with their postsurgical and post-injury rehabilitation. Oh...I also filled *a lot* of water bottles and taped up *a lot* of ankles. And you better believe I've still got the skills!

It was a rush, and I knew that's where I wanted to stay—working with athletes.

From there, medical school was unidirectional. The light at the end of the tunnel was to become a surgeon. I didn't even really have a backup plan. That seems super dumb while I write it out, but that was the truth. I had no other motivation than that. Orthopedic surgery. That's it.

My first stop was the College of Osteopathic Medicine at Des Moines University. Here I studied medicine and the practice of osteopathic manipulative medicine (OMM, or sometimes referred to as OMT). I had worked with two physicians in college, one an MD (allopathic physician or medical doctor) and the other a DO (osteopathic physician or doctor or osteopathy). Working alongside these two fantastic sports medicine physicians, I paid close attention to their individual skillsets and to the interplay relating to their training. These interactions kept me thinking as I went forward with my applications.

My goal to become an orthopedic surgeon would require good

hands-on medical evaluations and treatments. So when the MD told athletes that he wanted them to come back on the day that the DO was present, I paid attention, and I watched as this DO performed special manipulative techniques during office visits and evaluations. Techniques that the MD did not learn in his training program. And that is what I wanted. I wanted that additional tool, and I wanted that additional treatment modality.

Truth be told, I use this skill now more on my family and friends than anybody else! It is not as often necessary during my office visits with patients, but it certainly comes in handy when one of my kids has a headache or when one of the employees in the office complains of back pain. Using those treatment techniques brings me great joy, and looking back, I can confidently say that, if I wasn't blessed to have made it into a surgical program, I would certainly be utilizing those OMM and OMT skills in whatever type of practice that I would have found myself in.

Following medical school, it was time for my residency training, which took me to Ohio, where the next five years of my life—spent in Cuyahoga Falls, Akron, Cleveland, Cincinnati, Columbus, and touring several sports medicine programs on the East and West Coasts. I spent time at some wonderful hospitals and worked with many talented surgeons. This training took me to the Cleveland Clinic, Cincinnati Children's Hospital, University Hospitals, and Metro Health Trauma Center, and I also got to rub shoulders with some of the most talented sports medicine professionals in Pittsburg, Detroit, Virginia, Cleveland, San Diego, and Florida.

This was one of the most challenging and demanding periods of my life. It required an absurd amount of work and commitment, and those of us that had to ("got to") spend this time working and learning together are bonded in a way that very few people will ever understand. I was surrounded by fantastic people—and I am now a member of a comradery and fellowship that will last forever.

Very few people will ever understand what this required and what parts of ourselves that became lost. Needless to say, medical training is not for the faint of heart. It's brutal. But that made us who we are. And some of the recovery from those challenging years of sacrifice has continued to be a point of emphasis as I work on my own HealthSpan.

Lastly, to consolidate and complete my training, I was awarded a year-long sports medicine fellowship with Dr. James Andrews and his team of orthopedic surgery professionals in Gulf Breeze, Florida. These cutting-edge surgeons instilled in me the final sharpenings to the tools that I had spent years collecting and refining. And at the completion of this additional final year, I was ready.

I still send Dr. Andrews a happy birthday greeting every year, and he still asks me how things are going and that he wishes me well. His care and charisma is second-to-none, and I witnessed first-hand why he earned the right of being called the best in the business. Exposure to his expertise is the capstone experience that rounded out—exactly what I wanted and needed as a budding professional. And I left that final year well-versed in the management, evaluations, and execution of the treatment of athletic injuries and in the business of sports medicine.

Since then, it's been a whirlwind! I joined a practice and tried to build a name for myself. In addition to hosting a busy orthopedic surgery clinic and performing surgeries, I took calls at the local hospital. I provided my medical expertise to sports journalism and have appeared in interviews on ESPN and on various radio shows. I commented on the injuries of the local professional sports teams and discussed the questions from fans and the proposed rehabilitation that these athletes had ahead of them. And I did all of this while trying to provide for a family and while trying to cultivate a lasting and meaningful relationship with my children and close friends.

As continued opportunities presented themselves, I had to consider the effects of advancements in my career and their impact on my family. And in the end, I turned down some of the offers to advance my career into the realm of professional sports and more glamorous roles in the local orthopedic and sports medicine scene. I took a really long and deep look at my family, at my growing children, and at the time that all of these pursuits would cost. As I considered these pursuits, and the family relationships that I currently had in comparison to the family relationships that I truly wanted, I kept hearing Trevor's voice! And I kept getting pulled back into the life and goals of all our childhood dreams. He would say, as if on repeat, "When are we hanging out?" And I could hear his voice in my head almost every time.

And now, here we are! Trevor and I have both completely pivoted from the fast-paced and potentially glamorous working environments that we were in so that we could pursue this dream. So that we could pursue balance. So that we could pursue what really motivates us and what really brings us joy. So when are we hanging Trevor? Later this month, my friend! Let's make it happen! Let's make a plan! Let's do this! I absolutely love being able to say that to Trevor. He waited a long time to hear that! And he was patient and persistent. So now, when he calls me in the middle of the day, I pick up! Because Trevor is a person that will show you down a road that will actually bring you joy and peace. Because he believes it, and because he lives it.

So there you go. We have, in fact, made it happen...again. And this book is proof!

TREVOR'S INTERJECTION

My turn to brag about you, Caleb. Reading between the lines of your career, we can say plainly that your natural inclination is to help others. That's where it begins and ends. I'll give the world a specific example.

When one of my children tore their meniscus, you were the only one I wanted to operate. Understandably, you were a little uncomfortable operating on a member of your family, but you did it anyway. When we flew out, you did everything to make my child comfortable. You made them laugh. You talked them through what to expect and how to attack the pre- and postsurgery periods to maximize their recovery. You did it in a way that made them feel like a collaborator, someone with agency in their own HealthSpan. You were, in a word, *you*.

Now, multiply that by the thousands of individuals you've served, and perhaps that multitude is one way to understand the true scope of your caring soul. Between the list of your accomplishments are countless grateful human beings—grateful that you came into their lives to help them, medically or otherwise. You can count me as one of them.

LEGAL DISCLAIMER

The content in this book is for informational and educational purposes only, and (1) it does not act as professional financial advice, nor does it create a fiduciary relationship, and (2) it does not act as medical diagnosis, prescribe treatment, create a physician-patient relationship, or provide intended or unintended medical advice. You are advised to challenge the presentation of this work and to consult a licensed professional for all of your personalized strategies in relation to your WealthSpan and HealthSpan.

The information contained in this book does not purport to be a complete description of the securities, markets, or developments referred to in this material. The information has been obtained from sources considered to be reliable, but we do not guarantee that the foregoing material is accurate or complete. Any information is not a complete summary or statement of all available data necessary for making an investment decision and does not constitute a recommendation. Any opinions are those of the author and not necessarily those of RJFS or Raymond James. Expressions of opinion are, as of the initial book publishing date, subject to change without notice. Raymond James is not affiliated with and does not endorse the opinions or services of Caleb Pinegar or any mentioned organization. Neither Raymond James Financial Services nor any Raymond James Financial Advisor renders advice on tax issues; these matters should be discussed with the appropriate professional. Investing involves risk, and you may incur a profit or loss regardless of strategy selected, including diversification and asset allocation. Prior to making an investment decision, please consult with your financial advisor.

Be advised that investments in real estate and in REITs have various risks, including possible lack of liquidity and devaluation based on adverse economic and regulatory changes. Additionally, investments in REITs will fluctuate with the value of the underlying properties, and the price at redemption may be more or less than the original price paid. Real estate investments can be subject to different and greater risks than more diversified investments. Declines in the value of real estate, economic conditions, property taxes, tax laws, and interest rates all present potential risks to real estate investments.

There are special risks associated with investing with bonds, such as interest rate risk, market risk, call risk, prepayment risk, credit risk, reinvestment risk, and unique tax consequences. To learn more about these risks and the suitability of these bonds for you, please contact your financial advisor.

Unless certain criteria are met, Roth IRA owners must be fifty-nine-and-a-half years of age or older and have held the IRA for five years before tax-free withdrawals are permitted. Additionally, each converted amount may be subject to its own five-year holding period. Converting a traditional IRA into a Roth IRA has tax complications. Investors should consult a tax advisor before deciding to do a conversion.

Dividends are not guaranteed and must be authorized by the company's board of directors.

Securities offered through Raymond James Financial Services, Inc. Member FINRA/SIPC. Investment advisory services offered through Raymond James Financial Services Advisors, Inc., Paramount Private Wealth LLC, and ApexFlow Wealth Management are not a registered